This Book is unique. Not merely another dust-choked, stodgy and lusterless panoply of biographical data, *My Friend Lenny* is a living, breathing chronical of a very intimate and personal nature. And this is what makes it so eminently readable: with its direct and garrulous style, Ouida's memoir scales the entire gamut of antipodal emotions, from waggish wit to full-blown wisdom.

You may ask if it really is possible to care enough about the private lives of others. This straightforward volume will unequivocally answer, 'Yes.' Because, in the greater scheme of things, what affects one person affects us all. Or as Ouida's cherished father so tersely wrote in one of his fine epigrams, 'No one is worthwhile who cannot appreciate the worth of others.'

Eleni Traganas
Concert Pianist, Author and Artist

"My Friend Lenny" is an intimate portrait of Ouida Mintz's fascinating life. Her fluid and sentimental style of writing evokes vivid pictures of a musical life in the 20th century, which we relive through her words. This is not just a collection of memories, but also a true account of a talented musician and teacher! Readers will especially enjoy Ouida's sense of humor and enthusiasm as they travel through time and meet all of her friends and family. She has been able to preserve precious mementos of her friendship with Leonard Bernstein and shares with us a side of his personality that few people knew. Since reading "My Friend Lenny," I feel even more special playing my Baldwin Grand since it once belonged to Leonard Bernstein and bears his signature!

Alexander Peskanov
Concert pianist and composer

Dear Ouida,

　　I appreciate your writing, your comments about me, as well as all the good things about me and my friend, Lenny.

　　Good work!

　　　　　　Lukas Foss

　　(Distinguished American composer, conductor, pianist and close friend of Lenny Bernstein from their Tanglewood years when they both studied with Koussevitzky)

Dear Ouida,

　　Your book, "My Friend Lenny," is destined to become an important contribution to future historians in their search for detailed information about our musical life.

　　　　　　Morton Estrin

　　(Professor in the Music Department of Hofstra University for over thirty years and an important Sony Classical recording artist who has performed in many famous halls across the country)

My Friend Lenny

A Memoir

of my life in music,
with personal stories about
Leonard Bernstein, Mike Wallace,
Paul Simon, and others.

by

OUIDA BLATT MINTZ

Bravura Books

Copyright © 2000 by Ouida Blatt Mintz

ISBN 0-615-11879-8

Library of Congress Catalog Number: 00-105955

Second Edition 2001

Printed in the United States of America

Bravura Books
417 Roslyn Road
Roslyn Heights, N.Y. 11577
1-800-769-4171
www.MyFriendLenny.com

DEDICATION

This book of memoirs is dedicated to my loved ones who are still living in our hearts but no longer on earth; my dad, William M. Blatt; my mom, Lucy Blatt; my sister, Jo Blatt Pall; my husband, Samson Mintz; my son, William Michael Mintz; my niece, Steffi Pall; and my nephew, William Blatt Pall.

TABLE OF CONTENTS

	Dedication	VII
	Acknowledgments	XI
	Foreword	XIII
1	Beginnings.	15
	Lenny Bernstein's dreams	
2	First Impressions.	24
	Family life - My dad's plays are produced	
3	Interesting People.	32
	We give marionette shows for adults	
4	Playing Violin with Mike Wallace.	37
5	Meeting Heinrich Gebhard and	40
	Leonard Bernstein - Slonimsky -	
	Abram Chasins	
6	Playing Concerti, and Letters from "Gebby".	53
	Lenny and I play concerti - Tanglewood	
	in the early days - My letters from Gebhard	
7	Mildred Spiegel Remembers Lenny.	73
	She teaches Beethoven's *First Piano Concerto*	
	to him - Lenny meets Adolph Green	
8	Lenny's Awesome Beginnings.	81
	On the Town, first musical - Koussevitsky	
	is upset - Lenny and Jerome Robbbins	
	receive an ovation for *Fancy Free* ballet -	
	Lenny meets Aaron Copland	
9	My Roots.	88
	The Romberg family had to flee Kharkov	
	under the Czarist regime and sail to Ellis	
	Island when my mom was only three	
	years old - Dr. Eli Romberg, my famous	
	uncle	
10	Why I Didn't Become a Concert Pianist.	97
11	My Very Best Friends.	100
	Some letters during lifetime friendships -	
	A few letters from "Gebby"	
12	I Meet My Husband, Samson Mintz.	116
	Contrasting forms of Judaism -	
	A surprising honeymoon	

13 Life in Worcester, Massachusetts.   121
    We have two boys and a girl - I sing in
    the chorus of the Worcester Music Festival,
    the oldest in the country, under Eugene
    Ormandy, with the Philadelphia Orchestra -
    I meet with Leonard Bernstein when he brings
    the New York Philharmonic to Worcester -
    Reuniting with Mike Wallace

14 We Move to New York   132
    Lenny looks at my songs at the Osborn -
    we adopt a cat

15 I Meet Paul Simon.   140
    He makes demonstration discs of my songs

16 Lenny, the Conductor.   149
    And composer of *Kaddish, West Side Story,*
    Candide, etc

17 How to Write a Song .   153
    Gebhard's last two letters - "Bach is the
    greatest of all," he says - Lenny's Intro. to
    Gebhard' s book on Pedaling

18 How I Teach.   162
    Tips on keeping kids interested

19 My Wonderful Students.   167
    With letters of appreciation telling what
    music did for them

20 Some of My Dad's Wit and Wisdom.   187

21 Loss: My beloved sister, Jo and Adored Son, Bill -   202
    Jo's unusual poetry, some deep, some
    deep, some humorous - The worst tragedy:
    losing a child

22 Trip to Europe and Israel with Sam.   235
    Visits with interesting relatives

23 Lucy in the Big City   241
    Her life in New York's theatrical center -
    Son, Jerry writes of his visit with Nana

24 Other Family Members.   253
    I'm so proud of their accomplishments

25 Other Trips and Cruises.   274
    On Eurail Pass for six weeks - Costa del Sol

26 Losing Sam and Saving a Life.   281
    Jerry's medical problems - alternative
    education

27 Answering ads for daughter, Lisa, and   285
        later, for me - "Getting Personal" by
        Ray Sandiford
28 Lenny's Swan Song.   305
        His birthday bash at Tanglewood,
        attended by ten thousand people -
        "Lenny's Last Rehearsal" by Jerry Mintz -
        Lenny's Memorial Concerts

APPENDAGES

Leonard Bernstein's Most Important   313
    Compositions.

Books by Leonard Bernstein.   317

More of My Dad's Wit and Wisdom.   318

David Mamet and Jerry.   328

This and That.   330

My Performing Friends at APTLI.   347

Post-Script   377

ACKNOWLEDGMENTS

Personal thanks to Alexander Bernstein, Mike Wallace, and Carol Montparker for reading the manuscript of this book, and writing such encouraging and complimentary words. I would also like to thank Carol for the delightful letter she wrote in the final chapter of the book.

My appreciation to "My Very Best Friends" for their letters: Bob Goldman, Dr. Byron H. Waksman and Sheldon Rotenberg, also to my nieces, Ellen Pall, and Freda Bright, both sucessful authors of numerous books. Thanks to Jonas Rosenfeld for his exquisite love letter to my sister, Jo, also to Howard Fast, the famous author, for his thoughtful letter about my dad's booklet, "Inklings."

Of course, I'm very grateful to be able to publish my beloved teacher, Heinrich Gebhard's warm and enthusiastic letters to me, as he had so many admiring students all over the country.

I also want to acknowledge the many artistic photos in the book.

Special thanks to my good friend and colleague, Mildred Spiegel Zucker, for her warm and perceptive remembrances of Lenny in Chapter Seven, also to my sister, Hester, for her interesting article on marionettes called, "Tony Sarg Magic and How it Touched our Family."

Most of all I want to thank my close friend, Ray Sandiford, for his recently self-acquired ability as a typesetter, as well as the designer of the cover for which my friend, Eleni Traganas, made helpful suggestions. Ray also wrote his own romantic story about how we met in the chapter, "Getting Personal." There, we give our first impressions of each other.

I want to give credit to my son, Jerry Mintz, who suggested several years ago that since I had known many interesting people in my life, I should write a memoir. I decided it might be fun. Jerry took my hasty scrawls to an educational assistant, Carol Morley, to transcribe. And so began this book, which turned into, "My Friend Lenny," who was the most illustrious of all my friends.

Jerry found a method to get me to write in a more dramatic way by asking pertinent questions and taking down my answers on the spot, which helped enliven several parts of the book.

One of these days I hope he will find time amid his many important meetings all over the world to write his own personal memoir. He certainly has a wealth of material to call on from his experiences as headmaster for many years of his own school of alternative education.

FOREWORD

This book is halfway between a memoir and a very personal diary, because the author has taken care to include everything from her life that is meaningful and dear. The nice thing about this surprisingly textured compilation of anecdotes and reminiscences is that a lot of it has a touching appeal and charm for the reader. Ouida has had privileged glimpses into the lives of some folks who are household names, and she comes from an unusual family; some of the choicest tidbits are from family members – most notably her father, William Blatt, and her sister, Jo, and from the renowned visitors who came through her childhood home.

She tells her tales – the tragedies and the courage of her family, as well as the delights – not only with an urgency to share every detail, but with sensitivity and a sweet freshness. How she remembers, with apparent total recall, all the particulars of her enviable childhood, is remarkable.

Carol Montparker, pianist,
author of "A Pianist's Landscape,"
and editor at Clavier Magazine

1

BEGINNINGS

This world is the most exciting place I have ever lived in.
William M. Blatt

"You know, Ouida, when I grow up I think I'm going to do something in music."

That prophetic, casual statement was made to me by Leonard Bernstein when we were teenagers. We were having refreshments after our monthly student recital at the home of our teacher, Heinrich Gebhard, in Brookline, Massachusetts. I had started studying the piano at eleven, after first taking up the violin at seven, even playing violin duets with Myron Wallace (later known as Mike Wallace, of CBS's 60 Minutes). His sister, Helen, was my first piano teacher. When Lenny was ten, his Aunt Clara stored her piano in his house, and he fell in love with it.

At the time he made the remark, we were both learning piano concerti. Lenny was learning the Grieg *A minor* and I was learning the Mendelssohn *G minor,* Gebhard playing the orchestral part on his second piano. I didn't think I was ever going to play with orchestra. Very few people get the chance.

I was already teaching piano. I started at fourteen, teaching Gebhard's daughter and my uncle's patients. At that time, Lenny was just beginning to develop his ability at the piano and he had learned a few pieces. His father was hoping that Lenny would

Ouida at age six

Ouida at age seventeen

join him in his cosmetic business. I never imagined that he would become one of the greatest musicians and musical influences of the century, or that I would play with orchestra before he did, and he would be jealous of little me.

But first, let's go back to the beginning of my life. When I was born they named me Pauline Louise Blatt, after my father's mother. I've even seen her stone with my name on it. But I've never been known as Pauline Louise. People know me as Ouida. Ouida comes from Louise. My father knew of the French author (Maria Louise de la Ramée, 1839-1908) whose little niece couldn't pronounce "Louise" and called her Ouida, which she decided to use as her pen name. She wrote, among many other novels, "Under Two Flags," later made into a movie with Claudette Colbert. "A Dog of Flanders" (1872), one of her stories for children has been filmed recently by Kevin Brodie in Belgium. It is the latest of several film versions.

You are probably wondering how old I am, but I'm not going to tell you. I think that people who tell their age and say they are "proud of it," are kidding themselves. So I'll just say, if you're really curious, that I'll admit to over seventy (although I hope I don't look it, and I don't feel as if I'm that old—I don't like it and I'm certainly not proud of it). You'll have to figure out how much over as the book goes on. My mother even made us promise not to tell her age in her obituary. People were always telling her how young she looked, so you can understand she didn't want anyone to know she was over eighty when she looked no more than sixty.

In the Jewish religion, one always names the baby after a deceased relative, but my dad's beliefs were non-traditional. So, being a rebel, he named me for his mother while she was still alive and could enjoy it. In fact, when I and my two sisters gave birth to three boys within a few months, March, April, and June, we named them all "Billy" for my dad. He was delighted and dubbed them B1, B2, B3 and he was B4 because, as he said, "I came before them."

My dad, William M. Blatt, was definitely the intellectual type and the guiding genius of the family. He was short and stocky with a ready smile. Many thought he was Irish. He had an immense supply of jokes that he had cut out from newspapers and magazines, and kept notebooks of them. They could fit almost any occasion, and though he claimed to have a poor memory, he never failed to recall one that was appropriate. He was born in East Orange, New Jersey, the only one of three boys to survive, and had two younger sisters. His mother, Pauline Louise Blatt, whom we called "Nana," was a very sweet, affectionate woman with a beautiful singing voice. I often think I might have inherited some of my musical ability from her.

My father had studied law at Boston University and was one of the founders of the New Century Club, although his real love was writing. However, he became a successful attorney and professor, and was president of the Law Society of Massachusetts for several years. Because of his wit and knowledge, he was the favorite master of ceremonies for their dinners.

Dad deplored the fact that he rarely had any time to spend with his adored children. I remember clearly one morning on a school day, he woke us up at five-thirty while it was still dark and said, "Get dressed kids, we're going out for a walk. Maybe we'll discover some haunted houses and pick some rare mushrooms." (He knew the difference between the poisonous and edible ones). We jumped at the chance to be with our dad who had to work day and night to make a decent living for his family.

I can still see the startling sight before us when we stepped out the door. There was a thin layer of newly fallen snow on the ground and on the surrounding trees and houses. It looked as if the whole world had been sprinkled with confectioner's sugar, and we loved inhaling the crisp morning air as we took this rare, memorable walk with our dad.

Dad was a struggling young lawyer and playwright when he met my charming mother, Lucy Romberg, who was a graduate of the Leland Powers School in Boston. A philanthropist, whose name was Murdoch, had helped with her education when he saw her picture in the paper. He sponsored many deserving young people to further their education. It must have given him a great deal of satisfaction when he heard her perform Tennyson's "Enoch Arden," a narrative poem of great length, put to music by Richard Strauss. She had the whole thing memorized. My dad was in the audience and was immediately taken by her beauty and charm. Since he was considerably older (eleven years) and a few inches shorter and wore a beard, Lucy was slow to respond to him, but as she was an actress, she admired his creative ability as a playwright. Lena, her older sister, advised her to marry William when he proposed marriage. Lucy did accept his proposal but almost immediately took off for New York to audition for an acting job, which upset her fiancée no end as he felt she should be with him at such an important time of their lives. Here is a letter expressing his feelings after not hearing from her for several weeks:

```
Lucy dear,
     Have a good time while you are in New
York but don't forget that there is
someone waiting for you in Boston.As I
write, I see that I must break my deter-
mination to send a cold-blooded letter.
     Of one thing I am sure, nothing can
ever make me care less than I do for
you. I have gone deeper than your talent
and your beauty.   I love you.
                         As ever, Will
```

```
And another letter:
```

```
Dear Lucy,
     Your first note to me after our en-
gagement will always be very precious. I
have read it a hundred times and it
always rings true - a perfect gem of a
letter, modest yet unmistakably tender
between the lines. Hereafter, though, I
shall expect a considerable change of
scoring - fortissimo, presto con
espressione, instead of andante
cantabile. Don't be afraid to cut loose.
You owe me that much for staying away.
Now let's have no more foolishness, but
pack up, telegraph me at the office, and
come back on the first train you can
take.
     Yours, very much exasperated, Will
```

```
    P.S.      I am more in love with you
than ever. My thoughts are with you
constantly. Can't you feel them? It
seems as if they were strong enough to
reach out and draw you close to me.
    With all the love I have,
                            Will
```

My mother finally returned to Boston to get married. I
don't think she was really in love with my dad. She admired him,
but I think she was more in love with the theater and the fact that
he was a playwright. She was very romantic, but unfortunately, he
was not inclined to be sentimental. When I grew old enough to
realize these things, I swore I would never marry anyone I didn't
love.

Their wedding took place on April 2, 1911, after which
they set up housekeeping in a dark green colonial house at 48
Francis Street in Brookline. I think most parents whose first and
second children are of the same sex, hope that the next child will
be of the opposite sex. As the third child, and a girl, I felt I was no
exception to that desire, and a disappointment. However, I was a
bit spoiled, being the "baby." Also, I never had to make my own
bed as my mother always managed to have a housekeeper, and we
had quite a collection of them in those depression days who were
happy just to get room and board and a little spending money.
Unfortunately, one of my mother's helpers got annoyed at something I did one day and hung me out the third floor window by
my ankles. I still remember the panic I felt when I saw the world
upside down and the ground so far below. I don't remember whether
I told on her. I was just glad to be alive. I guess child abuse had
been going on back then and even before that. I still remember
Claire, the ballet dancer, who fascinated me when she worked on
her costumes and toe shoes; Audrey, the red-headed black girl;
Ethel, the college student who helped me with my homework;
Kanako, the Japanese man who gave my dad massages; and Percy,
who used to polish our grand piano with infinite care because he
loved music so much. I got along very well with my mother since
she was hardly ever home. Most of her afternoons were spent shop-

ping in Filene's Basement to get bargain clothes for our family. All of our fancy gowns for concerts and weddings were purchased there, and had been greatly reduced in price. The salesladies would say to her, "See you tomorrow, Mrs. Blatt," as she often returned the merchandise she had bought the day before. Since we had to economize, my father insisted that she make a list of what she bought every day and how much it cost.

When I became a teenager, I was told I had the straightest nose in the family, which was considered an advantage, I guess, plus high cheekbones, which made some people say I resembled Claudette Colbert. Sometimes I was compared to Shirley MacLaine or Jennifer Jones. I knew I didn't have the figure of any of these movie stars as I was a bit on the chubby side, but I soon found out that wearing darker clothes, especially black, gave the illusion of slimness.

I grew up feeling inferior to my older sisters, as they excelled in school and received honors in many subjects. Jo was even president of the Honor Society in high school, and Hester, the oldest, was also in the Honor Society and a straight-A student.

Mothers are wonderful people. My mom had special ways of easing my feelings. I know that she directed my life in very subtle ways; she always took advantage of opportunities that came up, and followed through on them. It was she who maneuvered me into a fascinating career in music – with her loving ways.

Both of my sisters had shown unusual ability at a fairly early age and had "found" themselves. Hester had discovered the profession she was going to follow – chemistry. She had eclectic interests and was awarded a French prize when she graduated from Brookline High School. She was accepted at Radcliffe College in Cambridge and studied chemistry there, and she acted in school plays as well as in summer stock. After graduating, she worked as a research chemist in all the most important Boston Hospitals.

Our middle sister, Josephine, was the angelic one who never got mad at anyone. She had two adorable dimples when she smiled, and had been a recognized poet at the age of seven, having had her poetry published in the Boston Post. Josie got started on her literary career at a very early age.

Here is a poem she wrote at the age of six. It was published with several other poems as part of a newspaper article about her and her family:

TO A ROSE

Dear rose, will you open
Come out of your bed
Put on your green dress
And your bonnet of red
The robins are calling
The bluebirds are here
Dear rose, will you open
Now summer is near
The other dear flowers
They open quite soon
But cunning dear rosebud
You open in JUNE.

The publicity which followed must have been the reason she stopped writing in her mid-teens. She always felt self-conscious about it because she was very shy. She turned to art in her college years, at which she was equally gifted. In her sketches of people, she was able to capture the personality of the subject. For instance, when the mother of twin friends of mine asked Jo if she would do a picture of them, she agreed if they would pose for an hour. The result was a charcoal sketch of them in profile which brought out the personalities of each so perfectly that their family treasured it and displayed it for years on their living room wall. Jo attended the Massachusetts School of Art and then studied oil painting under the guidance of some fine teachers — Paul Wood of New York was one of her favorites. She turned out some beautiful paintings, running the gamut from realistic to abstract.

I feel it is important to tell the following story about my experience at a summer camp in order to prevent a family tragedy from happening.

At the age of seven, I had never been to summer camp, but my sister, Hester, was going to a camp in Sharon, Massachusetts, so my folks thought it would be a safe place for me to go. They didn't realize how dangerous it was that I couldn't swim, but thought it might be a good place for me to learn. However, they didn't count on my having an inexperienced counselor.

On the day I was scheduled to practice my newly learned swimming strokes, I was accompanied by a teen-age counselor who was to take me out to the raft, which was in water over my head. I managed to just about get to the raft, but was extremely out of breath when, to my horror, my supposed protector assumed her job was done, said good-bye and headed back to shore. She had neglected to help me get on the raft and figured I was OK.

I wasn't. As I sank down into the depths of the lake, thinking I would never come up again. I frantically waved my arms about and, to my surprise, I ascended to the surface, but I was a very scared little girl, as you can imagine. I had enough presence of mind to get to the ladder and climb up on the raft, even though I was exhausted. Luckily, I'm here to tell the tale.

I hope this is a warning that a counselor should never assume that a child is safe, and should always double check before he or she departs.

The Three Graces,
Hester, Josie, and Ouida

2

FIRST IMPRESSIONS

If flowers could speak, they would have children's voices.
William M. Blatt

My first memory of the opposite sex was about the age of three when I was playing in the sandbox with my childhood friend, Kenneth Rodgers. I was startled one day to see a stream of water coming from what I thought was a finger. It was many years later that I realized it wasn't magic but that he was just relieving himself in the sandbox. I used to stand on the back of his oversized tricycle and cling to him as he swung around the block of 48 Francis Street, Brookline, the house where we three girls were born.

My mother's former boyfriend, Dr. Albert Shapiro, who was an obstetrician, stayed the night when I was about to be delivered. He dubbed me P. (Pauline) Louise; I dampened his lap when he held me. He was an amateur violinist, and several years later he came to visit us with his wife and he brought his violin so that I could accompany him on the piano! It was a funny feeling to be making music with the man who brought me into this world.

When I was seven years old, we moved from our home on Francis Street to 359 Tappan Street, a four story orange brick apartment building which my dad had bought. My mom decided to let me have violin lessons with a woman who lived around the corner, so I could get there myself. I attended Runkle School, an alternative-type public school, which allowed me to pursue a project during geography class — a Chinese city carved out of Ivory soap that I later painted. This school is located in Brookline, which was considered one of the wealthiest towns in the country. It's where John Kennedy and his brothers and sisters grew up. I still remember some of the fancy names of my classmates: Whipple Withington, Woodbury Rand, Roger Wyman Halliday Dodds (one person), Nancy McCann (of the shoe family), and a girl named Mercedes. However, I never felt put down by these children of the upper class, even though my family was of moderate means, because the kids were so congenial.

The great Amelia Earhart visited our school at an assembly one morning when I was about nine years old. She shook hands with every child there. It made such an impression on me when I looked up at this tall, boyish-looking young woman with the tousled hair and warm smile. I could hardly believe she was a famous airplane pilot.

In the fifth grade, I was a dreamer and not very inspired by the teacher. On top of that, I contracted pneumonia and missed a lot of school. At the end of the year, I read on my report card that I was immature and should repeat fifth grade. It was quite a blow to my ego, especially since my sisters were always top students. It was hard to leave my familiar friends behind, but I was consoled by the fact that two of my best friends had to repeat the grade, also.

My dad asked if I could study some books in the summer and take a test in the fall. The principal agreed. The trouble was that I really didn't know how or what to study and was too afraid of failure, so I refused to take the test, preferring to face the consequence of "staying back." It affected the rest of my life. I never felt as smart as either of my sisters. Although I was at the top of my class the year that I repeated, I never felt much self-esteem. The following year, in the sixth grade, I was fortunate enough to get the best school teacher I ever had, Elgie Clucas, a tall, slim, not beautiful woman with a ready smile. I will never forget her as she was so sensitive, and appreciated the humorous poetry I wrote when we were studying about Greece:

ZEUS

The king of Greek Gods was named Zeus,
And one day this God raised the deuce;
His head -- it did ache -- till he thought it would break --
This mighty Greek God named Zeus.
The Gods they were greatly distressed,
And Zeus rather more than the rest,
So they sent for a man
Who cracked open his pan,
And out popped Athena undressed!
This Goddess, so thoughtful and fair,
With a quiet and scholarly air -- in Athens is found
Standing high on a mound,
And worshiped by all who are there.

I wrote the following poem when we were studying about Egypt:

THE SPHINX

The Sphinx is a statue widely known,
It bears the head of Kafra,
It is so very, very huge,
That it's bigger than
Sidney Kafka.

Sidney was the fat boy of the class, and when I finished reading the poem, Miss Clucas tried to conceal her laughter, but finally had to put her head down on the desk. Sidney was very upset, and after recess, he asked Miss Clucas if he could read his answer to my poem. All I remember is that he rhymed "Blatt" with fat, but said nothing about Egypt.

When I was eleven, my Mom decided I could quit violin lessons and study piano, which I had always longed to do. It didn't matter to Mom, but my dad objected. My two older sisters had been playing piano for years and had graduated from the Carl Faelton School in Boston and he thought two pianists were enough. Hester was more serious about it than Josie and studied with several piano teachers. Helen Wallace, my first piano teacher, also taught twin friends of mine — Eleanor and Estelle Levy. Helen lived on the first floor of her family's house at 169 Rawson Road, which was around the corner from me. She always wore a green coat with brown accessories. That became my favorite color combination. Her teacher was Hans Ebell. He came to our parties and always played the *Étude Mignonne* of Eduard Schuett. I asked him if he thought I could learn it and he assured me that of course I could. It has since then been in my repertoire. Helen, incidentally, was the big sister of Mike Wallace of "Sixty Minutes" TV fame. Mike and I had played violin duets at a concert on the stage of the Edward Devotion School when we studied with Harry Ellis Dickson as teenagers.

From the very first lesson, I fell in love with the piano and eventually I came to idolize my teacher, Helen, mainly because she had given me back my self-esteem. In one year I made so much progress that I was placed last at the students' concerts, the place for the best student. Helen's teacher, Mr. Hans Ebell, let me replace her at class lessons when she couldn't make it, and he encouraged me tremendously. I played one piece at each piano session which was meant to be only for technique, but since he wasn't my private teacher, he allowed me to play solos and gave me some valuable criticism. My folks used to ask Mr. Ebell to our home when we put on marionette shows, and he used to play the piano for the guests.

Hans Ebell was one of the greatest musicians I had ever met at that time, and was a real inspiration to me, so you can imagine my shock when I picked up the paper one morning and the headline said, "Hans Ebell, The Great Pianist, Killed by Ex-Wife and Lover." Ebell had tried to rescue his daughter who was sick at summer camp. His ex-wife and her lover got the girl into their car to drive her off to another town. Ebell tried to pull her out of the car and was knocked off the running board as they drove off at high speed. I was devastated; it was the first trauma I had ever suffered. When that happened, I vowed that someday I would write a book about him.

I was very young when I first heard fourteen year old piano prodigy, Elly Kassman, play the piano in my house. Our families were friends who lived on the same street in Brookline. At that early age I never realized what an inspiration she was to me. As the years went on, I decided that my ambition was to play the piano as well as she did.

Elly was born in Finland where her father, a former student of Leopold Auer, was concertmaster of the same orchestra in which her mother played violin. Elly began her formal music studies in the U.S.A. at the age of seven. She studied with the eminent Puerto Rican pianist, Jesus Maria Sanroma, who had become a Bostonian and acted as the principal pianist of the Boston Symphony Orchestra in addition to his large schedule of solo appearances. At fifteen, Elly, a slim charming brunette with a lovely smile, appeared in a joint recital with her father in Boston at Jordan Hall.

I still have one of her programs. She played the Schumann *Concerto* under the direction of Richard Burgin and the Saint-Saëns *G minor Concerto* under Serge Koussevitzky, who considered her to be one of the outstanding young American pianists. Elly continued to be my inspiration during my formative years in the thirties.

In these early years, my folks managed to go places without ever owning a car; in fact they did so for all of their lives. The street car (trolley) was the very convenient way we traveled from Brookline to Boston, where most of our activities took place. Surprisingly, the street car is in just as much use today in Boston, though it has been replaced by the bus in almost all American cities. When I took the street car in Brookline, it came every fifteen minutes or so - there were three or four bright orange cars hooked together which clanged noisily down tree-lined Beacon Street on tracks and under the overhead power line. Today the street cars are much quieter. As they approach Boston proper, they go underground into the dark subway after Kenmore Station and proceed to Copley Square for those who want to go to the Boston Public Library. After that comes Arlington, Boylston and Tremont Street, where my dad's office was located. When my friends came to visit from out of town, it seemed quite natural to go to Boston by street car to attend plays and concerts on dates.

My sisters and I commuted to our college by street car also: Hester, to Radcliffe at Cambridge; Jo, to the Massachusetts Art School; and eventually, I attended the Boston University School of Music, which was located at Copley Square at the time.

My dad was a most versatile gentleman, and though he had to work very hard as a lawyer and judge, he was determined to pursue his first love, writing. For years he managed to turn out thirty five three-act plays by writing in the early morning. My Mom acted as his agent because Dad didn't seem to care what happened to his plays; he enjoyed the creative process. The opening paragraph of Dad's essay, "How Far Ambition?" showed his feelings about pride of authorship:

Ambition is the source of many woes. When too great, it inevitably produces frustration, bitterness and despair. It overcomes all triumphs, it takes the joy out of all achievements. It makes every day a Yom Kippur and every event a calamity. Unbridled, it stops at nothing. All the past is forgotten. Nothing in the present is good enough. Each success is only a notice to do better. Defeat is tragedy. A returned manuscript is a little death. A critic's dissatisfaction is a criminal conviction. A period without public praise is a prison term. Happiness is impossible.

Mom actually got some of his plays produced. I remember seeing "Over Here" at the Apollo Theatre in Atlantic City. I was very young at the time. Later on, I saw one of his plays at the Copley Theatre in Boston. "After the Curtain Falls" was an added final act to Shakespeare's "Merchant of Venice," making Shylock the good man. It was all in blank verse, published by Baker, and was performed a great deal, especially in England.

One of my dad and mom's best friends was a Chinese scholar who had graduated from Oxford. It was quite unusual to hear a Chinese man with an English accent. His name was Tehyi Tsieh (Tayhee Shia). One day he asked my dad to give a talk to a club that he belonged to in Chinatown. Dad complied and spoke on "Humor." He noticed as he proceeded that the Chinese audience was strangely silent and hardly laughed at any of the many jokes in his talk. After he finished, the audience applauded politely and Dad sat down, thinking that he had failed to reach them. His friend, Mr. Tsieh, spoke next and Dad was puzzled to hear many outbursts of uproarious laughter throughout his talk. Later he asked his friend, "What were you talking about that made them laugh so much?" Tehyi replied, "I was just translating your speech!"

Dad also gave many lectures on law, the Bible, politics, oriental rugs, humor, mushrooms, and Shakespeare, etc. Once, at the Statler Hotel in Boston, he was emcee for the American Bar Association and I was featured as the entertainment segment. (I was using the pseudonym of Ouida Lieff, as my teacher liked the sound of Lieff better than Blatt; blatt translates as leaf in German.) It was a successful performance though I had studied only a few years. I played the Sibelius *Romance* and a Chopin *Waltz*. I was about sixteen. It was exciting, as there were 2,000 people there — mostly lawyers and judges. I wore a long, slinky gown. After I played, I was given a dozen long-stemmed roses. My dad came back on stage and announced, "I'm glad you enjoyed her, but I have to listen to her practice every day. You see, she's my daughter." The Boston Globe critic wrote, "Nearly 2,000 guests, members of the American Bar Association and their families, were entertained at a concert in the Imperial Ballroom of the Hotel Statler last evening by Ouida Blatt. She is a gifted artist and was given cordial recalls after she finished her last number."

My dad always had a witty response for everyone he talked to. One day, when he was over eighty, we met some friends while taking a walk. At the end of the conversation, one of the women said to my dad, "I hope you live to a ripe old age." He answered, "What do you mean? I'm rotten already!"

Ouida, Lucy (mom), Josie, Bill (dad), and sister, Hester

Dr. Tehyi Hsieh, our Chinese
Oxford-grad friend

Ouida at the house where she was
born in Brookline

Elly Kassman, the concert
pianist who inspired Ouida

3

INTERESTING PEOPLE

*If you are not in the big parade you can
still get lots of fun out of watching it.*
William M. Blatt

When I was a teenager, we lived on the first floor of a two
family house on Lanark Road. Many interesting people were invited to our home for dinner. My mom loved to cook and she had
some great specialties like blintzes, sweet and sour stuffed cabbage, little hot dogs and sauerkraut. David Glazer, the well known
clarinetist, and his brother Frank, the pianist, came to dinner so
frequently that we girls called them "our adopted brothers." They
came from a large family in Milwaukee. Frank taught at the Longy
School in Boston and he played the Brahms *Second Piano Concerto*
with the Boston Symphony Orchestra. His review in the New York
Times was excellent. The eminent critic, Warren Story Smith,
wrote, "Frank Glazer, with Dr. Koussevitsky to aid him, played
this greatly exacting work with a maturity of conception and ex-
ecution that might have characterized a much older head and pair
of hands. When vigor was required he had it to give, yet never was
the tone forced or hard, and the more expressive portions were
played in the true Brahmsian spirit."

The brothers often brought their friends to visit us. I remember Paul Tortelier, the great French cellist, came to the house
and loved my mother's cooking. Also, Al Capp, who did the L'il
Abner comic strip, limped in with his wooden leg; he lost his leg
in childhood and he was known for helping veteran amputees.
Mr. Al Capp was an authentic reactionary who appeared on Johnny

Carson's Tonight Show many times, where he got big laughs at the expense of some politicians. He talked and looked somewhat like L'il Abner, tall and husky, and had a slight drawl even though he was born in New Haven, Connecticut.

I was fortunate to have been brought up in a family where I had the opportunity to meet so many interesting people. Picture a musical background of Ravel's *Jeux d'Eau* set to a marionette show with my teenage sisters and me standing on a table backstage, manipulating the dolls that we had made ourselves. Josie, the artist of the family, made the most intricate marionettes. One of them resembled Marlene Dietrich, and she could move her mouth and tap her toes as well as move her arms and legs.

There was always an audience of our friends from all fields- law, politics, the arts, etc. We called upon some of them to participate in Shakespeare or one of my dad's plays by reading dialogue back-stage. Being out of sight, they could perform without being self-conscious and could fulfill any dreams they may have had of being actors. My dad was the director, sometime author, and producer, and my mom performed as well. My older sister, Hester, wrote a piece about marionettes much later for the Nantucket newspaper:

TONY SARG MAGIC

How it Touched Our Family

by

Hester Blatt Shapiro

(As published in "Historic Nantucket," the quarterly of the Nantucket Historical Association.)

For years my mother tried to sell my father's plays – long distance – to a Broadway producer. She did succeed five or six times, even to the point of advance royalties, but each time something happened – like a war, the crash, the depression – to prevent a Broadway opening. Finally, when one of his plays had been "doctored" mercilessly, my father was so frustrated that he exclaimed to his four female fans, "Let's have our own theatre! We'll have a marionette theatre and produce whatever we want to." We, in our early teens, agreed it was some kind of solution.

The first big problem was how to make the marionettes. In the not too distant past, puppeteers had been secretive about their methods. My father searched the libraries, asked around, found no practical directions. He began to experiment. What an ordeal for a lawyer-poet who couldn't turn a screwdriver without scraping a finger.

One day, however, he came home with a new book by Tony Sarg. Sarg's instructions were clear and workable. From those diagrams came our own marionettes, about fourteen inches in height, modeled after Tony Sarg's.

Our theatre was sturdy and handsome because it was custom-made by a builder, one of my father's clients. He owed him a legal fee and offered to build the theatre as payment.

My father and sister, Jo, an artist and poet, made the marionettes. I did the sets. Lucy, erstwhile actress, was casting director and coach. From the audience of thirty or more, Lucy might choose a judge, a doctor, a musician, a singer , to read the parts backstage, but not before she gave them a whirlwind lesson in elocution. (They invariably became "instant" hams.) My sister, Ouida, an accomplished musician, played piano interludes before the show and during intermission. All of us, except Lucy, worked the marionettes. Among our repertoire were reveries after three Shakespeare plays and a verse play by Billy Blatt, An Arabian Night's Tale, a Lord Dunsany one-acter. According to my father we had nearly ten thousand guests (no repeats) during the eight years that we presented the shows.

Eventually we did, of course, go our separate ways. We teen-age daughters went on to the dating game. I went into theatre in the summer and biochemical research in the winter. Ouida became a piano teacher and concert performer, and Josie did commercial and fine arts in New York City. Mom and Dad, lacking their family staff, sought other involvements.

Too few today - with the exception of those in puppetry or theatre arts - know the name, Tony Sarg. His books, his scripts, his part in our country's artistic history, should not be lost, nor should that of any prime artistic mover. Why aren't there accessible spots (notwithstanding the Library of Congress) where historic books are preserved and available to everyone. It's a shame that library shelves are over-crowded or that libraries lack funds to maintain historically important books. It's maddening to discover that books are "out of print" (at least in the five sizable libraries in which I searched). A fertile, productive future depends upon knowledge of the past. Even today, Sarg's directions would be wondrous to young people who want to experiment.

In fact, I, myself, recently found answers to some puppetry questions in a remarkable book that should never be "out of print." I refer to "The Art of the Puppet" by Bill Baird. The photographs are superb, the text engaging. Baird, an early associate of Tony Sarg gives a comprehensive view of puppetry, past and present, including anecdotes and little known facts: puppetry, an ancient art, hundreds of years old, developed in unbelievable corners of the world. Puppets were even found in Nazi concentration camps.

During the nineteenth century, traveling troupes emphasized "magic tricks" in their shows and jealously guarded their technical effects from each other as well as from the public. But by the twentieth century it became clear that puppetry could do more than simply surprise audiences.

Today, puppetry is a high art; the dramatic impact of the story and the characters is as important as theatrical effects. Tony Sarg played a crucial role in this transition to sophistication. He experimented and pioneered on his own. His audiences were stimulated to appreciate the range and scope of marionette theatre.

George Bernard Shaw and Arthur Schnitzler wrote for puppets. Paul Klee, Wassily Kandinsky, Gian-Carlo Menotti, George Sand, and many other great artists expressed themselves through puppetry. Puppetry answers man's urge to recreate life. A many-layered art, it is more diverse than painting, sculpture, dance, song or story, for it has something of all of them.

Since my mother, Lucy, was born in Kharkov in the Ukraine, I may have inherited her love for Russian music. One night, after attending a concert of the Red Army Chorus in Jordan Hall, we invited a group of the singers to come to our apartment for a midnight snack. After they had enjoyed Lucy's specialties, they all settled down and made themselves at home.

Soon they started to sing the *Internationale* and some of their folksongs. It was unbelievable to hear such beautiful voices emanating from every part of the house, all singing their songs in unison!

One friendly singer taught me how to say "I love you" in Russian (Ya Tia Bia Lu Blu). I also learned "hello" (Drasvacha) and "goodbye" (Dosvidania).

Once we had a party for some members of the Group Theatre. Lee Jay Cobb, the actor, was there and I remember playing the piano for him. He requested the César Franck *Symphonic Variations*, which was a favorite of his, and I played the solo part for him. He was very appreciative and thanked me many times. Leif Ericson, the film actor, also was there with the star, Frances Farmer, and they seemed very much in love.

The Blatt family Marionette Theatre

MY SILENT ANCESTORS

For years I played the piano and practiced for a silent audience of my ancestors who graced the walls of the living room in my family home in Brookline.

There were five life-size paintings of my father's mother's father and other ancient relatives, some of the men are wearing yarmulkes. These were some of the first paintings of Jewish immigrants to be done by American artists.

I remember practicing day after day for this stern audience who surrounded our mahogany grand piano. If I could play for this solemn room-full of people, I could take on the worst of critics. It was an excellent place to rehearse for a concert.

Since we three girls showed no interest in owning these valuable art works, my dad offered them to the Jewish Museum in New York City, where they now reside in all their glory.

4

PLAYING VIOLIN
WITH MIKE WALLACE

We are such stuff as dreams are made on,
And our little life is rounded with a sleep.
Shakespeare, "The Taming of the Shrew."

The "60-Minute" star, Mike Wallace, whom I knew as Myron, played a duet with me in a concert when we were students of Harry Ellis Dickson. Dickson is the father-in-law of Michael Dukakis, and was also assistant conductor to Arthur Fiedler at the Boston Pops. One time, Mike and I were supposed to play a duet at a recital at the home of our new teacher, Mr. Budd. We took a long street car ride to go there for the rehearsal. I must admit it was not easy working with Mike as he was very particular about getting the music just right. When the day of the recital arrived, on a beautiful Sunday in August, my parents gave me an option: would I like to go to Winthrop Beach with them to visit friends and go swimming, or would I prefer to play the violin duet with Mike at the recital? Well, of course, since it was a lovely summer day, there was not much choice as to which would be more fun. I suspect they would feel obligated to attend if I decided to play. Recitals are mostly for the purpose of allowing parents to observe the progress their children are making in their music lessons. I doubt that my folks wanted to attend, as they didn't drive and it would be a difficult trip. My mother called Mr. Budd who most accommodatingly agreed to play my part with Mike. I still felt guilty, but I guess that, with the participation of my folks, I came out looking like a spoiled brat.

I played first violin in the high school orchestra, but I was never an outstanding violinist, although I studied with two violin teachers during one year. It was rather confusing; my mom thought I'd learn twice as fast! One teacher played in the Boston Symphony Orchestra.

Now, these many years later, I have so much admiration for Mike Wallace's accomplishments. I always watch him on "Sixty Minutes," the award-winning news show on CBS, with a great deal of pride that I knew him when we played violin together, and later when we attended Brookline High School. We continued to play violin in the high school orchestra. I recall that when he was quite young he had a tendency to stutter, as did his sister, Helen. She later married the eminent first violinist of the Boston Symphony Orchestra, Alfred Krips. By the time Mike was a senior, he was chosen to take part in several of the high school plays. He spoke flawlessly, which in retrospect seems to have been a portent of his future role on TV.

When he was in college he discovered that broadcasting was the medium for him. He wanted to be an announcer and do commercials, which he later did at WXYZ Radio in Detroit, and was the announcer on the "Green Hornet." During World War II he joined the Navy and was shipped to Australia where he acted in training films, in one of which he sold insurance to sailors.

After the war he went to Chicago where he did a radio series called, "For the Love of Mike." That was when he had decided to change his name to Mike, which fit him better than Myron. Among his many pursuits at that time were voice-overs on radio commercials, as well as announcing the Colgate Comedy Hour in 1951. Eventually, he graduated to television and did a show called "Nightbeat" where he did interviews. He said the show fit him like a glove. Some of the people he interviewed were Rod Serling, William Buckley, Adam Clayton Powell, and Hugh Hefner. When he asked "Hef" if he respected girls who would pose in the nude in his magazine, he answered, "Of course I do." Later Mike admitted that he must have been a prude for asking that. He also interviewed John Kennedy, Kirk Douglas, and Jack Benny, with whom he did a skit in which Mike grilled Benny about why he continued to earn so much money. Benny cowered in defense and said pathetically with his hands raised, "Because I haven't got it all!"

Mike said that Salvador Dali was the weirdest celebrity he ever interviewed, and Louis Farrakand, the wildest. Vladimir Horowitz was very agreeable when Mike interviewed him in his home and got him to play many pieces including his own arrangement of the *Stars and Stripes Forever*. A few minutes before he played, he had protested that he couldn't remember it, but then proceeded to play it flawlessly.

CBS Photo

Mike Wallace

5

MEETING HEINRICH GEBHARD
AND LEONARD BERNSTEIN

*Life is a series of doors. We open one and expect
to find truth, but all we find is another door.*
William M. Blatt

My mom's philosophy was that it is a privilege to strive,
and she pursued it to the hilt. One Friday afternoon after a piano
lesson, Helen Wallace mentioned to my mother that she was able
to get an audition with the great pianist and teacher, Heinrich
Gebhard, who was a disciple of the eminent teacher, Theodore
Leschetizky. Among Gebhard's most prominent students was the
prolific composer, Alan Hovhaness, who wrote the "Mysterious
Mountain" symphony. That's all Mom needed. She subsequently
called Gebhard and made an appointment for me to play for him.
I was very impressed with the way he put me at ease so I wouldn't
be nervous. Gebhard was very encouraging and said he could hardly
believe I had only studied the piano for less than two years. He
told us that he had never taught anyone so young and inexperienced, but he would like to have me study with one of his assistants, Helen Coates, with the understanding that I could study
with him eventually. The next day, Mom called Gebhard and told
a white lie. She said I hadn't slept all night as I was very upset that
I had been rejected. She made a deal with him: if he would teach
me, she would give expression lessons to his only child, Peggy, and
my sister, Jo, would give her lessons in making marionettes. He

couldn't resist a deal like that and promised to start my lessons in the fall. I was sworn to secrecy when he said that he would teach me for only three dollars a lesson; his usual rate was a high one for those days - fifteen dollars per hour. There I was, a little fourteen year old girl ready to be taught by one of the country's finest teachers, all because of that clever agent — my mom. Of course my sweet sister, Jo, was willing to help out by teaching Peggy how to make marionettes. What an angel she was to teach her every Saturday morning for two years. Gebhard was very generous with his time and would often extend a lesson to as much as two hours if a student was inspired. One summer, he even gave me the keys to his house so that I could practice on his fine Mason & Hamlin piano. I was then preparing for an important concert with orchestra.

Heinrich Gebhard

Gebhard's home,
where Ouida met Lenny

Heinrich Gebhard came to the United States from Cologne, Germany, as a boy of eight. He studied piano with Clayton Johns in Boston until he was seventeen. He then went to Vienna where he completed his piano studies under Leschetitzky, while also studying composition under Heuberger. Gebhard returned to Boston where he made his debut as a soloist with the Boston Symphony Orchestra in 1900. His solo career took him to all of the great orchestras of this country and abroad for appearances that spanned close to forty years. He introduced Loeffler's *Pagan Poem* and D'Indy's *Symphony on a French Mountain Air* to this country in concerts with the Boston Symphony and played in many solo and chamber music recitals. He played the *Pagan Poem* sixty-six times with nine different orchestras.

Gebhard also introduced his own *Fantasy for Piano and Orchestra* with Mengelberg and the New York Philharmonic, as well as his *Divertissement for Piano and Chamber Orchestra* in Boston under Nicolas Slonimsky, who was a unique man of music. My mother and I used to hear Slonimsky lecture regularly, and he was always very amusing; he could play the piano with his back to the keyboard, and he hit most of the right notes. One night he surprised the audience by playing Chopin's *Black Key Etude* with an orange, rolling it with his right hand on the black keys while his left hand played the harmony. This orange trick made a vivid impression on me as a kid. He could also play the Chopin *Minute Waltz* in forty three seconds.

He wrote a fascinating life story called, "Perfect Pitch," which begins, "When I was six years old my mother told me I was a genius," and he describes his adolescence of longings for immortality, sex and death. His "Music in America since 1900," was another successful book. He longed for a career as a great concert pianist, composer and conductor, but never reached his goal. However, he stumbled into a distinguished career as a famous musical lexicographer; he edited the Baker's "Biographical Dictionary of Musicians."

Slonimsky married Dorothy Adlow, who was the art critic of the Christian Science Monitor, and they had a daughter, Electra. Dorothy's brother was the well-known judge, Elijah Adlow, who was a very good friend of my dad's.

He organized a chamber orchestra which was recruited from members of the Boston Symphony. It was called the Chamber Orchestra of Boston. Gebhard's *Divertissement for Piano and Chamber Orchestra* was featured at their first performance. Slonimsky was so self-conscious that he could hardly concentrate on the music. These Boston players were able to perform with an inadequate leader because of their years of experience. Gebhard played his piece brilliantly and Slonimsky followed his tempo. H.T. Parker, the Transcript critic, who was known from his initials as "Hard to Please" and "Hell to Pay," gave it a devastating review under the headline, "Modern Concert Conductor Clearly at His Beginning. Mr. Gebhard's Piece Saved the Evening."

Aaron Copland and George Gershwin were very good friends of Slonimsky's. It's interesting to note that in the spring of 1927, Copland played his own *Jazz Concerto* with the Boston Symphony under Koussevitzky. Philip Hale, the prominent Boston critic, panned it in his review, but in the Boston Transcript, H.T. Parker suggested that Copland may be a representative of a new and genuine American music. Because Koussevitsky championed his music, it helped Copland become one of the greatest composers of this century.

During an intermission at a New York Koussevitzsky concert, Slonimsky introduced Copland to Gershwin. This was a historic meeting as both composers were innovators who combined classical music with jazz.

Slonimsky went backstage after the first performance of Gershwin's opera, *Porgy and Bess*. Gershwin, being in a lighthearted mood, recited a satirical ditty about four fiddlers, Jascha, Mischa, Sascha and Toscha, "whose tone was sour until a man, Professor Auer, came right along and taught 'em all how to pack 'em in Carnegie Hall. They were not lowbrows, they were not highbrows, they were Hebrews."

One of the unspoken secrets of Koussevitzky's tenure with the Boston Symphony Orchestra was that Nicolas Slonimsky was an invaluable help to this great Russian conductor on a daily basis. Koussevitzky invited Slonimsky to leave Rochester's Eastman School of Music to be his bilingual secretary, as well as his rehearsal pianist for the big sum of fifty dollars a week plus meals, which was considered quite generous in 1925. Slonimsky also went to Paris with him in the summer.

Koussevitsky needed help in the conducting of Stravinsky's *Le Sacre du Printemps*, and because it was so complicated, Slonimsky rebarred the score to simplify the conducting. Lenny Bernstein used the same score when he conducted *Le Sacre* with the Boston Symphony Orchestra. On Slonimsky's ninetieth birthday, Lenny wrote a letter to his friend, acknowledging the work he did, and said he "admired and revered him."

Although Koussevitzky never finished his formal education, he founded the Berkshire School of Music at Tanglewood, Massachusetts for young people who wanted to study singing, various instruments, or conducting. Leonard Bernstein and Lukas Foss are among its distinguished graduates.

Serge Koussevitsky, unlike most foreign conductors, championed the work of American composers, introducing symphonies of William Schuman, Roy Harris and David Diamond. Aaron Copland's *El Salon Mexico* was given its American premier in 1938 by Koussevitsky and the Boston Symphony Orchestra. It was received with great acclaim and described as an "American Bolero."

Koussevitsky also introduced Bernstein's *Jeremiah Symphony*, and later on, the Koussevitzky Foundation commissioned works such as Lenny's *Kaddish Symphony* in 1955. Also when Sibelius's symphonies were being neglected, he scheduled them on his regular BSO subscription concerts.

Koussevitzky died in 1951 and was buried in Tanglewood. The previous year, he had conducted several concerts in Israel and seemed proud to be Jewish, although in earlier days he appeared to cover it up. Later, he even signed "Shalom" at the end of his letters.

In 1956, a sudden piece of luck came Slonimsky's way in the form of a TV Quiz show called "The Big Surprise," similar to the "Sixty Four Thousand Dollar Question."

Mike Wallace was the MC and Lenny's sister, Shirley, was the producer. Slonimsky had a fund of knowledge which almost enabled him to reach the top prize of $100,000. He became recognizable to the public after being on the show for two weeks, and he actually won $19,000 after taxes, which was a windfall for him. At last, Slonimsky became a celebrity of sorts - something he had never achieved during his long lifetime in music.

He was considered a martyr for the cause of new music, which he conducted most of his life - and because of that, he was thought of as a dangerous musical revolutionary. He is remembered for his promotion of the works of modern composers, namely, Edgar Varese, Charles Ives, Paul Creston, Wallingford Riegger, Henry Cowell, William Schuman, Elie Siegmeister, Arnold Schoenberg, and Frank Zappa.

At the time my mother and I attended the lecture series of Slonimsky, I had just started studying with Heinrich Gebhard. I recall being so excited that I was sitting in the front row of Symphony Hall in Boston and hearing my teacher play Vincent D'Indy's *Symphony on a French Mountain Air* so magnificently with the Boston Symphony under Koussevitsky. He was in his sixties at the time and this was also his last performance with orchestra; from then on he devoted his time to teaching and composing. Olin Downes, in the New York Times, wrote of Gebhard, "--- there are few who equal him in musicianship and the finer qualities of interpretation."

ano teachers of the last century. He was born in Poland in 1830 and died in Dresden, Germany in 1915. I always tell my students that we go back to Haydn, who taught Beethoven, who taught Czerny, who taught Leschetizky. I say to my students, "This wonderful musician, Leschetizky, taught my teacher, Gebhard, who handed down this heritage to me, Ouida Mintz, who is now teaching you," and I mention the student's name. Beside Gebhard, Leschetizky taught Ignace Paderewski (he later became premier of Poland), Elly Ney, Mark Hambourg, Ossip Gabrilovich, Ignatz Friedman, Benno Moiseivich, and many other notable pianists. Leschetizky also composed forty-nine piano pieces as well as two operas.

I believe that Leschetizky was similar to my teacher in that he taught according to the needs of each student, but he was much more demanding than Gebhard and had a gruff manner. He gave regular concerts at which his students played, a practice that my teacher followed; they both felt it was the only way to get used to performing. At the end of each program, a student played a well-known piano concerto with the teacher playing the orchestra part on a second piano, which in Gebhard's case was a Mason & Hamlin, the piano he preferred most of all because of its rich tone.

Leonard Bernstein was then a young aspiring musician living in the Boston area who had decided he wanted to study with Gebhard. He auditioned but was rejected because, as Mr. Gebhard explained to me, he had talent, but hadn't practiced enough and was "faking some of it." Gebhard recommended that he study with Helen Coates, his assistant. It wasn't long before Helen reported to Gebhard that Lenny had great talent and that he should be studying with him, which he soon did. Little did Lenny know at the time that Helen would eventually give up her work in Boston to become his life-long secretary in New York.

The first piece that Gebhard assigned to me was the third movement of the *Moonlight Sonata* which was quite a challenge but very good for the technique. I went on to play the Beethoven

Opus 10 #3 Sonata which I performed at one of his recital classes.

At Gebhard's recitals, Lenny, his friend Mildred Spiegel, and I usually sat together when we weren't performing. After the concert we would adjourn to the dining room for light refreshments. I still have etched in my memory Lenny's casual remark at about age fifteen, when he said he thought his career would be in music.

I progressed with Gebhard to the point of learning the Mendelssohn *Piano Concerto in G Minor*, among other works of great composers such as Chopin, Bach, and later, Brahms. I was happy just to be able to play the Mendelssohn *Concerto* with Gebhard doing the orchestra on the second piano, which we also played at one of Gebhard's home recitals. My mom and dad were very impressed that I could play a major concerto after only four years of study.

At that time I used to listen to Abram Chasin's radio program every week on WQXR, the classical station in New York, of which he was the music director for many years. On the program, he played solo piano pieces and discussed the interpretation of them. Sometimes he played his own compositions. I had to put my ear up to the radio to hear, as I lived in Brookline, Massachusetts then — quite a distance from New York City. I wrote to Mr. Chasins about how much his music (especially his own theme song) inspired me, and surprisingly I received an immediate answer. After I wrote to him again, we soon became pen pals; I still have his cards and letters.

One day, when my family was visiting New York, my dad decided to treat me to the show in person. He explained to the man in charge that we were friends of Mr. Chasins, so he let us sit in the balcony and watch. Surprisingly, no one else was there and we enjoyed hearing him with his student, Constance Keene, later his wife. I noticed we got some stares from Mr. Chasins; as it turned out, he never allowed anyone to attend his program. After the show, we went downstairs to talk to him and he was very cordial when he learned that I was his pen pal from Brookline.

Here are two of the postcards he wrote to me in response to my questions:

Oct. 15th, 1936

Dear Miss Blatt:

Many thanks for your interesting letter and it's enclosures. I was very glad to hear of your activities and accomplishments. In Mr. Gebhard you have a distinguished master. My programs are arranged pretty far in advance, but I found room this coming Sat. for one of your Chopin requests, the *F minor Nocturne*. Some fifty people from every corner of our country requested it within two weeks. Strange, and gratifying! I shall try to do the Beethoven *C minor Concerto* with a second piano that should be interesting, and I would spread it over two sessions. With best wishes and thanks,

Sincerely,
Abram Chasins

May 3, 1937

Dear Miss Blatt:

Will answer you at greater length when I am less pressed for time, but now will answer your question.

One can easily keep all three pedals down - the Sostenuto and the left pedal taken by the left foot slanting toward the body. A little practice will make this an easy stunt, one that you can use to enormous effect - more than you can at the moment realize.

Sincerely yours,
Abram Chasins

This special pedaling was used in his *Prelude in E flat minor*, the theme song of his show.

About five years later, I renewed my friendship with Abram Chasins at Tanglewood, and I remember standing next to him listening to the Tschaikowsky *1812 Overture* being played by the Boston Symphony Orchestra. He exclaimed, "This is one of the greatest masterpieces ever written." Incidentally, Chasins was quite a composer himself. He wrote a great deal of piano music, one of his most popular being *Rush hour in Hong Kong*. It's still one of my favorite piano pieces as is his *Prelude in E flat minor*.

Meanwhile, I had been teaching Gebhard's daughter, Peggy. She hadn't done well with his teaching assistants, so her dad decided to try me out as her teacher, as she had become too grown-up for marionette lessons with my sister. She progressed very well and learned the Sibelius *Romance* among other pieces. We began a life-long friendship and I spent two weeks with her at Bailey Island, Maine; "Gebby" composed there in a little cabin in the woods. When the piano was played there, the woods resounded with the most beautiful tones you could imagine. I can still hear my friend and fellow student, Norma Bertolami, playing *Notturno* by Respighi with its haunting harmonies wafting through the air.

After I had performed the Mendelssohn *Concerto* at Gebhard's monthly concert, with Gebhard at the second piano, my mother thought I would like to play it with orchestra. She called Harry Ellis Dickson, my former violin teacher, who conducted a small orchestra on the radio and asked if I could audition for him, which I did shortly afterwards, but he could never believe I had become an accomplished pianist in such a short time.

Abram Chasins and his wife, pianist Constance Keene.
He was a radio pioneer, music director of WQXR
in New York, a fine pianist, author, and composer

I soon had an opportunity to take part in a performance of a very different kind.

SNOW WHITE AND THE SEVEN PROFS

*One bite of the artistic bug and you never again
will have a normal temperature.*
William M. Blatt

My dad was afraid I couldn't make a living in music so he insisted that I take a secretarial course in the last year of high school. I did this under protest. I found the course extremely boring and hated hearing a roomful of people hitting keys and making only a tremendous clatter instead of music. I used my typing and shorthand skills for just one summer when I took the place of the main secretary at Boston University College of Music, who was on sabbatical leave. It was hectic being secretary, not only to the Dean (Marshall), but also to the Registrar and any other professor who needed a letter typed. Though I had studied Gregg shorthand, I used my own abbreviation-type shorthand just to be sure I got the words right. My touch typing was more dependable.

At the end of the summer session, the Boston University faculty put on a show called *Snow White and the Seven Profs*, a take-off on the Disney story. I was Snow White and had to sing duets with my prince charming, who was to become the Dean of the Boston University Business School — Professor J. Wendell Yeo. At the end of the show, the "professor dwarfs" and the audience watched as Snow White and the Prince rode off down the aisle on a tandem bike singing *I Have But One Song*.

There was dancing after the show, and it made me feel so happy when the people I danced with told me how much they enjoyed the show, and of course my mom had the Boston Globe there to report and take pictures for the morning paper.

Boston University Summer Session

ANNUAL FAREWELL PARTY

Thursday evening, August 4, at 8 0'clock

SODEN BUILDING, Exeter Street, Boston

I.   Piano solo ....Allegrine Guez

II.   Reading ....Miriam Cahalan

III.   Impersonations ....Mary Jayne Wheatley

IV.   Snow White and the Seven Profs

Snow White ....Ouida Blatt
Prince Charming ....Professor J. Wendell Yeo
Grumpy ....Professor Rufus Stickney
Bashful ....Professor William G. Sutcliffe
Sleepy ....Professor Charles P. Huse
Happy ....Mr. Charles Palumbo
Sneezy ....Professor John M. Harmon
Doc ....Professor George B. Franklin
Dopey ....Professor Noel P. Laird
Accompanist . ...Elinore E. Cole

V.   Dancing ....Bill Higgens Orchestra

Entertainment Committee

Carla Passke   Co- Chairmen
Dr. Noel P. Laird

Prof. Rufus Stickney   Eleanor R. Moselely
Prof. William G. Hoffman   Prof. William G Sutlciffe

Music by Dizzy __ Verses by Everybody __ Script by Somebody
Gags by Nobody __ Suggestions by Everybody __Rehearsals by Proxy
Worry by Mosely & Passke __ Gowns by CBA Bookstore __ Props by
WPA Subway Project __ Coaching bye and bye __ Exits by Request

6

PLAYING CONCERTI, AND LETTERS FROM "GEBBY"

Start the job, and power and joy will come to you.
William M. Blatt

One Sunday afternoon, my mom heard the State Symphony Orchestra concert at the Brookline shell under Alexander Thiede (Teeda), a young, talented conductor. At the end of the concert, she went up to Mr. Thiede and told him that she had a talented sixteen year old daughter (me) who would love to play the Mendelssohn *Concerto in G minor* with him. Upon learning that Gebhard was my teacher, he asked my mom to have him write a note about my qualities and then he would set up an audition in Gebhard's house using his second grand piano for the orchestra part.

Two weeks later, the day arrived for the big audition. I was so nervous because this was my first opportunity to play a concerto with orchestra under a fine conductor. When I first started to play, I noticed that my fingers were trembling a bit from the excitement of the moment. Fortunately, I came through with flying colors, and Thiede accepted me. Gebhard was determined to get me into perfect shape for the scheduled concert and gave me many extra lessons to prepare me. The concert took place in a tremendous hall, Nevins Memorial, in Framingham, Massachusetts. My sister, Jo, was backstage to comfort me with her moral support. Before I went onstage I peeked out to see how the concert grand was placed. When I suggested to Mr. Thiede that the piano should be turned more toward the audience, he answered by saying, "Young lady, I don't care if that piano is on the ceiling, your job is to go out and play it!" I needed that tough attitude because I was so nervous that he literally had to push me onto the stage.

As far as the audience was concerned, it was a fine performance, but, in fact, at the end of the first movement during the dozen or so measures of trilling with the orchestra, I accidentally left out two of them. To my surprise, Mr. Thiede immediately conducted in double time so that the orchestra was with me on my next phrase. He warned me not to make that mistake again. The Framingham News said, "The soloist looked like a little girl in a long dress. She displayed a masterly technique .... The applause was prolonged and the young musician returned for several bows." Not bad for only four years of study.

I was booked to perform the concerto again at the same outdoor shell in Brookline at Dean Road Park where my mother had first heard Thiede. Gebhard was on vacation and not able to attend this performance, but his sister and Peggy did, and she reported to Gebby. Here is his note from Bailey Island, Maine:

                                        Aug 17, '36
My Dear Ouida,
     With heavenly joy I read your letter and
all the programs and the postal card included.
     Congratulations on your big success!
     I even received a short letter from my
sister who told me even more- that the
audience applauded tremendously at the end
of the concerto and that the orchestra applauded and Mr. Thiede immensely pleased, -
and you really played wonderfully. You see,
you were too modest in your account of your
own performance.

I am simply delighted, and you deserve every bit of your success.

It was lovely of you to write me such a minute account of everything - including your suffering! But this was your first time, - it will be easier each next time.

I am proud of you, and now at Dean Road I want to be just as proud, and I know I shall be.

Here are best wishes for Tuesday night! I'll be with you in spirit!

Your teacher and friend,
Heinrich Gebhard

After I repeated my performance of the Mendelssohn *G Minor Concerto* at the Dean Road Park, I received this letter from Gebhard:

Heinrich Gebhard
"The Restabit"
Bailey Island, Maine

Sept, 18, 1936

My Dear Louise,

During the last week I received both of your long letters. Many thanks! It was charming of you to write me at such great length. I read it all with great interest.

You are very modest about your performance at Dean Road Park. Mildred Spiegel and others wrote me that you did wonderfully! So once more congratulations! — Meanwhile I feel you should learn the Beethoven *C Minor Concerto*. It will suit you. You may also study the Cesar Franck *Variations* at the same time!—-

It was very charming of you and
your family to ask Margaret (Peggy) and
Marguerite for supper. I am sure they enjoyed the evening with you very much. What
you have "thought out" in connection with
the lessons you are giving Margaret, is fine.
As soon as I see you I will arrange a time,
outside of your lessons when I'll tell you
still more about how to teach her - I know
you will be excellent for Margaret. Please
tell your splendid father that I read over
most carefully his "Introduction to Boston."
I think it is written in most fascinating
style and I learned a lot which I never
knew!

Kindest regards to you and all your
family.

Your,
Heinrich Gebhard

I never expected to get a call from my conductor, Alexander Thiede, one day, asking me if I would like to play the Mendelssohn *Concerto* again - this time at the famous Jordan Hall of the New England Conservatory of Music. I was very excited at the mention of this hall where I had heard some of the greatest artists in the world; lieder singers, string quartets and pianists like Myra Hess, and Jan Smeterlin, the Chopin specialist, as well as violinist Nathan Milstein. I remember what a thrill it was to meet Harold Bauer, the virtuoso pianist, to whom I was introduced by Gebhard back-stage after a concert.

I even surprised myself when I suggested to Mr. Thiede that I play the Beethoven *Third Piano Concerto*, which I was work-ing on at the time and would have a couple of months to master before the concert was scheduled. I felt that this would be a greater challenge to me, and Mr. Gebhard fortunately agreed. It was won-derful of him because it meant he would have to give me extra lessons, mostly at night, in which he played the orchestra part on his second piano, so I would know where the piano entrances were, and also to become familiar with the orchestra part. But that wasn't all he did, of course. I had to go over and over the difficult passages and play them the way Gebhard wanted them to sound.

He always gave me the feeling that I had the ability to accomplish this without praising me too much. I had had so little experience at the time; I was just eighteen years old. It would be only the third time I played with orchestra, and in such a prestigious hall! I didn't feel I was ready for this with only one rehearsal. It was also scary to know that the critics were poised to write down their honest opinions for the morning newspapers.

I remember how I felt the day I was to play. I thought, "I don't HAVE to do this. How easy it would be to jump out of my third floor window and avoid all the turmoil going on in my brain." It was the most frightening thing I had ever experienced. When I got to the hall I thought, "How am I going to do it?" Would I be able to remember the entrances? It also helped to remember what Gebhard once said to me, "It may help you to relax if you think of the audience as a bunch of cabbage heads."

As usual, my sister, Jo, was backstage to give me moral support. Good old dependable Josie. "Gebby" and some of the top critics were in the audience. Lenny was backstage chanting, "Ouida's (Weeda's) going to play with Thiede (Teeda)." He had never, up to then, experienced the thrill of playing with orchestra, and I expect he was a bit jealous. Even Harry Ellis Dickson, my former violin teacher, who had turned me down at my audition for playing with his orchestra, was a violin soloist in the same series (sweet revenge).

I walked shakily onto the tremendous stage in my taffeta, fuschia gown, gave a low bow with my head down, as I had been taught, and sat down at the nine foot concert grand. It seemed to me that the orchestral introduction to this concerto took an endless amount of time, but it was probably about three or four minutes -- just enough time for me to survey my awesome surroundings -- the audience, orchestra and conductor, all waiting to hear my opening notes. Before I knew it, I was sailing along and finally came to the cadenza, the solo part where my playing was completely exposed with no orchestra to back me up.

It was especially hard as I was playing without my glasses for the first time, something Gebhard had suggested. Even though I had no need to read music, it was a pretty daring thing to do as I had never tried it before. I think it might have helped me as everything looked so hazy, and I guess it kept me from the reality of it all.

At the moment of performance, I was immersed in the intense feelings which Beethoven might have had when creating this masterpiece. It was almost like being in a hypnotic trance. My memory came through, with my fingers almost playing by themselves all that I had been practicing for so many months. It's beforehand that one is nervous, but when I actually started to play, that feeling almost disappeared. I got carried away with the music and even forgot that I was on stage in front of a large audience and several critics. About one hundred instrumentalists in the orchestra depended upon me to inspire them to play their hearts out.

When the first movement ended with loud chords, the audience applauded, although that is usually frowned upon. I had to stand up to bow in response. I always thought there was nothing wrong in applauding to express your feelings after an exciting first movement of a concerto, and Mr. Gebhard felt the same way.

The whole thing went fine and took about one half hour. When it was over, I was still in a daze. I couldn't believe I had played those thousands of notes with all the interpretation, crescendos, diminuendos, pedal and feeling that was demanded.

Fortunately the critics liked it too. The Boston Transcript reviewer wrote of my performance, "Ouida Blatt, who was soloist with the State Symphony Orchestra in Jordan Hall playing the Beethoven *Concerto in C minor*, displayed an uncommonly good talent for proper pacing; and she succeeded through this ability, in capturing the more delicate nuances- particularly in the Largo where her carefully executed pianissimos were outstanding." The Boston Globe had this to say, "Miss Ouida Blatt was soloist on an ambitious and satisfying program. In the first and last movements (the *Allegrò Con Brio* and *Rondo Allegro*) Miss Blatt performed with expertness. The orchestra's accompaniment was admirable. To Mr. Thiede and Miss Blatt an appreciative audience offered eloquent approval."

I realize now that it took at least three people to make it possible for a young kid like me to accomplish a dream - my mom, who asked a conductor named Alexander Thiede to audition me (he had the guts to take a chance on an inexperienced young pianist), and my patient and dedicated teacher, Gebhard. They made it all come true.

After this tremendously emotional experience of the most important performance of my career so far, I couldn't help but ask myself the question: Did I want to spend the rest of my life preparing for concerts and traveling all over the place with all the tension and stress it involves, or did I want to be a normal person who settles down with the ideal husband and raises some adorable children who, of course, will be music lovers, or perhaps even musicians. I'd have to think about that.

While we were still teenagers, Lenny and I tried out for a contest at Jordan Hall in Boston. The prize was a Mason & Hamlin grand piano. Before our turns to play, we were holding hands and shaking with anxiety. Lenny played his main piece at the time, *Malaguena* by Lecuona; and I did the Chopin *Scherzo in B flat Minor*. Neither of us won the prize. Even now I can remember the name of the winner, Edith Stearn. She was a fine pianist who was a good friend, and went to Boston University College of Music with me.

Another contest we entered several years later took place in Boston Garden under the sponsorship of The Boston Herald and RCA Victor Records. The idea was to be able to recognize recorded excerpts from the classics which were played for the audience. Lenny and I received high marks on the written answers and were eligible for the second and third parts which took place in Boston Symphony Hall.

Before the finals, I decided to bone up in the Boston Music Store on Boylston Street. I spent one whole day playing records and memorizing melodies. By this time I had met my future husband, Samson Mintz. I wanted Sam to meet Lenny, so we invited him and his sister, Shirley, for a day at Revere Beach, a Coney Island-type amusement park. Lenny gathered all the little kids he could find on the beach and played games such as London Bridge is Falling Down. Then we went on the highest roller coaster I had ever seen. If I had known how terrifying those twists and turns, ups and downs, were going to be, I would never have taken that ride. I was fighting it all the way and became sick as a dog when it finally landed. But Lenny decided to go back on again, and he turned himself around in the seat and rode backwards for a new thrill. I found out later that roller coasters were a passion with him.

While sitting on the beach, Lenny asked me to sing some melodies I had learned from my day in the music store. One that I hummed for him was the slow movement of the Brahms *Violin Concerto*, which he had never heard. Sure enough, it was one of the excerpts played in the finals, and Lenny got it right. It was a trick question because it had a long orchestral introduction, and the solo violin doesn't enter for ten minutes. My research served me well also; our pictures were in the papers the next day. What is so ironic is that quite a few years later I saw him conduct that same Brahms *Concerto* with Jascha Heifetz, who was considered the greatest violinist of the day.

I placed highest among the women and won several record albums. In those days it was accepted to differentiate between men and women, as the feminist movement had not arrived. Lenny won second prize which consisted of a trip to Tanglewood. Since he already had a scholarship to study there, they substituted an alternative prize – to conduct a concert of the Boston Pops Orchestra at the Esplanade, replacing Arthur Fiedler. This was his first experience conducting an orchestra; he got an ovation and was he elated! He had invited all the friends he had ever known to come to this big event to share his joy.

It just occurred to me that I gave some impetus to his career when Sam and I took him to that contest which led to his first conducting experience. Because I studied with Gebhard before Lenny did, I had the opportunity to play the Mendelssohn and Beethoven *Concerti* with the State Symphony under Alexander Thiede. As a matter of fact, it wasn't long before he played with the same conductor and orchestra in Jordan Hall, as I had done the year before. I played the Beethoven *Third Concerto* and he played the Beethoven *First* later on.

One afternoon at Tanglewood, while a few of us were sunning ourselves at the lake, Lenny, whose head was resting on my lap, looked up at me and said, "I have a problem. I can't decide whether to be a pianist or a conductor. If I made a career of being a pianist I'd be one of many, but if I were to be a conductor, I'd have a chance to study with Koussevitzky and become more important. Koussy wants me to change my name to Leonard S. Berns, because he thinks I would be more successful with that name rather than Bernstein, which is too Jewish sounding." I knew Lenny was proud to be Jewish when he said, "I'll keep my name and become both a conductor and a pianist,"

Incidentally, he was a stickler on the pronunciation of his family name. Once, someone mispronounced his name and called him "Bernsteen," which he hated. He retorted, "Did you ever hear of an Albert Einsteen?"

Later, Dmitri Mitropoulos, gave encouragement to Lenny's decision to be a conductor. One night there was a reception for Mitropoulous at a private home after he conducted a concert of the New York Philharmonic. Mitropoulous heard Lenny play a Chopin *Nocturne*, and he was so impressed with his interpretation that he urged him to consider conducting as a career. I wasn't there, but Lenny told me later about how excited he was that Mitropoulous was so enthusiastic.

In the early days of Tanglewood, my sister, Hes, and I hung out with Lenny, Lukas Foss, Harold Shapero, and other aspiring musicians. We ate meals together in a local restaurant where there was a tinny upright piano that we liked to play. Lukas Foss was a prodigy who started composing when he was very young. I came across one of his piano pieces in a music book which he wrote when he was fifteen. It was amazing how professionally this piece was written.

After Lukas and his family fled Nazi Germany and came to this country, he and Lenny followed similar paths. They both attended Curtis Institute in Philadelphia and studied conducting with Fritz Reiner, and piano with Isabelle Vengerova (Slonimsky's aunt). Lukas Foss then continued with Koussevitzky at Tanglewood and Paul Hindemith at Yale.

Foss is an innovator in music and founded The Improvisation Chamber Ensemble. He also wrote *Time Cycle*, which his friend, Lenny, conducted with the New York Philharmonic, and even repeated after the first performance.

Lukas Foss

After that "First Performance" *Time Cycle* received the 1961 Critics Circle Award, and was recorded by Columbia Records.

Foss has been Music Director of the Buffalo Philharmonic and the Milwaukee Symphony, and for many years of the Brooklyn Philharmonic, where he conducted the music of living composers as well as some of his own works, such as *Baroque Variations* for orchestra in 1967, *Echoi, Paradigm* and *Solo Observed* for chamber ensemble, considered to be very important additions to contemporary music.

He has been composer-in-residence at Harvard University, Tanglewood, The Manhattan School of Music, Yale, Carnegie-Mellon and Boston Universities.

In 1983, he was elected American Academy and Institute of Arts and Letters. He is now a Vice Chancellor of that prestigious Instute. Foss also holds eight honorary doctorates.

Lukas Foss has been a guest conductor of the New York Philharmonic, the Boston Symphony Orchestra, the Chicago Symphony, the Cleveland Orchestra, the Los Angeles Philharmonic, the Philadelphia Orchestra, and the San Francisco Symphony.

Abroad, he has conducted the Berlin and Tokyo Philharmonic Orchestras, the Leningrad and London Symphony Orchestras and the Santa Cecilia Orchestra of Rome.

Mr. Foss lives in New York City with his artist wife Cornelia, and their son and daughter.

Charles Munch, French
conductor of the BSO

Bohislav Martinu, eminent
Czechoslovakian composer

Ruth Posselt, concert violinist,
wife of Richard Burgin,
concertmaster of the BSO

Jorge Bolet, a great pianist, signed
this for Ouida at Tanglewood

66

Jerome Robbins, who died of a stroke in July 1998, became famous at about the same time as his good friend and collaborator, Leonard Bernstein. It all started with the success of the ballet, *Fancy Free*, which featured three sailors on the loose in New York City. Oliver Smith, its designer, suggested that Lenny and Jerry expand it into the musical that resulted in *On the Town*, which became a hit on Broadway in December, 1944. Audiences needed some relief from the devastating war that was going on at that time, and this story about sailors on leave did the trick.

Later in 1946, I saw Robbins' ballet with Bernstein's music, *Facsimile*. It almost led to Robbins' marriage with its female star, Nora Kaye, but the engagement was called off, and he never married.

Jerome Robbins' name was changed legally by his dad in the forties from Rabinowitz to Robbins. He grew up in New York City surrounded by a great deal of culture, as many Jewish families did. His older sister, Sonya, took modern dance lessons with Felicia Sorel and Gluck Andor. Jerry took some lessons and was very impressed with Sorel's imagination and her focus on the audience. Robbins felt that classic ballet would make a comeback, though modern dance was predominant in the thirties. He went to NYU majoring in chemistry, but left in a year as he ran out of money, because his dad's corset business began to go downhill.

Jerry Robbins had two distinct sides to his personality; he could be gruff and exacting on the one hand, and at other times he could be warm and relaxed. Chita Rivera said of him after he died, "I loved and adored him; I've lost a father, teacher, and an eternal friend." He launched Chita's career when he directed her in *Call Me Madam* and later in the blockbuster, *West Side Story*.

Robbins felt that in the art of dance, technique was not the most important element, but the telling of a story was everything. He always selected dancers who could act and vice-versa. The look of spontaneity was of utmost importance to him.

Although he had the reputation of being difficult, he could be easygoing if people understood what he wanted. After all, that's a big part of what made him who he was – a genius of the dance.

Betty Comden and Adolph Green are two names that are usually mentioned together, as they make up one of the most successful teams ever to create hit shows on Broadway. Lenny was fortunate that his friend, Adolph, introduced him to the *Reviewers*, and especially to Betty Comden, as they played such a big part in his success on Broadway – with *On the Town* and *Wonderful Town*. So many hit songs have come from their shows, but *New York, New York* is one of their biggest with its clever lyrics about the subway being "a hole in the ground." In the song, *I Get Carried Away* in *On the Town*, these two creative people made it sound operatic, which was a great idea and it stole the show. Putting it in a minor key did the trick, and they performed it sensationally.

In *On the Town*, Lenny had the good luck to get George Abbott to direct and supervise the show. It made all the difference.

Lenny used to come to our house for my family's celebrated parties. He loved to sing Gilbert and Sullivan *Operettas* and we were amazed that he knew all the parts and could sing them from memory. One night, he played his own piano arrangement of Aaron Copland's *El Salon Mexico*. It was the first time he had tried it out on anyone, and he played it to the hilt with all the fortissimos. The neighbors, not realizing a future wunderkind was playing, complained to the police about the racket, and the cops came knocking on our door. That was the end of that soirée. Later on, after this work was published, he was asked why he made a transcription for piano of this orchestral work, and he replied, "Because I love Copland's music and felt this would be an exciting showpiece for a piano recital. I got sick and tired of hearing every recital end with a Liszt *Hungarian Rhapsody*."

I remember when Lenny was still living at home with his family. His father wanted him to help in his cosmetic business, but neither Burton, his much younger brother, or he, ever considered it. A few years later, on December 7, 1941, my fiancée, Sam, and I were visiting Lenny in his Boston studio. He had just heard on the radio about the Japanese bombing at Pearl Harbor. We were all very upset at this terrible news, but especially Lenny, who wanted to be drafted to help his country. However, because of his emphysema, he was turned down. I sometimes think how fortunate it was that he never had to fight for the U.S.A., as we might have lost him and never would have heard *Fancy Free*, or *West Side Story, Candide, Chichester Psalms* (my favorite), or all of his "Omnibus" TV shows. Just think what we would have missed if we never had him as conductor of the New York Philharmonic and of the Young People's Concerts, which influenced so many children and gave us the music audiences of today; not to mention his immense store of recordings that have enriched the world.

Lenny adored Mahler and did much to bring his music to the public when interest was waning. He told me once that he felt as if he were Mahler, himself, conducting at times, and that he even felt he was Mahler reincarnated. In the Mahler Sixth Symphony, there is a steady march-like feeling which seems to predict his early death at fifty. Even though he was happy and fulfilled with his wife, Alma Gluck, he had suffered the blow of losing his five year old daughter to scarlet fever. He was also told by his doctor that he had a serious heart problem. The last movement of the Sixth did not lighten up as most of his symphonies did at the end. Incidentally, Alma also married two other distinguished men: Walter Gropius, the architect, and writer, Franz Werfel. She was not only a flirtatious personality, who attracted these intellectual men, but she was also a very accomplished composer herself.

One very hot summer's day in July at Tanglewood in the 1950s, Lenny was to rehearse the Boston Symphony Orchestra. He did something so spontaneous seeming that I couldn't tell if it was planned or not. He sat down at the piano and played and sang much of the opera, *Carmen*, singing all the parts himself -- even doing a falsetto voice for Carmen. He tried to act with his arms while playing and singing the parts of Don Jose and Escamillo, the Toreador. The audience ate it up and gave him an ovation. This all took place before he got down to rehearsing the orchestra for the Sunday program. Where he got all this energy, I'll never know. He was very elated when the rehearsal was over and all his friends rushed up to congratulate him. I got my usual big hug and kiss.

I received this letter from Lenny when he was on his honeymoon with his wife, Felicia, in Mexico:
sexuality; perhaps she thought he might change. She was a very beautiful and charming woman who was a fine actress and certainly could have married most anyone she desired.

```
            Humboldt 53
          Cuernavace, Mo
             Mexico
                  25 Oct '51
Dear Ouida and Sam,
        Your warm felicitations did not
by any means go unnoticed; but the
enormous time involved in getting
here by car has postponed all corr-
espondence. You were very sweet to
think of us, and we thank you warmly.
        We are now settled in a fine big
house with a great garden and pool,
and life is now reduced to a happy
winter in the sun, with much com-
posing, I hope. It couldn't be nicer.
        Affectionate greetings to you and
all the family.

                    Lenny
```

Incidentally, I recently learned that Rabbi Rabinowitz, a close family friend, who presided at my wedding and those of my sisters, was also the rabbi at Felicia and Lenny's wedding. What a coincidence, that our two families were so closely associated with the same rabbi, and I never knew about it!

The couple had many happy years together, but Felicia knew what she was getting into when she married Lenny. Evidently her love and admiration for him made her overlook his bisexuality; perhaps she thought he might change. She was a very beautiful and charming woman who was a fine actress and certainly could have married most anyone she desired

His infidelities with young men finally got to her, and they separated in the seventies. The children, Jamie, Alex, and Nina seemed to be unaware of what was going on in their parents personal lives, as they were used to living in a very busy household. Felicia was active as a TV actress while they were growing up, and the kids were accustomed to having their dad out of town and abroad conducting much of the time.

Eventually, when Felicia contracted cancer, Lenny felt very guilty and thought he might have caused it due to the stress she must have been under. He returned and tried to make up for his neglect, but came to realize it was too late.

Lenny at Tanglewood

****

ANOTHER LETTER FROM "GEBBY"

> *And to hear with Music,*
> *In your depths we deposit*
> *Our hearts and souls;*
> *Thou hast taught us to*
> *See with our hearts.*
>   Kahil Gibran

Letters tell much about a person, and that's why I use them in this book. I feel very fortunate that I have saved many letters from my teacher because they depict so much of his contagious personality. These letters are very important to me, and should be to anyone who loves music or who is interested in one of Leschetizky's most important disciples. I found that there are a dozen biographies of Leschetizky, and none about Gebhard, although he became one of the most important teachers of this century and his students came from all parts of the country to study with him.

Every year, on Mr. Gebhard's birthday, July 25, I would send him a gift to show him how grateful I was. It was usually a book about a musician he admired, or might have known. He was so delighted that he always responded with fascinating letters, most of which I have managed to save.

The first book I sent him was about Beethoven, written by Schauffler. This is his response:

Heinrich Gebhard
Manchester Road

July 26, 1941

My Dear Ouida,

Again you have surprised me in the most
beautiful way! Do you never forget my birthday? Many,many thanks for the book!-

This Beethoven by Schauffler I always
wanted to possess. I have read the first
fifty pages. It is a very unique approach
and a unique style. And I shall be intensely
interested to read his analytical survey of
how "Beethoven freed music."- Beethoven did
"free" music and made it the most democratic
of the arts.-

Please tell your nice fiancé that he is
marrying the best girl in the USA.-and she
is marrying a very fine man.-Once more many
thanks for the lovely gift, and my best and
deepest good wishes to you and "Sam" for a
most happy marriage!

Yours ever faithfully,

Heinrich Gebhard

7

MILDRED SPIEGEL REMEMBERS LENNY

No one is worthwhile who cannot appreciate
the worth of others.
Willliam M. Blatt

Lenny had been seeing a fellow student of Gebhard--
Mildred Spiegel. Contrary to some of his biographers, the chemistry between them was tremendous. They went to Boston Symphony concerts together and played duets. Lenny dedicated some
of his piano music to her. They had a lot of fun, in particular they
enjoyed mimicking Gebhard's thick German accent, especially his
use of "By Jove!" as punctuation.

Mildred was a colleague of mine in the days when we both
studied with Heinrich Gebhard. Lenny, Mildred and I used to sit
together at Gebhard's monthly recitals in his home. She played
the Beethoven *First Piano Concerto* with orchestra and taught piano for many years. Mildred formed the Madison Trio which gave
weekly recitals on WGBH radio in Boston and played at the
Gardner Museum and other halls in Boston. Lenny wrote two trio
compositions for his good friend, Mildred, which her trio played
at Harvard. He also dedicated piano compositions to Mildred which
she performed frequently. She later studied piano with Sasha
Gorodnitzki in New York.

I was reunited with Mildred through Henry Levine who
gave me her address when he performed for the Piano Teachers of
Long Island, and Mildred and I became very close again. I realize
that I was very fortunate to have such a good friend who was also
a closer friend to Leonard Bernstein during the early years than I
was, so I have asked her to write the following story:

Mildred

LENNY AND MILDRED

by

Mildred Spiegel Zucker

It is a great pleasure for me to recall my close, musical, and joyful friendship with Leonard Bernstein, whom I met in the fall of 1932 when he came, after school, from the Boys Latin High School in Boston to my school, Roxbury Memorial High School for Girls. I found him playing *Malaguena* by Lecuona on the Steinway grand in a long, empty auditorium surrounded by a small group of admiring students. I was astonished at his sense of drama, stupendous enthusiasm (mentally and physically) and his creative genius in the realm of sound. His playing sounded like an orchestra. It was love at first sight. We quickly became musical friends, playing lots of duets and two piano pieces almost every Tuesday, alternating between the Harvard Musical Society and the New England Conservatory, where we would meet under the heroic bronze statue of Beethoven. Sometimes he arrived late. I was so amazed and moved by his sight-reading, rhythmic vitality, memory, musicality, dynamics, attacks and releases, that at age sixteen (in 1932) I informed Lenny that he was a genius and would one day be famous (I wrote it in my diary). He replied, "Do you really think so?" After rehearsals, he bought a five-cent chocolate Nestle bar and a two-cent portion of halvah, which he loved.

We were a very popular couple and were invited to many parties in the mid-30's where we entertained. I would imitate a coloratura soprano singing *Je veux Vivre* and *Sempre Libra*. Lenny accompanied me at the piano. Our favorite keyboard duet was *Rumbalero* by Morton Gould, which was originally written for two pianos. We played it on one.

Lenny often visited me at home without advance notice. He'd bounce up the stairs, run into the kitchen, give my mother a bear hug and lift the pot covers to see what was cooking. The growing adolescent was often hungry, enjoyed my mother's cooking, and she liked to feed him. This was his second home. He would run into the living room, pound on my new Baldwin Grand Piano, and a few times broke the strings which the tuner had to replace. His playing was unpolished and undisciplined.

I was the official pianist of the Boston Public School Senior Symphony. Many of the members were music majors and later joined the Boston Symphony Orchestra. Lenny admired my polished command of the keyboard and asked me to show him how to practice and acquire it, which I did. He had a subconscious feeling of inadequacy and I always gave him praise, encouragement and confidence. At his home he was misunderstood and got resistance from his father, who resented Lenny's being serious about a musical career.

In 1932, Lenny was fourteen and had an audition with the distinguished artist teacher, Heinrich Gebhard, who felt that Lenny was not prepared for him. He advised Lenny to study with Helen Coates, one of his assistants. Helen recognized his gifts and taught him etudes and technical studies as well as repertoire during the first lesson hour. The second hour Lenny played opera scores, which fascinated him. Helen Coates later became his devoted secretary.

I attended one of Helen's student recitals when Lenny played Beethoven's *Sonata Op. 13.* I urged him to study with Gebhard as he was a more advanced teacher with an artistic imagination and had more to offer. At age eighteen, when he entered Harvard, Lenny studied with Gebhard, who enlarged his repertoire and musical perception. Lenny acquired a better tone and interpretation.

In 1933, I played the Beethoven *First Piano Concerto* in public with the Boston Public Senior Symphony Orchestra. Lenny rehearsed the orchestral part with me, fell in love with the music, borrowed a copy and returned it in tatters. Several years later, when he conducted and played it with the Boston Symphony Orchestra, he told everyone in the green room that he "learned it from Mildred."

Lenny dedicated a four-page piece to me for my twenty-first birthday which he signed, "With all my heart, Leonard Bernstein, June 12, 1937." He also dedicated another four-page piece to me in 1938, *Music for the Dance No. II.* He signed it, "For Mildred on her twenty second birthday in friendliest affection." This was played by Lenny and me as pupils of Gebhard, as well as his *Music for Two Pianos.* He also wrote a piano trio for my Madison Trio, which we played at Harvard.

At the Gebhard classes, we met Mrs. Robinson, his student, and a lecturer who conducted a State Extension Music Appreciation Course in Haverhill, Mass. She asked Lenny and me to play the works of the composers she was speaking about. Each Monday night we would board a train and go to a large high school auditorium where the lectures were held. When the course was over, she invited us for a weekend at her summer home on Canobie Lake in New Hampshire. At an amusement park we visited, there was a roller coaster. It was raining and there was thunder and lightning, but Lenny made me go on it against my will. Sometimes he did crazy things.

As a teenager, he directed the *Mikado* during a summer

in Sharon. He was Nanki-Poo and his sister, Shirley, was Yum-Yum. I played the entire accompaniment. The following summer in Sharon he directed *H.M.S. Pinafore*. It was performed at the Town Hall there. Tickets were ten cents and proceeds went to the Sharon Ladies Aid Society. Lenny was Captain Corcoran and I was Little Buttercup. The piano was in the wings near the stage. When he sang solos, I accompanied him. When I sang solos, he accompanied me. When we sang duets, a local resident accompanied us. In appreciation, Mrs. Bok, the president of the society, presented him with a gift: a large box which had a bathrobe in it. After the show there was a cast party at Dutchland Farms where he put on the robe and paraded around the restaurant.

In 1937, when Dmitri Mitropoulos was guest conductor of the Boston Symphony Orchestra, he invited Lenny to a rehearsal. Lenny invited me to join him.

When Lenny was a music counselor at Camp Onata in Pittsfield, Mass., he would visit Camp Allegro for Girls across the lake to entertain at the keyboard, which he loved. The director asked him to recommend a music counsellor. He thought of me and sent a telegram. I accepted, and we had a great time visiting each other's camps.

Once, after a concert, Lenny drove me home and asked if he could sleep in my house. I gave him my bedroom and I slept on the living room sofa.

When eating out after some concerts, he ordered cinnamon toast and tea. Lenny never forgot his old friends. When we moved to New York in 1970, he invited us to several concerts he conducted, and any rehearsal I wished to attend.

On June 4, 1951, Lenny came to Boston for Koussevitsky's funeral. We met for dinner. He told me that he missed Felicia, his fiancée, when touring and was planning to marry her. I was taking a Sabbatical from teaching and Lenny advised me to go to Israel, where I met and married my dear husband.

In September of 1951, Gebhard's students had a testimonial dinner to celebrate his fifty five years of teaching. I was not his student at the time but was asked to play Gebhard's original two piano works with another student. Lenny did not come. His wedding was to take place the next day.

He sent me a New Year's card every year and invited me to his wedding, and later to his son's Bar Mitzvah. When he received an honorary degree at Harvard, I was the only Boston friend who attended.

In 1978, I heard him at Tanglewood and went backstage. He held my hand during the conversation and told me that on his way back to New York, after conducting in Providence, R.I., he had asked his chauffeur to drive him by my former home in Roxbury where we spent our early years playing duets and demonstrating solos for each other. He was "filled with nostalgia."

Lenny had an intense passion for music and was very dedicated to the piano, his first love, as he indicated in his piano piece, *Touches*. The sounds of the keyboard obsessed him. He hammered out tunes and drove the family to distraction at all hours, even late at night. His father asked him to stop. He did not feel that music was a good vocation. He thought that Lenny would be impoverished playing in a lounge with a dance band. He wanted him to join his successful business. They clashed and had a constant conflict over music. His father was religious, intelligent, ambitious, and wanted his children to love learning and to have a comfortable life. During the depression, his dad owned two cars and two beautiful custom-built homes.

While at Harvard, he invited budding poets, writers and musicians to spend the weekend in Sharon. His father did not like it and called his friends "crazy artist nuts."

One of these friends was Adolph Green, whom Lenny met at Camp Onata. Lenny was fascinated with Adolph's humor and knowledge of music. They sat around the house for hours inventing musical parodies. Lenny's father said, "Who is that guy? I want him out of the house." He never understood their talents. Jennie did; she was a perfect mother for Lenny — never pushed and was very proud of him.

My cousins, Mr. and Mrs. Morris Goodman of Brookline, Mass., made a large party for Lenny in April 1949 when *The Age of Anxiety* was premiered by the Boston Symphony.

Koussevitzky and many Symphony members came. Lenny was oblivious to everyone except Adolph.

Lenny was fond of Lewis Carroll's "Alice in Wonderland" and enjoyed quoting from it. He especially liked:

> He thought he saw an albatross
> Fluttering around the lamp.
> He looked again and found
> It was a penny postage stamp.
> "You'd best be getting home," he said.
> "The nights are very damp."

Lenny had always loved to read and never passed a bookstore without going in. He sometimes bought a second-hand book, and once he advised me to buy two volumes of "From Beowulf to Thomas Hardy." In his late teens he said that someday he wanted love, marriage and children; also that he was going to try everything in his lifetime. In 1939 he told me that he did not know what sex he would choose — "that the pendulum was swinging back and forth." He always liked athletic activity—tennis, swimming, skiing, and he worked out at the Harvard gym. Driving his car, he would sing themes and pump the gas pedal in time with the music. He had a clear, concise, colorful power of expression. Lenny had a sensitive stomach and nerves, and was sometimes moody and depressed. His allergies, asthma, and smoking always dogged his life. Lenny had a natural inclination for the spotlight. He was magnetic, outgoing, fun-loving, and surrounded himself with many friends from all walks of life. He had sex-appeal, charisma, contagious enthusiasm, and an endless source of creativity. He needed the freedom to be spontaneous, and liked having many projects going on simultaneously.

Lenny was the best friend that one could ever hope to find and I was always touched by his presence. He had a strong religious outlook, a great love for his family, and a profound spiritual connection with mankind.

Lenny sent eighty four letters and postcards to me over the years, especially when we were young, and we exchanged letters when he went out of town. They are still in my possession. Only Aaron Copland received as many letters from him.

There never was and never will be another Lenny.

A Friday afternoon custom that I, Lenny, Mildred, and other serious young musicians never missed was to wait in line to hear the Boston Symphony Orchestra concerts in Symphony Hall.

I used to sit for hours on the floor of the lobby on newspapers with my friend, Luise Vosgerchian, and when the bell rang, we ran as fast as we could up many flights of stairs to claim our seats which cost only fifty cents and were called "rush seats." This friend, I'm proud to say, became a distinguished professor of music at Harvard.

In 1971, she also became Naumberg Professor Emeritus of Harvard. She was a student of Slonimsky, Vengerova (Lenny'a teacher at Curtis), and the great Nadia Boulanger, who was teacher of many of the finest composers.

1986, The Luise Vosgerchian Teaching Award was established to perpetuate her values of teaching in the world. She was piano soloist with the New York Philharmonic and the Boston Symphony Orchestra, and many chamber groups in Europe and North America.

She recorded many of the great masters such as Brahms, Schumann, Debussy, and Bartok. She has spoken many times for the BSO Lecture Series, at the Museum of Fine Arts and the Isabelle Stuart Gardner Museum. She has taught at Tanglewood, Dartmouth College, and Brandeis University.

A few years ago, she spoke at length on television about music during intermission at a performance by the Boston Symphony Orchestra. She was very impressive when asked many complicated questions about music.

Since I hadn't been in touch with Luise for so many years, I decided to write to her. Surprisingly, she answered my letter with enthusiasm, recalling my smile that she remembered, and the unusual opportunity students like us were given to hear magical composers weave their spell under that outstanding conductor, the great Dr. Serge Koussevitzky.

8

LENNY'S AWESOME BEGINNINGS

The world's moral leaders are the men and women
who refused to mind their own business.
William M. Blatt

In December, 1944, Leonard Bernstein's first musical, *On the Town*, opened in New York City to rave reviews. I had been at the try-outs in Boston and felt in my bones that it would make it. The New York Times critic said, "There can be no mistake about it: *On the Town* is the freshest and most engaging musical show to come this way since the golden day of *Oklahoma*. The Adelphi Theatre on West Fifty Fourth street is the new Utopia."

Jerome Robbins' idea for this show came from his ballet *Fancy Free*, and he supplied some great dances. George Abbott did his usual imaginative job of directing. Betty Comden and Adolph Green did the clever book and lyrics, and also acted and sang together for the first time. Sono Osato made a spectacular dancing debut, and Nancy Walker launched her career as a top comedienne. Recently, a revival of *On the Town* was a great success on Broadway.

Lenny described his songs for *On the Town* as simple, and with a melodic line that he tried to develop. My favorite songs in the show are *Lucky to be Me*, with a memorable melody, and *Lonely Town*, also very beautiful and torchy. Koussevitsky tried to convince Bernstein that he shouldn't divert his attention in other directions if he wanted to grow as a conductor. However, Lenny still wanted to write many other works plus an exciting new opera with a modern libretto. "Winterset" was a possibility, he thought.

Koussevitzky came to see *On the Town* at the Boston try-out and said he liked it, but was still upset that Lenny was neglecting his conducting. He gave him a long lecture the next day. Little did "Kousy" know that Lenny had no intention of giving up his many other interests in the theater, mainly composing.

A few months before in that same magical year – April 19, 1944 to be exact – Lenny and Jerome Robbins received accolades for their ballet, *Fancy Free*. In the New York Herald Tribune, the critic, Edwin Denby raved, "Leonard Bernstein, the young composer of *Jeremiah*, wrote the score for *Fancy Free* and conducted it brilliantly. It has complex nervous rhythms and violent contrasts of thick and thin orchestral textures. I liked best the *rhumba* for Robbins' solo."

In the Spring before this opening, Lenny received the Music Critics Annual Prize for the best new composition of the year for his *Jeremiah Symphony*. The *Lamentation* of the symphony is Jeremiah's hymn of sorrow for the destruction of Jerusalem. "How long more wilt thou forsake us. Turn us unto thee, oh, Lord" This was Lenny's way, he said, of "striking a blow to Fascism." *Jeremiah* was premiered in Pittsburg under his early conducting teacher, Fritz Reiner. Lenny conducted the symphony in Boston, New York, Chigago, St. Louis, Detroit, Rochester, Prague, and Jerusalem. In most of these concerts Jennie Tourel, the great soprano, and Lenny's good friend, was the soloist.

In Boston, Lenny was honored at a dinner by the Joint Anti-Fascist Refugee Committee at the Copley Plaza Hotel. A large sum was collected to aid the Spanish victims of Fascist aggression. I was thrilled to hear Lenny praised highly for being sympathetic to victims of cruelty and oppression. I am proud that he is among the great artists who sing of democracy and freedom.

During those years, I saw Lenny every summer when he conducted at Tanglewood. I remember one time, back-stage after a concert, he was surrounded by a group of admirers, sitting in his bathrobe, holding a drink in one hand and a cigarette in the other, talking to one person while everybody else hung on intently, listening to every word. He happened to look up and spotted me in the crowd and said, "Ah, Ouida," I came over and he stood up to give me a big hug and kiss.

Surely, the real turning point of Leonard Bernstein's career happened when the misfortune of Conductor Bruno Walter's illness became Lenny's good fortune. It was the evening of Saturday November 14, 1943 when Lenny, who was then the assistant conductor of the New York Philharmonic, got a call from Bruno Zurati, the orchestra's assistant manager, warning him that Bruno Walter was ill and he might have to take his place on Sunday afternoon in Carnegie Hall, but it seemed unlikely.

That night Lenny attended a concert by his good friend, Jennie Tourel, who introduced his song, *I Hate Music*, the highlight of the evening. They went out to celebrate their triumph. When he got home at two thirty Sunday morning he found the startling message from Bruno Zurati that he was indeed scheduled to conduct the orchestra without rehearsal at the afternoon concert.

Lenny stayed up until four thirty in the morning studying the scores while sipping coffee to stay awake. Later that morning, Bruno Walter graciously coached him for an hour from his sickbed. Lenny's family just happened to be in town that weekend and were planning to leave early that afternoon, until Lenny presented them with tickets for the program.

The historic concert was not only heard by several thousand people in the hall but also by millions in the radio audience across the country. The next morning the New York Times carried rave reviews on the first page. Olin Downs, the Times music critic, said, "He was remarkably free of the score, which he followed confidently, but without ever burying his nose in it . . . He conducted without a baton . . . was to the point, alive and expressive of the music . . . It's a good American success story. The warm, friendly triumph of it filled Carnegie Hall and spread over the airwaves."

Thus was launched the conducting career of the young fellow, who only a few years before had told me very innocently that he thought he would pursue a career in music.

My husband and I saw Lenny that summer in Tanglewood in Massachusetts where he returned as Koussevitzky's assistant in conducting at the Berkshire Music Center. We had our usual warm reunion - only this time it was special after his spectacular conducting debut. It was hard to believe that at this exciting time of his life, he was a bit jealous because I had my first child and he wasn't married yet. He wrote as much when he signed the photo I asked for, which said, "For Ouida and her rapidly enlarging family, with affection, Lenny Bernstein."

In 1945, when Lenny was still the assistant conductor of the New York Philharmonic, and had already made his surprise debut, substituting for the ailing Bruno Walter, he was asked to be guest conductor of the Boston Symphony Orchestra at Symphony Hall. Among the pieces he conducted were Aaron Copland's *El Salon Mexico*, and the first local performance of his own *Jeremiah Symphony*.

Lenny

These years, during his twenties, were to prove to be the most important of Lenny's lifetime.

A WAR OF INDEPENDENCE

Lenny was in Israel for two months in 1948 during the Arab-Israeli war when thousands were killed and many more were wounded.

In October, the Israeli army pushed into the Negev Desert and conquered Beersheba, an important town described in the Bible. When the U.N. ordered the Israeli Army to withdraw, Lenny persuaded the authorities to allow him to give a concert for the soldiers who refused to leave. The following day, he conducted and played three piano concerti outdoors with a group of hastily gathered members of the Israel Philharmonic. He played Mozart's *B flat Concerto* and Beethoven's *First Piano Concerto*, as well as Gershwin's *Rhapsody in Blue*.

This was a crude place to perform — on a makeshift platform surrounded by high stone walls. Lenny had trouble keeping steady while he played, and when his piano stool started to shift under him, someone had to come to his rescue and shore it up. He felt this hastily prepared concert was worth the trouble of transporting these dedicated musicians across the desert, as it made the Egyptians pull back their troops that were about to threaten Jerusalem.

Leonard Lyons wrote in his New York column that Egypt must have thought this concert gathering was a military maneuver because "who'd take time out in war to listen to a *Mozart Concerto?*"

Much earlier, Sam's older sister, Mary, had moved to Avichael, Natanya, which was a part of Palestine, with her husband, Aaron, when they were married in the thirties. He was a real pioneer, as he had fought as a member of the Jewish Legion in the twenties, and had bought a good sized piece of land there. Mary's family (Sam was her youngest brother) was very unhappy when her husband insisted that they settle in Palestine, as they couldn't see her often.

LENNY MEETS AARON COPLAND

The common man grows silent in his pain,
but God gave the artist the ability to say what he suffers.
Goethe

Perhaps the most influential person in Leonard Bernstein's life, actually his mentor, was Aaron Copland.

One night in 1937 at a ballet concert, Lenny, who was then nineteen, found himself sitting next to "an odd-looking man in his thirties, a pair of glasses resting on his great hooked nose and a mouth filled with teeth, flashing a wide grin. When the poet Muriel Rukeyser introduced us, 'Aaron Copland — Leonard Bernstein,' I almost fell out of the balcony."

Lenny had known and loved Copland's music for so many years, he had pictured him as a bearded Old Testament prophet. The first piece of Copland's that he fell in love with was his *Piano Variations*. After Copland met Lenny, he soon became his adviser. Lenny said, "He taught me a tremendous amount about taste, style, and consistency in music.

Aaron Copland was born on November 14, 1900 in Brooklyn. He picked up what he could from his older sister who was an amateur pianist. Aaron was a rebel from the start, though he studied with the conservative, Rubin Goldmark. Later on, he left for Paris to study with the legendary Nadia Boulanger, and he produced such unforgettable works as *Appalachian Spring, Rodeo,* and *Billy the Kid.* The finale of *Appalachian Spring* was built around the old Shaker hymn, *Simple Gifts.* An admirer exclaimed that the title of the ballet was so perfect that it brought images to mind of the real Appalachia. Copland replied, "That's interesting, because it was named by Martha Graham after she had heard my music." In 1944, the year he was starting to make his mark in the musical world, Copland was awarded the Pulitzer Prize for that composition.

"Composers differ greatly in their ideas about how American you ought to sound," Copland said in 1985. "The main thing, of course, is to write music that you feel is great and that everybody wants to hear." For fifty years, Copland lived up to his ideal, and American music will never be the same.

9

MY ROOTS

I wouldn't be here if it hadn't been for the Russian Czar and the evil he caused.

This is the story that was told to me by my aunt Lena. My mother, Lucy, and her four siblings, Sarah, Fanny, Lena, Eli, and their parents had to flee the town of Lebedin in the province of Kharkov in the Ukraine on twenty four hours notice. An edict had been issued to expel all wealthy Jews from Russia.

In previous years, the family had a beautiful lifestyle. My grandfather, my mom's dad, whom I never met, ran a successful brewery, and in a contest for the best beer in Kharkov, received a bronze medal. Their only son, my Uncle Eli, treasured it and showed it to everyone. On one side of the medal was the face of Catherine the Great.

My mother's family of seven, the only wealthy Jewish family in Lebedin, lived in a large white house with green shutters and a spacious lawn, surrounded by apple, pear, and cherry orchards, "so plentiful that one had but to extend an arm to a branch to be rewarded with an armful of luscious fruit." The cellar was laden with freshly churned butter, cheese, crocks of heavy cream, shelves filled with hundreds of jars of preserves, and barrels of sauerkraut. There was a constant turnover of guests who were invited by the family to share their abundant life.

My mother's oldest sister, Fanny, was given the greatest advantages. Beside attending school, she had tutors at home. She guided the destinies of the family who thought of her as a judge whose word was final. Fanny was wise and understanding. She had an uncanny power of knowing what were the right decisions to make. She was also very sweet and caring. I remember seeing her postcards in my mailbox, having come all the way from the Ukraine to Brookline, Massachusetts. She never forgot our birthdays and began her notes to us with "Dear Ones." I always wanted to meet this special person but I never did. Russia was too far off and too expensive for us to visit.

My mother often told me all about the sleigh rides in winter. "The children were dressed in furs from head to toe, all covered by a fur blanket up to their eyes," as Russian winters could be cold. Away they would go in sleighs driven by four spirited horses for miles and miles over the glistening snow. Afterwards, there would be tea drinking from the steaming samovar. The glasses were filled with lump sugar and lemon, consumed with strawberry preserves spread over black bread - all very warming after a great sleigh ride.

Most of the Jewish people lived terrible lives in Russia under the Czarist regime. My mother's family was worried, even though they were able to afford a luxurious life. Sure enough, the Czar aimed the decree directly at the family of Henry Romberg, my grandfather, the wealthy brewer. The family had to decide within twenty four hours where to emigrate. My grandfather had to leave immediately to avoid prison, or worse. Fanny, the all-knowing sister, decided the family should go to America and make a new start. My mom, Lucy Romberg, was three years old and her younger brother, my uncle Eli, was only nine months at the end of the nineteenth century. Unfortunately, Fanny, because of an earlier commitment, had to return to Russia and eventually married her very persistent suitor, Samuel Smollianoff, who fell deeply in love with her, though she never felt the same toward him, intellectually or otherwise.

The family went on their sad journey by train to Hamburg, Germany, where they were met by very kindly German Jews who helped the adults and children get cleaned, fed, and settled in barracks in preparation for the long eighteen day boat trip to America. On the boat, the Jewish refugees were assigned to the crowded steerage in the bottom of the ship, where there was little food to eat. Beside that, the voyage was an exceedingly rough one "with the terrible lurching of the boat and lashing waves." Most people, including my mother's family succumbed to the dreaded seasickness. Worse still, my mother and her sister, Lena, contracted measles and had to be detained in the ship's hospital. It was horrifying to be told that they could have been deported if they didn't recover before docking time in New York. However, when they arrived at Ellis Island and were still sick, Lucy and Lena were allowed to go to the hospital there to recover.

Ellis Island

Eventually, the family went to the home of their cousins, the Sandbergs in Boston, who were expecting them. My grandfather had to find some kind of employment and through contacts he found work in Portland, Maine, in a men's hat factory. In his next job he learned to fix broken umbrellas and went from door to door doing that menial work. The family was forced to scrounge around for used clothing and shoes. What a change from the luxurious life they lived in Russia! Meanwhile, back in the Ukraine, Fanny sewed clothes for the children, even though she was busy teaching English in the Russian schools.

Fanny and her husband raised a family of children who grew up to be doctors, but, sadly, we heard that they had died of starvation, which was common in those days of sorrow.

In America, my mother married her Shakespearean teacher, my dad, William M. Blatt, who was born in Orange, New Jersey. His mother, Pauline, for whom I was named, was born in New York City - quite a contrast from the beginnings of my mother's family, who finally found the freedom they were looking for in the new land across the ocean. My mother's sisters, Lena and Sarah, married well. Lena had one child and Sarah had eight. Lena's daughter, Esther Byer Milner, my favorite cousin, lives in Chestnut Hill, Massachusetts, and I am still in touch with her.

Ouida at intermission while singing in chorus with the
Philadelphia Orchestra in Worcester, Massachusetts

Music is very important to the Russian people, and I feel very lucky to have inherited their love of music and the arts, including ballet and choral singing. I remember, especially when I was a young pianist, how enthusiastic my aunt Lena was about music. She always asked me to play her favorite pieces when we came to visit. This gave me some much needed self-esteem which influenced my decision to pursue the study of piano even more.

My uncle, Eli, who became a well known pediatrician,was like a second father to me. I recall that he took me at a very early age to a violin recital in Symphony Hall, Boston, by the ten year old Yehudi Menuhin, who played with amazing technique and a beautiful tone. He impressed me so much that I remember at the end of the performance, after several encores, the young Yehudi came back onstage dressed in a blue bathrobe to convince the enthusiastic audience that he was finally through playing encores. Menuhin, born in New York City in 1916, made his debut at seven with the San Francisco Symphony. He then studied in Paris with Georges Enesco, the famed Romanian violinist, teacher and composer. At eleven he appeared with the Berlin Philharmonic, and since then has played with leading orchestras of the world. He has recently been the conductor of the orchestra in Bath, England. His sisters, Yaltah and Hepzibah, were fine pianists. Hepzibah, who died several years ago of cancer, played duo concerts with her brother all over the world for many years. He was devastated by her death. He confessed on a recent PBS TV show that he wished he had realized how much she needed more love and understanding from him as she was a very intellectually needy person. She tried to make up for it by helping others as much as she could. He also felt she had a great natural talent and played beautifully without a lot of practice. I was greatly saddened to learn of his death.

When I was a small child, I heard the great Rachmaninoff at Symphony Hall. This tall, gaunt figure with a shaved head walked out on the stage toward the piano and never cracked a smile. The technique and feeling which he displayed in his performance made me realize that he was as great a pianist as he was a composer. He played Chopin and other composers as well as his own *Études Tableaux*. At the end of the recital, the applause and cheering was overwhelming and he played several encores. When Rachmaninoff was ready to leave the stage, the enthusiastic crowd yelled, "Play *IT!*" which meant they wanted to hear his famous *Prelude in C Sharp Minor*. He played it even though he had come to abhor it, because it was an early work that he had been forced to play entirely too many times. He received no royalties whenever he played it, since he had sold it for practically nothing when he was young. I was so impressed with his playing that I summoned up all my teen-age courage and went backstage. There in the Green Room, he sat at a desk signing autographs with a glove on his right hand. At my turn, he signed his name, but a year later, in my childlike innocence, I felt that more was needed; when I attended his next recital in Boston, I brought the program he had already signed and asked him if he would write "Sincerely" over his name, to which he replied, "Okeh." I have that signature framed in my den.

My piano students go back to when I was 14 years old, starting with my teacher's daughter, Peggy Gebhard. My next students were young patients of my Uncle Eli, who recommended me to them. Dr. Eli Romberg, pediatrician at Harvard Medical School invented "The Romberg Test," named for him, which was a neurological test for balance. He was also an accomplished caricaturist and magician. I recall how he loved to amuse his little patients by pretending to take quarters out of their ears. In a way, he was the Patch Adams of his time.

Dr. Eli Charles Romberg

When Ray ane I found ourrselves in Israel as part of an eastern Mediterranean cruise. I asked one of my relatives (I have at least twenty five) to get in touch with my first cousin, Henry, Eli's son. He was exceedingly happy to talk with me, but we were unfortunately unable to visit him and his family in Jerusalem as we had to get back to our ship. I promised to send him a copy of this book because it contains a great deal about his family background.

Elissa Lee Romberg, Henry's sister, who lives in Virginia and has two beautiful married daughters, was told by her brother that she should get a copy of "My Friend Lenny." She took his advice and ordered one on Amazon.com. Ellissa was so very excited to read about her family that she wrote a long letter to me . That was the beginning of a wonderful friendship because I hadn't seen her since she was a baby - over half a century ago. During our phone conversations she mentioned that there was a favorite radio talk show of hers that she had listened to for years on WBZ-AM in Boston. The show is hosted by Jordan Rich whom she admires greatly because of his charming personality and his wide range of interests. Elissa sent an e-mail to Rich, telling him how enthusiastic she was about the book. He responded in a very positive way, saying that he was anxious to have Ray and me on his program. We are tremendously excited that he will be interviewing us on WBZ shortly.

When I was a child, if any of my family took sick, my uncle Eli visited every day to take care of him or her. He came to dinner every Sunday afternoon and would take me out with him on his rounds. Uncle Eli's marriage to Natalie at the age of fifty produced two children, Elissa and Henry. Henry moved to Israel, practices medicine there and has several children. He became an orthodox Jew in Israel, even though his father was not a religious person. I believe he turned orthodox because he thought it would give him answers to why he felt so lost, as his parents died when he was very young.

One of my uncle's fellow students at Harvard was Henry Levine who came to be a fine pianist, teacher and arranger. Many years later I met him when we were both students of Gebhard. He studied with him in his maturity to perfect his technique and interpretation. Levine also simplified symphonies and concerti for piano students to play. He specialized in kinesthetics and wrote a book on the manner in which the fingers move on the keyboard. I was reunited with Henry at a meeting of my Association of Piano Teachers of Long Island where he was the guest artist. When I introduced myself, he was amazed when I told him who I was, as so many years had passed since we were students of Gebhard, and I'm sure I must have changed a lot. He played his arrangement for four hands of Chopin's *Etudes* with Bernard Kirchbaum, a veteran member and former Program Chairman of APTLI. I wrote Henry a letter after his appearance and thanked him for coming, by sending him a book of my dad's epigrams. Here is his reply:

```
                    Henry Levine
              134 West 58th Street
              New York, N.Y. 10019
                    March 25, 1976
Dear Ouida,
     Many thanks for the copy of your father's
"Inklings." They are gems of philosophical
reflection. My friends too get a "kick" out
of them - wisdom, in capsule form.
     My wife and I were interested in Peggy's
new marital status and her new address. So
far, all of the other Gebhard students you
mention I have lost contact with, except
Mildred Spiegel. She is now Mrs. Mildred
Spiegel Zucker and lives in White Plains,
N.Y. She teaches at a Westchester Conserva-
tory of Music.
     I knew you would enjoy having the program
I sent you. What a happy coincidence of
those who participated.
```

On Tuesday morning a pupil of mine and I played my duet arrangement of all twenty four Chopin *Études* at the Mannes College of Music. Great success. Lovely to have met you at Hempstead. A great reunion.

With great affection from,
Henry

On the next page is the program he sent me. It's such a coincidence that Leonard Bernstein, Henry Levine, Mildred and I are all on it together:

Pupils of

Heinrich Gebhard

SIXTH CLASS
SEASON 1938

Sunday 3 P.M.
JUNE 12, 1938

Program

Etude C sharp minor . . . . .Scriabine
Pavane pour une enfant défunte . . . . Ravel
Fantasia in C minor . . . . Bach
Mazurka A minor Op. 17- 4 . . . . .Chopin
Sacre Monte . . . . .Turina

Ouida Blatt

Music for the Dance No. 1 . . . . Bernstein
  Allegretto
  Vivacissimmo
Music for the Dance No. 2 (for Mildred)
  Moderato
  Allegro non troppo

Leonard Bernstein

Music for Two Pianos No. 1 . . . . Bernstein

Mildred Spiegel
Leonard Bernstein

Sonata in B minor . . . . .Liszt
  Lento Assai
  Allegro Energico
  Recitativo
  Adagio
  Allegro
  Andante - lento assai

Henry Levine

10

WHY I DIDN'T BECOME
A CONCERT PIANIST

The train of events must have an engineer.
William M. Blatt

The expectation of anyone who had the great fortune to study with Heinrich Gebhard was to have a concert career. There is a natural desire to be a concert pianist, especially if the individual feels he's got what it takes. I didn't start piano lessons until I was eleven, having played the violin from the age of seven. Actually, most successful concert pianists start lessons at the age of three or four. The overwhelming ambition to become proficient by practicing six or seven hours a day is most important, and I did that as a teenager. I also had a teacher who was dedicated to me when I had the opportunity to play with orchestra; he gave me several extra lessons a week free of charge.

It is very important to have the physical ability such as a large hand with strong fingers and a long little finger to enable one to play big chords. Arthur Rubinstein, for instance, used to hold his hand up on television to show that his little finger was as long as his other fingers and claimed half jokingly that this was the reason for his success. I didn't have a little finger like that and my hand stretched only a bit over an octave. Alicia de Larrocha, who is only five feet tall and has short fingers, did hand stretching exercises which produced excellent results. She is an example of a very talented and ambitious artist who also has the stamina to continue an active concert career into her seventies. Horowitz, Horszowski, and Arthur Rubenstein also stayed active into their eighties and nineties.

Ouida

Incidentally, Arthur Rubenstein (formerly known as Artur Rubenstein) was often mistaken for the great pianist-composer, Anton Rubenstein. Once he received a letter from a fan mistakenly addressed to Anton Rubenstein, asking for his autograph. Arthur responded with this letter:

```
Dear Madam,
    I would have been glad to send my sig-
nature, but unfortunately I have been
dead for many years.
                    Anton Rubenstein
```

My sister heard Rubenstein give a concert in Puerto Rico when a storm came up and all the lights went out in the hall. Rubenstein wasn't fazed a bit and kept right on playing to the end of his program. He was, and still is, my favorite pianist, never putting technique above interpretation, especially when he played his beloved Chopin *Mazurkas*, written by a fellow Pole.

Gebhard used to tell me that my biggest asset was my expressive interpretation of the romantic composers, but I felt that was not enough to warrant a concert career.

A young woman usually has the basic instinct and the natural urge to become a wife and mother. This can interfere with her career ambitions as it did with mine. I didn't have time to have a social life. I felt it was important to find the right partner with whom to spend my life and to have children while I was young. Also, I did not want to travel from city to city as it would take me away from a growing family, which was more important to me than a career.

Unfortunately, a serious piano student hopes to have a career as a concert artist, but it is very difficult to break into the field, and he usually has to settle either for teaching in a university, or privately.

I wasn't the type of person who liked to plan my life. I just let things happen, and never realized when I was teaching Gebhard's daughter, Peggy, that it was the beginning of my teaching career, but that's what it turned out to be.

Later, I did have another chance to play with orchestra after I got married and had my first son, Jerry. I was invited to play the César Franck *Symphonic Variations* with the Worcester Orchestra. At first I was excited and agreed to do it, but since I was pregnant and had started to have the usual unpleasant symptoms, I eventually had to refuse. I wasn't that upset about it because it was too scary to think about playing when I was pregnant. My husband, Sam, was disappointed as he loved the *Symphonic Variations*, and besides had never heard me play with orchestra.

11

MY VERY BEST FRIENDS

Short words are longest remembered.
William M. Blatt

Bob Goldman, whom I met in a street car in Boston on the way to a concert, became my musical brother for life. We attended concerts and music lessons together. He was one of the most charming and caring people I ever met, and he became a very talented jazz pianist and songwriter. We corresponded all the years I lived in New York. Here is a letter I received from him in 1988:

Dear Ouida,

I can't let '88 expire without getting some written word to you!

Your last communique sounded exciting re: Lenny's birthday party. He sure has had a fabulous career. Weren't we lucky to have had him to ourselves- and free, yet! -

I remember his getting *Carmen* from the Brookline Library - (I had a card to their open-shelf music section)- coming to my house where he spent the entire afternoon performing and with commentary. What is even more astounding is that he was only fifteen years old at that time, and the TV lecture he gave some fifteen years later on *Carmen* contains much of what he showed me - almost to the very letter - at the age of fifteen! (There's no explanation for genius??)

Other than my car radio, music has centered
about a series of chamber concerts that Barbara
and I subscribed to and have found satisfying to
our musical hunger. I remember - circa 1940-41 -
your excited announcement of having heard - or
going to hear - a Beethoven quartet. I must
admit that I, at that time, couldn't empathize
with your enthusiasm, and it's only now in my
more "mature years" that I appreciate these
gems. (You always were eons ahead of me in
taste).

Jerry's recognition for his endeavors, which
sound so noble for these times, are most
enheartening. The Blatt genes always did have a
high degree of social awareness.

Love to all and don't let my delinquency in
writing infect you. I'm always delighted to hear
about the Saga-of-Ouida.

Bob

I also met Arthur Rosenheimer, Jr.,
who became Arthur Knight, the famous movie critic, but since he
lived in Brooklyn, New York, we couldn't get together very often.
Jo had met him and decided to introduce him to me when I came
to New York to visit her. Esther, a beautiful, tall, blonde friend of
mine from high school accompanied me. Arthur and I met at a
house party and became interested in each other immediately because of our mutual passion for music. He found a recording that
he wanted me to hear. It was Delius' *The Walk to the Paradise Garden* and was very romantic. Josie had not been able to get a date
for Esther, so Arthur and I had to take her with us, and since it
was New Year's Eve we went to Times Square. I would never again
go there on New Year's Eve, as it was impossible to move among
the throngs. We escaped to see a movie, "The Lady Vanishes."

Arthur and I held hands and fell madly in love, though
Esther, who sat on the other side of him, didn't know what was
going on. We dated for a year — mostly by letters. He came to
visit me a few times, and I was in heaven. Usually we went to a

movie, which was his favorite diversion, and when it was time to go to bed he wore his black silk pajamas, and he looked so handsome in them that I couldn't resist crawling into bed and cuddling with him. I had no intention of going any further and when things started warming up, I got out of bed and announced that we had better say goodnight. That's the way things were in those days; maybe it was for the best. In fact, I'm very glad that my husband and I were still virgins when we were married.

Arthur was very career-oriented and wanted to be a movie critic. He said it was a lifelong dream of his. He wrote long letters which included movie criticism and reviews of concerts he had attended as well as the romantic phrases which showed his affection for me. He told me that before we met, he used to look at Charlie Chaplin's picture before he went to sleep at night, but since he had met me, it was <u>my</u> picture he looked at.

It always amazed me that at the age of twenty, Arthur had announced that he intended to be a film critic. He took out a book of his clippings of well known film critics and showed them to me. At that time, I must admit, I was very skeptical that he would ever realize his dream. A couple of years later, he was up for a job at the film library of the Museum of Modern Art. He wrote in his letter to me "Cross your fingers, light a candle, say a prayer!" Lo and behold, he got the job and he was on his way. He used the name "Arthur Knight" and he became very successful as a film critic. Much later, I remembered his phrase and wrote a song titled, *Cross Your Fingers, Light a Candle, Say a Prayer!*

It was impossible to keep a relationship going between Boston and New York. His letters became less and less frequent and I finally decided not to torture myself. When I was visiting my sister in New York, I couldn't resist calling him. He seemed happy to hear my voice and invited me to the gala opening of a Van Gogh exhibition at The Museum of Modern Art. I accepted, but later changed my mind. I called and told him that I wanted to spend the last day of my visit with my sister, even though I desperately wanted to go with him. My instinct told me that I shouldn't pursue the relationship because marriage with him would be a mistake. He was so handsome and brilliant, but very conceited, and he even admitted it.

My sweet sister, Jo, tried to cheer me up by writing this letter of advice:

```
Dear Ouidy-ley,
    Here is the special Dear Abby letter I
have been promising you.
    No. 1 - Is the guy worth trying for?
(opinion later)

    No.  2.- If so, how shall I bag him?
                    (signed)
                "MISERABLE"
```

```
Now, about point number one, I feel
fairly strongly. I know you don't have any
doubt about it, but I do, and I am the one
who first introduced him to you. I thought
he was very swell, but I must say that I
never met a boy who was more vain about
talking to me. He has apparently a most
independent nature which would not be the
best thing to be married to. He absolutely
snubbed me - and I never had anyone do that.
And I don't think any boy has a right to be
so conceited as to think no one is worth
talking to unless he knows her. This trait
is apparently again showing up in him, as he
thinks he can get away with ignoring someone
he has been nice to. Now I don't say he has
a right to worry about getting involved in
an early marriage, but that he hasn't the
courage to come right out with his stand,
instead of hurting you by not writing, I
cannot condone. I think it is selfish,
childish, and inconsiderate.
    However, just to give him the benefit of
the doubt, let us assume that he is really
busy - and not given to letter writing.
```

Alright, then, I will ask him if he wants to
come to Boston next time I go, and you can
then ask him bluntly what he is waiting for,
if he likes you - and why he takes the
chance of losing you by not writing. In the
meantime, you can show you are not a piece
of fish by standing on your own feet and not
letting one piece of conceited humanity
spoil your fun.

You are now in the formative period of
your life, and could be showing yourself to
be quite a person. Don't think that Arthur
is the only guy you would have got so attached to. It's just the time that you would
be doing so, and I'm sure it would be someone else if not he that you waited for letters from. I know, because I realize that
there are three men, just as cute as the one
who turned you down, who would be glad you
turned up.

Love XO,

NOT MISERABLE

Years later, after I moved to New York with my husband
and three children, I heard Arthur on his radio show and decided
in a moment of weakness to write him a letter and asked if he was
the same Arthur I used to know. He said that indeed he was and
would very much like me to call him when I came to the city. I
was afraid to tell my husband that I intended to call Arthur because I feared his reaction. When I got to the city I hesitated, but
finally made the call. I was so excited to hear Arthur's voice after
all those years, and he seemed to feel the same way. After I told
him that I was a songwriter, he scoffed, "I hope you didn't write
The Purple People Eater," which was the ridiculous hit song of the
day. He invited me to come to his apartment for a cocktail. He
explained that his wife was away in Europe writing a novel, and in
the next breath he derided her for doing it. I decided then and
there that I had been right in the first place: he would have been

bad husband material. I refused his invitation and went on my way. Eventually I did tell my husband about my experience and, surprisingly, it didn't seem to bother him a bit.

Recently, I heard Goldie Hawn quote a review she got from Arthur Knight, "Goldie's performance was as flat as her chest." She seemed to be amused but not very happy about that.

Byron Waksman, the son of Selman Waksman, who coined the term "antibiotic," and received the Nobel Prize for his discovery of streptomycin, became my lifetime friend. I met him in Woods Hole, Massachusetts, where his father was the director of research at the Marine Biological Laboratory, and was introduced to him by my sister, Jo. He looked very handsome in his white suit and I was immediately attracted to him. I had gone with my family to visit my older sister, Hester, who was doing chemical research at Woods Hole. Byron and I went to a Saturday night dance and after dancing a while, we decided to go outside in the balmy summer air to get acquainted. We talked until the wee hours, analyzing our relationships, and he tried to talk me out of my infatuation with Arthur Knight, saying that New York men made terrible husbands. He was going with a girl called Kelly and was rethinking his relationship with her. He was attending Swarthmore at the time and later he went to the University of Pennsylvania, where he became an M.D. Byron had an enormous passion for learning and loved to practice his Chinese writing, and reading books in the original Greek. When he heard me play a piece that appealed to him, he would immediately start to learn it and eventually, without assistance, could play it passably well. One of these was the Brahms *Rhapsody in B minor.*

Byron and I kept in touch through the years and he visited me in Brookline during vacation times instead of going to his family in New Brunswick, NJ. Incidentally, he loved my mother's cooking, and used to ask for the recipes of his favorite dishes. I was impressed with his ability to speak a dozen languages fluently, and when he reached the top of his profession, he gave lectures in several of them. His father worried that Byron was spreading himself too thin because of his many interests. He studied viola with Marcel Dick and later played in amateur quartets made up of doctors he knew at Harvard Medical School, where he became a professor of bacteriology and immunology in 1949. When we were teenagers, I took him on a tour of Harvard University and the Aggasiz Museum with its displays of glass-blown flowers. Little did I know that he was to become a scientist in neurology at Harvard as well as a professor of microbiology at Yale. Some of his most important research was done for the National Multiple Sclerosis Society. He still is connected with Woods Hole where he is director of a course in science writing at the Marine Biological Laboratory, and lives with his wife, Joyce.

It's unusual for teen-agers to remain friends through the years. Here is an example of the correspondence we had more than thirty years after we met:

2/24/63

Dear Ouida,

You see what a bad correspondent I've become. I enjoyed getting your letter and hearing about Sam, your children, and your mother (and yourself too).I think you have every reason to be happy and proud of your children. It seems to me nowadays that the stream of time moves on so rapidly that one almost has to snatch pleasure as it passes, and for a long while children are our best pleasure. For some people they seem to become the only pleasure, but that is a bad mistake. We are having a checkered life just now. We all went to Europe last July, took a brief trip in Spain, then settled down in Paris, where I started to write a book. It won't get finished for quite a long time, I fear. Both Nan and Peter are in French schools, and doing very well indeed. I think they are getting an enormous amount out of it and I'm very glad we did this.

Both kids became quite addicted to opera, even in this short time. They are now skiing in the Alps at the moment - imagine!

I like my laboratory and the younger people around me. We've done some important work in the last several years, and I get to travel around quite a bit, giving speeches and whatnot. I also enjoy my teaching of medical students.

At the moment we are in some mental turmoil trying to decide whether to stay here at Harvard where we now have well formed roots, but still no permanent status, or to move to Yale where I've been offered a fine position with full professorship and all the rest of it.

It seems so long since we've seen each other. It is almost as if we had moved into two different universes. I haven't lost sight entirely of our youth, but they are gone, I fear, never to be recaptured.

Dear Ouida, please greet Sam and all your children, who do not know me. A big kiss for you

from,

Byron

P.S.- My folks are quite well, traveling in Mexico at the moment. You must also give your mother a kiss for me.

I encouraged him to make the move to Yale as I thought it would be advantagious. He eventually did and it turned out be a smart move. This is a more recent letter from him:

Byron H. Waksman, M. D.

1/20/91

Dear Ouida,

I felt like writing after you sent the copy of the lovely newspaper article about your connection with Lenny Bernstein and Aaron Copland, carrying with it the news about your going to three Bernstein Memorial Concerts with Jerry, and Lisa's getting married. It all must have been incredibly exciting.

The picture of you as a music student in Boston is one I have, of course, from a time when we were a lot closer than "best friends." Ah me!! You were a lovely young woman indeed. I think it's great that you are still playing and teaching and having joy in your kids.

I don't know whether I'm being a bit of a damned fool to do all the different things I am doing. It seems like an awful lot, but it has the virtue that I have no time to be bored. I think I told you about my German professorship. I have been using all my waking hours for that. Specifically, there is to be a meeting on May 27th in Heidelberg and I am responsible for the program, the speakers, the guest list, and finding some money to pay for the whole thing. All journalists, you understand, science journalists from newspapers, radio, TV, and free-lance. A challenging task, but it will get done.

So, Ouidee, keep well and keep having a good time.

Your, Byron

Even more recent:

9/30/94

Dear Ouida,

It was good to see you & spend time
talking family & music. I am glad you're
getting on with life.

We are OK, tho more and more creaky in
the joints. Joyce is in the last year of
study in her psychotherapy program at
Masterson Institute & I am still busy
coaching journalists about science writing (in Woods Hole and Munich). The kids
are fine, grandchildren fantastic. One even
is a good pianist!!

How about coming to have dinner with us
in Manhattan. Would love to see you.

Your, Byron & Joyce

I met Sheldon Rotenberg at one
of his uncle Harold's art exhibitions. Sheldon was a violinist who
was already playing *concerti* with orchestra. We became close friends
and were always there for each other backstage when we gave concerts. When he was in the Army in Europe he managed to study
with his idol, Georges Enesco. Eventually he became a first violinist in the Boston Symphony Orchestra, and remained there for
about forty years. When the Boston Symphony Orchestra played
each summer at Tanglewood, we got together at intermissions to
catch up on our family lives. The following is a letter he wrote to
me just before his retirement:

Sept. 23, 1991

Dear Ouida,

I was very happy to find your lovely,
newsy letter (and picture) waiting for me
when I returned from my final BSO tour of
Europe. The last concert in London was a

momentous and very moving event for me, which I will not soon forget. I have been living in the clouds for four months and suppose that I will have to return to planet earth one of these days, but I'm in no hurry to do that just yet!

It was great to see you again in our old stomping grounds, Tanglewood, a wonderful, heady period in our lives, never to be forgotten.

Love,
Sheldon

--- with Sheldon Rotenberg

I must also mention my high school friend May Carlin Homonoff, who stuck by me through my intense practice days when I was playing concerti with orchestra.

She still lives in Boston and is on AT&T Broadband Cable TV interviewing medical authorities on a weekly show called "Senior Spectrum." She is former Chairman of the Advisory Board of the South Shore Elder Services.

ANOTHER GOOD FRIEND?

Too bad that marriage, the most important decision in life,
must be made when we are mentally immature.
William M. Blatt

When I was in my late teens I had a very good friend named
Danielle. She lived in my neighborhood and we used to take walks
together. One day she introduced me to a friend of hers, Franz,
who was visiting her family. Franz was a doctor and he told me
how much music meant to him.

I got a call from him a couple of days later, and he asked if
he could visit me at home. I had thought he was Danielle's friend
but figured he probably wasn't serious about her since he had called
me. It wasn't long after he said hello to my family that he sat down
at the piano and started to improvise some of the most beautiful
music I had ever heard. Franz said he loved to write music as a
hobby, because medicine kept him so occupied. He asked me to
play the piano, and seemed quite impressed when I did.

I was attracted to him and knew he was an immigrant from
Vienna. He had a charming accent, which appealed to me, and he
was good-looking with a pleasant face and gold rimmed glasses.
Classy, I thought.

At any rate, he got serious much too soon for my taste, and
when he proposed after the third date I was appalled – especially
since he expected me to give him an immediate answer. Franz explained that he had decided if I didn't accept his proposal, he would
marry Danielle, as he wanted to settle down. Of course, that decided it for me – let Danielle have him; he must have had an
ulterior motive to be in such a hurry – perhaps citizenship.

Well, he did marry Danielle, and guess what? Danielle never
spoke to me again - she must have thought I tried to take him
away from her.

This story reminds me of a devastating experience I had in
high school. I had a close friend named Sarah. We always walked

home together, and one day she had to stay after school, so I walked home alone. Her mother, unfortunately, happened to see me when she was out driving and asked. "Where's Sarah?" I told her she had to stay after school. Later I got a call from Sarah. She sounded real mad and asked what I had said to her mother. When I answered, "Nothing much," she announced, "Ouida Blatt, I will never talk to you again as long as I live." P.S. She never did. Imagine what a lack of judgment that was. Apparently, her mother made it sound worse than what I had told her. I'm sure Sarah was just as miserable as I was because of her foolish decision. We constantly came in contact with each other during our four years of high school and it was quite a disaster for both of us.

****

In 1940 I decided to send Gebby a Christmas gift. I asked Josie if she would paint my portrait in watercolor, and she very sweetly obliged. Here is his response:

```
          Heinrich Gebhard
          Manchester Road
                    Dec 31, 1940
My Dear Ouidy,
     Your Christmas gift to me certainly was a
lovely surprise!—
     It is an exquisite picture of you. Josie
is a fine artist.You look extremely lovely,
and it does not flatter you in the least!-
     I am delighted to have the picture,- all
beautifully framed too,- and with the most
charming inscription!
     Many thanks to you. I have the picture in
my study (library) and I look at it often
every day!-
     A VERY HAPPY NEW YEAR, and many good ones
to come, to you -  from
                    Your,
                    Heinrich Gebhard
```

The following letter was sent to all of Gebhard's students:

Heinrich Gebhard
33 Manchester Road
Brookline 46, Massachusetts
July 6, 1944

Dear Ouida,

You have always known that I am a pupil of Leschetizky. I studied with him for four years in Vienna, when I was a very young man (after having been prepared, as a boy, by Clayton Johns here in Boston). The music-world at large has acknowledged Leschetizky as the greatest instructor in piano-playing the world has seen. He taught upward of 500 pupils, who came to him from all parts of the world. Many of the most eminent international concert-pianists were his pupils - such as Paderewski, Gabrilowitsch, Schnabel, Friedman, Brailowsky, Ethel Leginska, Moiseiwitsch, etc.

You may be interested to know that about seventy-five Leschetizky pupils are still living in the various sections of the U.S.A. About three years ago most of these banded themselves together and founded the "Leschetizky Association of America." I joined the Association a year ago and have been made the third vice-president of the society.

The object of the Association is "to perpetuate the ideals and principles of Theodor Leschetizky in piano-playing and teaching, and to honor his memory." The activities of the club include: The annual Paderewski Dinner, in New York City, on November sixth, the annual meeting in May, four or five lectures and recitals in New York each year, with discussions and forum on pianistic problems, and the publication of the "Lechetizky Bulletin" twice a year, containing news of members and articles of special interest to pianists.

Beside "Active Members," who are those that studied with Leschetizky at least one year, our organization has "Associate Members" who are pupils of Leschetizky. These have the same privileges of enjoying all the activities as the Active Members. But, since a good many of such Associate Members may find it difficult to go to New York several times a year, there are being formed local clubs outside New York City.

I have started to form a "Boston Chapter of the Leschetizky Association," composed of pupils of mine. We will meet three times a year at an easily reached studio in Boston City. I will preside and each time will lecture for a half-hour on some phase of piano-playing or teaching, and follow it by a voluntary forum, e.g. those who wish will ask questions and we will discuss them.

The cost of belonging to the Association - which includes belonging to the Boston Chapter - is two dollars a year.
WON'T YOU JOIN?

If so, please send your name to me and I will notify the Secretary of the Association in New York, who will then send you an application blank (for you to sign) and a bill for $2.00.

Yours for the upholding of our ideals of beautiful piano-playing, and with cordial greetings,

Heinrich Gebhard

--- with Byron, early

---with Byron, recently

Bob Goldman

12

I MEET MY HUSBAND, SAMSON MINTZ

Love is not in itself a virtue
but it breeds two of the highest virtues,
understanding and forgiveness.
William M. Blatt

In Brookline, I was a member of The 25 Club, which consisted of socially active young people who met at a temple on Beacon Street. In Worcester, Massachusetts, there was a similar club with the same name. During one season, these clubs exchanged dinners, and I took my date to the one in Worcester. Later the Worcester group came to Brookline and as I had another party to go to that night, I had to leave early. As I was walking up the stairs, I heard a voice from below asking if he could give me a ride. It was Samson Mintz, a tall, handsome, well-built man who looked to be quite a few years older than I was. He evidently had noticed me at the dinner in Worcester, but I was not aware of him. Apparently he had his eye on me all night and was too shy to approach me until he saw that I was leaving. I accepted his offer as it was a cold, snowy night and I thought he might be good for my sister, Hester. Before he dropped me off at my destination I asked him if he'd like to come to a party at my house at 117 Lanark Road, Brookline, the following Saturday. Josie, who was then married to David Pall, was to come from New York City to visit the family.

I was surprised when Sam actually turned up at the party.

He came with his best friend, Dave Chafitz, and looked very hand-some smoking his pipe. As I had planned, I indroduced him to Hes. When he was leaving, he asked if I'd like to go to dinner and a movie the following week. I accepted reluctantly because I had expected that he would be asking Hester for the date. A week later he picked me up for our first date and we went to Dinty Moore's in Boston for a fancy steak dinner under candlelight. It was very romantic, and after dinner we went to a movie to see Ginger Rogers in "Kitty Foyle." After the movie, I asked Sam how many sisters and brothers he had, and I noticed that he seemed reluctant to give me an answer, but he knew he had to confess that he had two brothers and six sisters. It came as quite a shock that I was going to have to cope with such a big family if we were to get serious. On our second date we went dancing, and from then on I was hooked. As we danced, Sam said to me, "We fit so well together, don't we?" He sure had a great technique and I fell for it. Actually, he looked a lot like my first love, Arthur, when we were driving at night. He was a Burt Lancaster type, with wide shoulders that led down to a narrow waist, an all-round sportsman who had been a star basketball player in college. After our third date, I knew he was very serious and I thought I would surprise him with a pro-posal. Sam told me much later that he had decided, long before we met in person, that I was the one he wanted to marry. How someone can know just from a glance that a particular person is the right partner for a lifetime, I'll never know! He seemed very pleased with my proposal but had some reservations because I was a concert pianist, and his great interest lay in sports and games, especially tennis and bridge. (He eventually won many tennis tro-phies and became a lifemaster bridge player). As a matter of fact, it didn't help that his sister, Nessie, said to me, "I can't imagine what you have in common with my brother." I had heard that Nessie was very frank, and it often got her in a lot of trouble, but I tried not to let her opinion bother me. Sam really knew how to make me feel special, and convinced me how sincere he was. How-ever, I knew what Nessie meant. Sam had been going with a girl for seven years who shared his love of sports, but they had had a disagreement. I hardly knew the difference between football and baseball, and never played his favorite sport, tennis. Sam was no musician, but he loved opera more than I did, and I figured I could introduce him to music by subscribing to concerts. Since we had so little in common, and he was worried I might change my mind, he insisted that I continue to date other men, in order to make sure that he was the one. A fellow I was dating was a doctor. He called me one night for a date and when Sam heard me accept, he pointed his finger at the phone as if he were shooting at it. He had obviously changed his mind about my dating others, and that was the last time I dated anyone else.

The next day he sent me the following acrostic to show how he felt about me:

OUIDA
by
Samson Mintz

O is for Ouida, synonymous with sweet
U is for unselfish; she's really a treat
I is for intelligence; she has the Quiz Kids beat
D is for dearest; such dearness is a feat
A is for adorable; the most adorable on Vesey Street

The honeymooners

Even though we were both of the Jewish faith, we were brought up in completely different ways. He was orthodox, and I was a Reform Jew. My dad was very interested in religion but he was not a follower – an agnostic, in fact. Sam made it clear that if we married, I would have to keep a kosher home; separate dishes for dairy and meat. I assured him that I could do it. Little did I know what trouble I was getting into; my folks had no experience with this sort of thing and they were to visit us often.

Six months later we were married. Our honeymoon was a pretty short one, as Sam was given less than a week for it, even though the people he was working for at the time were cousins of his in the scrap metal business.

Our first honeymoon stop was Atlantic City where Sam was worried that the hotel where he had reserved a room was not suitable for this special occasion. He decided to get a room at one of the fanciest hotels on the Boardwalk. We parked our rented car in front of this gorgeous hotel while Sam went in to inquire if a room was available and I waited in the car. As he told me later, he asked the man at the desk if they had a beautiful room with a double bed. The man said, "You're in luck. A couple has just vacated the only room left in the hotel," whereupon Sam responded, "Just a minute, I have to go out to ask my girlfriend." On the way out he realized that what he had just said out of force of habit was the word "girlfriend," which must have seemed to him to be emblazoned in the sky. He said, "I'm afraid, sweetheart, we can't go back in there after what I just said." Unfortunately, we ended up in a much less appropriate hotel, located on a side street. This speaks volumes about the manners of the time.

I must say I was in for a surprise on our wedding night. Believe it or not, we were both virgins. Sam, for his part, had never been intimate with his former girlfriend. I guess he must have taken a lot of cold showers during their seven years together. (Incidentally, she had met with Sam one night in order to return trophies he had won, but had used the occasion to beg him to come back).

To get back to the all-important wedding night, I'm afraid I felt so much pain when the big moment arrived that I was still a virgin at the end of the honeymoon.

Our first home in Worcester was at 126 Copperfield Road, on the first floor of a two family house. Another newlywed couple, who were friends of ours, lived upstairs. Incidentally, Worcester was the hometown of a popular singer of the time, "Her Nibs, Georgia Gibbs."

We had a very blissful marriage during the first few months, but then I discovered that my charming husband had a big temper when provoked. He had been clever enough to conceal it before our marriage. It was upsetting to my parents; however, I remembered that my dad had a pretty big temper on occasion, so I was used to it. It also helped to hear Sam say "I adore you" at the most unexpected times.

I began to realize that passionate people are the ones who have tempers; I guess we have to take the bad with the good.

One day my folks were visiting our kosher home, where the meat and dairy dishes were supposed to be kept separate. They got all the dishes mixed up when they were helping me prepare dinner. A big argument ensued and I soon realized that I could never continue with this unfamiliar way of life if I wanted to stay on friendly terms with my folks. These religious customs seem to keep some people apart. Sam and I eventually came to an understanding when we realized that our love for each other was more important than some ancient customs which I found too difficult to follow. I did try to observe the most important holidays. For instance, during Passover, I eliminated bread and substituted matzos for a week, but I didn't change to the Passover dishes as I was supposed to do for the holidays. Actually, Sam wanted me to keep kosher out of respect for his mother's wishes. I don't think he felt very religious himself. For instance, according to the Jewish law he and his family were not to drive on Saturdays or holidays, but in fact, they parked their cars around the corner from his mother's house so as not to offend her. Later, his mother and I became the closest of friends, and when she ate in my house she even closed her eyes to the fact that I didn't keep strictly kosher.

13

LIFE IN WORCESTER, MASS.

A diaper is a damp nuisance.
William M. Blatt

We were beginning to adjust to married life and were learning more about each other when we discovered we were going to be parents. Fortunately, I had a normal pregnancy and continued to teach a few piano students. When I was ready to give birth, I almost didn't make it to the hospital in time. We lived on top of a very high hill and Sam's car was unavailable at the time. It was a blizzard of a night and the roads were icy when suddenly my water broke. What were we to do? Sam made many frantic calls to get a cab. Finally, he found a sympathetic taxi driver who put chains on his cab in order to make the hill. The driver told us he was the father of seven children and was happy to help us. In our haste we forgot to take the bag which I had packed a month before and actually tripped over it at the front door. As I hobbled up the hospital steps, Sam tried to calm me down when he jokingly asked, "Honey, are you sure you want to go through with this?" In the hospital I was helped into a wheelchair and received the inevitable questioning. It didn't matter that I was having acute labor pains; the nurse insisted on filling out the entrance form before I was allowed to be taken to my room. I was trying to be brave and cooperative, even though Sam was not allowed to accompany me. When my nurse arrived, I knew by her manner that she was going to be very unsympathetic. I asked her for some medication to alleviate the pain and I was horrified to hear her gruff voice saying,

"Absolutely not." I suffered for the next several hours until my obstetrician, Dr. Hart, arrived. Shortly after, the miracle happened. Dr. Hart, who was also an anesthesiologist, gave me a spinal injection and the pain stopped dead in its tracks! I was able to see the complete birth as if it were happening to someone else. The epeseotomy with the surgeon's knife allowed my first born son, Jerome Alan Mintz, to practically fly into the world. The doctor caught all seven pounds of him as if he were a football, and Jerry was born at 10:15 A.M. Back in my room, we were presented with this fluffy-haired pink and white newborn baby which up to then was the most miraculous happening in our lives.

When I was due to have my second child three years later, we had moved to 99 Longfellow Road. I was feeling a few dull pains one morning, but it was nothing unusual, so I sat outside on my front step as it was a beautiful, mild April day. A neighbor of mine joined me and said she doubted I would give birth that day as I seemed too calm. I was scheduled to go to the Fairlawn Hospital, a rather small private one, unlike the last one, thank goodness, which had seemed in retrospect like a concentration camp. I gave Sam his lunch and we drove to the hospital to register. After the usual preparations for the delivery, all hell broke loose as the pains started to come at a rapid pace. I screamed when the head started to show while I was on the delivery table. Fortunately, they allowed Sam to be with me, which was rare in those days, and I squeezed his hand for dear life because the pain was so intense. Since my doctor hadn't shown up by then, my nurses told me not to push. Finally, after what seemed like hours, the doctor arrived and hurriedly gave me that miracle shot in the spine. My second son, William Michael, was born shortly after, and I witnessed the whole thing with no pain. Later, I did have post partum depression, however, probably due to the anxiety I had when my doctor didn't arrive on time.

As one might imagine, I went to a different doctor for the birth of my third child - a Dr. Stern. He was a charming man who promised I could have the same kind of spinal injection that I had had with my other deliveries. When it came time to give birth, I was examined in the St. Vincent Hospital and Dr. Stern said it might be hours before I would deliver. Just as he walked out the door, I felt a tremendous pain and I hollered for him to come back. When he saw that the head was showing, he rushed me into the delivery room while saying, "There's no time for a spinal," and I was given a whiff of gas. Before I knew it, Lisa Meryl was lying beside me on the delivery table, and Sam joined us in the room. It felt as if I were in heaven when he kissed me, as the gas must have been starting to take effect, but we sure were delighted that we got our wish for a baby daughter.

This is the announcement we sent to our friends:

WORCESTER GAZETTE

CONCERT REVIEW

LISA MERYL MINTZ, young lyric soprano, daughter of Ouida and Samson Mintz, made her operatic debut for the benefit of the St. Vincent Hospital fund on Sunday April 30, at 3:50 PM.

Miss Mintz's initial solo was technically sound, lusty, and expressive despite her extreme youth and diminutive size (6 lbs. 12 ozs.).

She was ably assisted by Dr. Arthur Stern,

OBM

After Billy was born and I was nursing him, four year old Jerry wanted attention and was making a pest of himself. I snapped at him, "Someday you'll have trouble with your child and you'll know what it feels like." Jerry answered, "Mom, isn't it hard enough to have bad children without having bad grandchildren too!"

One day while having lunch with friends and their kids, something Jerry ate didn't agree with him and later he threw up for the first time. He told a friend what happened, "I opened my mouth and my lunch fell out!"

The Worcester Music Group gave people an opportunity and an incentive to practice and perform for others at an informal meeting which took place every month.

We met in the homes of the members and served light refreshment after the concerts. In the course of a dozen years, I was able to review most of my repertoire while taking care of a house and three children. For the three years that I was president, I was forced to learn how to speak in front of an audience, which up to then I had always tried to avoid doing. I did research for the talks on the music that was to be played at the meetings, consisting of the classics - solos and chamber music.

One of the most colorful members was a Czechoslovakian cellist, Bedrich Vaska, who looked to be ninety but had to be younger in order to perform as well as he did. He was all bent over from playing the cello for so many years. I believed him when he told me that he had actually played quartets with Dvorak, one of my favorite composers. Incidentally, when my older son, Jerry, was at Goddard College in Vermont, he was amazed to find that Vaska was teaching music there. Jerry spoke to him and said he remembered hearing him play in Worcester when his mother was president of the Music Group. What a coincidence!

The oldest music festival in the country takes place in Worcester every year in the fall, where a world famous symphony orchestra is brought in for a week of concerts. When I was living in Worcester, I was a member of the chorus that sang with the Philadelphia Orchestra under Eugene Ormandy. We all felt that it was a privilege to be rehearsed by the great Boris Goldovsky, assisted by the young, talented Sarah Caldwell, who was much later to become the first woman to conduct at the Metropolitan Opera in New York.

My husband encouraged me to take Tuesday nights off for these rehearsals. Among the great works we performed were Beethoven's Ninth, the Verdi and Brahms Requiems, etc. When I hear those masterpieces performed today it takes me back to those early exciting days. It was so much fun for me and my friend, Rhoda, to go out for coffee after a concert with a group of musicians from the orchestra including Abe Torchinsky, "Torchy", who played the tuba, and Isidore Schwartz, "Izzy", a first violinist. Izzy's daughter, Susan Starr, who was only eight years old, played a Mozart Piano Concerto incredibly well for such a young child, at one of the concerts. When I suggested to Izzy that it was cruel to force a young child to practice for hours every day, he answered, "If I don't make her practice now, she will never forgive me when she is older." He proved to be right. She won several contests, including one in Russia, and became a successful concert pianist.

Once I met William Kincaid, the great flutist, backstage. During our conversation I thought I'd take the opportunity to ask him if he had ever heard a melody which I had written words to, and called, "Lullaby." I had shown it sometime before to Lenny Bernstein. He thought it was beautiful, and said, "If you wrote that song, you are a fine composer." When I sang it for Mr. Kincaid, he thought it sounded Norwegian. Sure enough, one night when I was listening to the radio, I was startled to hear "my melody." I could hardly believe it when the announcer said it was by Jarnefelt, and amazingly was called *Lullaby.* I had sung this melody to my children as they were growing up, and they even refused to go to sleep until I had sung it for them. When Jerry was older he loved to play it on the violin.

I remember one night when Lenny and the New York Philharmonic came to the Worcester Auditorium to give a concert. I wanted to go backstage to see him, but I was stopped by a security guard who said he had orders not to let anyone backstage. I asked him if he would give Mr. Bernstein a message. Just say, "Ouida is here to see you." It worked like magic. After he checked, I was immediately escorted in to see him, and we had a great reunion during which I congratulated him on a fine performance. We were talking about old times while surrounded by members of the orchestra, when a percussionist came over to ask him how one of the passages went in the score. Without any hesitation, Lenny beat out the time of the part in question - "dah dah dee dah dah dee dum." It seemed very complicated to me, but he had it all in his head, as he had most of the scores he conducted. At that time, he knew that he was being accused by the critics for exaggerating when he conducted, even jumping up and down on the podium. He explained that it was spontaneous because he loved the music so much that he almost felt that he was composing while he was conducting it. When he came to the end of a work, he often would bow automatically, and not realize where he was, not even what country he was in. It was only then that he knew he had given his all.

During our conversation Lenny admitted that whenever he travelled to a new city he liked to go on the local rollercoaster. It seems he always liked to take chances, and that carried over to his professional life. He had enough confidence in young people to come through in a tight spot when he asked the sixteen year old André Watts to substitute at the last minute for an ailing performer. Sure enough, it became an auspicious debut for the young boy which he never forgot.

I'm also reminded of an event that happened in 1963. Lenny happened to meet the great pianist and teacher, Rosina Lhevinne, when he was auditioning one of her students, Abbott Lee Ruskin, for a New York Philhamonic Young People's Concert. When the audition was over, Lenny asked the eighty two year old musician why she had never played with the Philharmonic, and she replied modestly, "Because nobody ever asked me." Evidently Lenny had heard that she still played very well, as shortly afterword the managing director of the orchestra called her to say they wanted her to play three days consecutively. What a chance Lenny was taking! Suppose she missed a run or had a lapse of memory - it would blow the whole thing!

She decided to play the extremely difficult Chopin *E minor Piano Concerto* which she had performed years ago at the Moscow Conservatory. When the concerts were scheduled, the dress rehearsal had to be open to the public, as there was such a demand for tickets. The concert I attended seemed to be crowded with students. They couldn't all be hers I thought, although I had heard she had a full teaching schedule at Juilliard. Before she came out you could feel the tension of the audience, wondering if she could do it. Of course, she was an overwhelming success. The New York Times critic wrote, "She got better as she went along . . . . with the brio of a young virtuoso."

When Mike Wallace and Buff Cobb, his then wife, had the CBS television show "All Around the Town" in 1952, I wrote a letter to him and asked if he would play the violin on his program. During the show he made a telephone call to me in Worcester, Massachusetts. We spoke and reminisced about old times and then he took out his violin and played unusually well, considering that he probably hadn't practiced for years. It brought back happy memories of some of the experiences we had, and I was surprised to receive a Bulova watch a few days later for my participation in the show.

Although Mike has always been primarily interested in journalism, which he studied at the University of Michigan, he did start his career as an actor in radio in the late 1930s and later in early TV dramas, such as the ABC police show, "Stand by for Crime" in 1949. Also in those early TV years Mike did his first interrogations on the ABC "Majority Rules" show, but at that time he was quizzing contestants instead of interviewing well-known people, and was still known as Myron Wallace. During the next few years, Mike's popularity grew as he acted as either host or panelist on a variety of game or quiz shows, and as an interviewer of many celebrities, and correspondent for CBS News. Mike got a reputation for being rather sharp and to the point when he interviewed anybody, even Gorbachev. It didn't really matter how important the person was, that was his style. All of these activities earned him a number of Emmy and Peabody awards as well as a Robert Sherwood award, a DuPont Columbia Journalism award, and the Thomas Hart Benton award. In 1968, when he and Harry Reasoner launched the extremely successful CBS "60 Minutes" show, his ambition to become an outstanding journalist was finally realized. Recently he received honorary degrees at the University of Massachusets and the University of Pennsylvania.

At the age of 79, Mike Wallace was honored on a CBS News Special in prime time on September 11, 1997. It was a retrospective of his thirty years on "60 Minutes," in addition to his thirty year career before that in the entertainment business. During those earlier years, he became involved in the civil rights movement and was in contact with such people as Martin Luther King, who became his hero, and Malcolm X, who became a close friend after he came to realize that violence didn't solve the race problem.

Mike interviewed Jeffrey Wygand, the cigarette whistle-blower who told Mike that cigarettes are addictive. Mike said, "You put it in your mouth and you've got your fix, right?" Wygand nodded yes.

At a fairly recent interview, Mike asked Barbara Streisand why a successful person as she, with such a gorgeous voice, needed twenty seven years of psychotherapy, and why it took so long. Barbara eyed him rather resentfully and, after some hesitation, said, "I guess I'm just a slow learner."

Talking with Shirley MacLaine, Mike asked, "You really believe that you lived lives before?"

"Yes, Mike, there's no doubt in my mind about it."

Mike asked, "Do you even believe in extra-terrestrials?"

Shirley's pleasant expression changed, she looked at him accusingly and said, "That is what I was afraid of, Mike. It doesn't become you."

Mike and CBS wound up in court when he confronted General William Westmoreland with the fact that American forces were facing much stronger opposition in Vietnam than the general had led the country to believe. Eventually CBS and Mike won their case.

In 1967 and '68, he covered the campaign of Richard Nixon, who, Mike said, was very straightforward and never lied to him. The future president started out with high expectations, but unfortunately ended with evil doings and tragedy.

One of the saddest days for Mike was when his older son, Peter, who was a junior at Yale, lost his life when he fell from a rock in Greece that suddenly loosened under his weight and sent him flying a hundred feet down the mountain. Peter was a writer and poet, and Mike took the loss very hard. I can identify with him, having also lost my twenty year old son. Of course he takes consolation in the accomplishments of his son, Chris, who seems to be following in his dad's footsteps. Chris has said that his father gave him the following advice: it's not how you ask the question, but its the right question you ask that's important. Chris can't understand how his dad gets away with some of the bold questions he asks.

Mike Wallace has been fighting depression for many years, but has now overcome it with the use of medication, and especially with the help of his good friends, Art Buchwald and Bill Styron, who also had similar problems. Other celebrities who have had this condition have come forward to speak of how they have overcome depression: Rod Steiger, Nobel Laureate Salvador Luria, and Patty Duke.

****

July 25th arrived once more and I chose a book on the life of Sigmund Romberg to send to my dear teacher:

H.G.

33 Manchester Road

July 27, 1951

Dear Ouida,-

Thank you for the lovely book on the Life of Sig. Romberg. I know I will enjoy it very much. Also the card, and the clipping from the Worcester newspaper. It is wonderful. I see Jerome, in his tender years, is already getting famous. He must be very talented to have written his camp song at such an early age — talented mother and father!

I am enjoying my summer greatly. Am away visiting each weekend (Fri. Sat. Sun.). And in the middle of the week I give six to seven lessons.

Will be at Tanglewood August ninth to hear Leonard B.("Lenny") conduct the Beethoven *Missa Solemnis* in memory of Koussevitsky— Lots of love to you.

You are incorrigible about sending me a gift each birthday. You are too sweet.

Your,

H.G.

Ouida holding year-old Jerry

--- with Billy

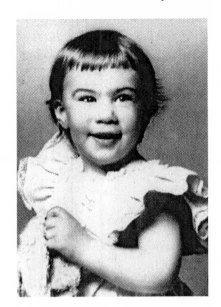

Daughter, Lisa Meryl, at two years

Billy at seven, Lisa at three,
Jerry at ten

14

WE MOVE TO NEW YORK

The ability to grow involves the ability to change.
William M. Blatt

When Sam had his own business, Universal Scrap Metal, he became successful enough to go into partnership with a New York "sharpie" who bought him out after a year. Part of the reason he "sold out" was that I had always wanted to live in New York to be near my sister, Josie, who lived in a charming community called the Country Club, where the homes were built on concrete slabs by William Levitt, of Levittown fame. Sam had picked a house out that was around the corner from Jo, so it didn't bother me that I had never seen it. The house cost $25,000 in 1955, when we moved in, and the value of the average house in the area had soared to $350,000 by the seventies, so it became the best investment we had ever made.

Included in the deal was membership in the Country Club, which consisted of an Olympic sized pool, several well-kept tennis courts (unfortunately for Sam, it was lacking a golf course), and the main house where we held receptions for two Bar Mitzvahs and one wedding, with delectable dinners for over one hundred people per affair.

In the last several years, many buyers of these homes have torn them down and built elegant mansions on the valuable tree-lined, manicured, one-third acre properties.

We enjoyed living in our new home, the first one we had

ever owned, especially since it was near my sister, Jo. But we never
had an inkling of what we were in for until we saw a small damp
spot on our new wall-to-wall rose colored carpet in the living room
one morning. At first we thought someone had spilled a glass of
water on it, but gradually the spot became larger and darker, and
we realized that it was a lot more serious than we had thought. My
sister told me, when I described it to her, that it happens quite
often in the Country Club, and we had better sign a contract with
our oil company to protect us. There was obviously a defect in the
radiant heating in the floor.

When the oil company people came, they rolled up the
wet carpet and padding, which had started to reek from the horse-
hair filling, and, to our horror, started to hack away at the floor of
our beautiful new home, leaving an excavation so big that we could
even stand in it. It was a shock, to put it mildly. However, for the
next several years we put up with more leaks and excavations because we were covered for it, and it was so delightful to walk bare-
foot on a warm floor in the wintertime. But finally we decided
that enough was enough, and we changed to baseboard heating.
We had to put up with a cold floor, but it was worth it not to have
any more floor leaks.

Molly Russek was one of the first persons I met when we
moved. She was responsible for an important chain of events that
took place in my life. Some people are born communicators and
Molly certainly was one of them. At a Jewish organization we belonged to, she introduced me to people as a very accomplished
piano teacher, and that is what got me started on my teaching
career in Roslyn Heights, Garden City, and Great Neck.

Molly's husband, Allen, who worked hard as an orthopedic doctor, was also an accomplished violinist, and was anxious to
perform with others in his free time. That was the signal for his
devoted wife to organize a local orchestra for him, which she did
by taking an ad in the Roslyn News. I decided to respond, as I was
curious to see if I could still play the violin after so many years of
neglect. The most important part of the story is that the pianist at
our first rehearsal at Temple Sinai, Ethel Weiss, became my close
friend and has been my soul-sister for the last forty years. My
mom, in her later years, thought of Ethel as another daughter

since we were together so much. We went to New York City every Wednesday to meet Mom for lunch and a matinée.

Moving to New York was a big adjustment for Sam. He had lived all his life in a rather small city and he had to give up his many friends. He was now going to work for Pall Corporation as a sales engineer for my brother-in-law, David Pall. This required driving into the city every day and fighting the traffic, something he was hardly used to. Many of his business trips entailed flights around the country. He managed to combine playing bridge at night with his daytime business appointments. Eventually, he got enough red points to become a Life Master in bridge.

When we started living in Roslyn Heights, Josie arranged for one of her good friends to take over for her when she was too busy to help me. After all, Jo was the wife of a very important executive, the mother of three young children, an artist who taught painting, and a promising writer. Hilda Brunswick was the friend who showed me the ropes. She helped me to arrange for Jerry's Bar Mitzvah, which took place only a couple of months after we moved in. There were so many things to think of, and Hilda was very helpful.

LENNY HEARS MY SONGS

When Rosalind Russell was playing in *Wonderful Town* in 1953, Lenny was very excited about it. The show had just opened and he thought it would be a big hit. I called him up in the morning because I wanted to bring him some songs I had been writing, and wanted his opinion about them. I had just moved to New York from Massachusetts and didn't know anybody. I thought he might be able to give me some contacts.

I went to his apartment in the Osborn. Sam stayed downstairs; he didn't think it was his business. The apartment was beautiful, with high ceilings and lots of pictures around of all the celebrities he knew. It was very impressive. Somebody brought him lunch while I was sitting there. He devoured it. He used to love to eat. Most artists do.

He listened very carefully to each song I played. He actually spent more time than I wanted him to on small details. It almost seemed as if he was storing certain phrases in his mind that he liked. He even mentioned certain ones. For example, in one song called *Don't let Trouble Trouble You*, there is an unusual interval, a whole step as in a modal scale. He said he liked it.

Lenny spent a couple of hours with me looking over my songs. We played with his daughter, Jamie, for a while. She was just a baby. Lenny was very excited bacause his wife, Felicia, was going to be on television that night in a play.

We went downstairs in the elevator. Up to that point, he hadn't given me any leads for my music. Sam was waiting for me. He asked if Lenny had given me any leads and I said he hadn't. Lenny finally gave me a name to contact. It was some kind of a bigshot, but it was never very useful.

I joined the Roslyn Music Group at that time, which was an organization that arranged for chamber music concerts several times a year at Wheatley High School where my children graduated. We heard some of the most prominent quartets including the Budapest, the Tokyo, and the Juilliard. There were also well-known soloists who gave concerts there, namely: Abby Simon, Leonard Rose, Ruth Slenczynska, Yalta Menuhin, Byron Janis, etc. After these concerts we had a reception for the artists and the Brunswick's graciously volunteered to have most of them at their home.

When the Juilliard performed, I decided to have the reception at my house because Raphael Hillyer, the violist, was an old friend of mine from Boston and was like a brother to me and my sisters. He used to call me "Ouidy," as my own family did, and once when I went backstage after he had given a concert, he recognized my voice when I asked to see him and called out from inside his dressing room, "Come in Ouidy." He married a German girl named Gerda, who had lost her family in the Holocaust, and they had three children. On the night when the Juilliard came to my house in Roslyn Heights for the reception, Raphael asked me to call his wife during the summer, but didn't say why. Unfortunately, I found out later why he was so concerned about her. I heard that while he was in London concertizing, this poor, disturbed woman jumped out of her hotel window and killed herself. Even though I hardly knew Gerda, I felt somewhat guilty for not having called her. I'll never know if it would have changed anything.

Whitestone Photo – Lenox, Massachusetts

For Ouida and all the Mintz's
Affectionately,
Lenny Bernstein

Heinrich Gebhard visits Ouida in Roslyn

One night Josie and I went to a piano recital at the new palatial home of the Norman Blankman family in Sand's Point, L.I. to hear a teen-age boy named Garrick Ohlsson, who was almost six feet tall. After hearing him play, it was obvious to Jo and me that he would make his mark in the musical world. Of course we now know he became famous as a Chopin specialist, having won the prestigious Chopin award in Poland. The home in which Ohlson played was unique in that it had a large tree sculpture of a colorful human figure that stood in the middle of the living room and rose up through the roof. The tree was sculpted by Alfred Van Loen. As Josie and I took our leave, I told Mr. Blankman and his wife that I hoped they'd be happy in their new home and he replied, "If we're not happy here, we won't be happy anywhere."

At that time our kids were quite young and anxious to have a pet, which we were not allowed to have back in Worcester, because of the landlord. Sure enough, a multi-colored cat (mostly yellow) padded into our house one day and we adopted it on the spot. We called her CATerpillar. Since she refused to be an indoor house-cat, we soon discovered that we were expecting a bunch of kittens. Caterpillar found a closet upstairs to await the birth of the cutest five kittens we ever saw: two pure white ones, one light orange, one grey and white, and a black one with white paws. They were all adorable. Mother Caterpillar took great pride in her kittens and rarely left their side, but when she didn't come home one day, we assumed she had been run over by a car. I had the job of feeding the kittens with a doll's bottle, and it worked very well. We easily found homes for all except the black one, so we kept him and called him "Bootsie." We all enjoyed his company for five years and, of course, I had most of the responsibility of feeding him. But he was worth it. However, he became sick and refused to eat anything but gefilte fish. The vet couldn't figure out what was wrong with him. Sam and I couldn't bear to tell the kids why he disappeared one day, but we were forced to put him to sleep when he refused to eat anything. We told a white lie, saying that he had just run away.

****

It's that time again, July 25th, and I am sending Gebhard a book about the life of Pablo Casals, the great cellist.

Aug 10, 1957

Dear Ouida,-

The Casals book arrived and I cannot thank you enough. You have sent me in all these years many fine books. But this is one of the finest - many thanks!

I don't know whether you knew that twenty five years ago I had lunch with Casals and Mr. Loeffler (my great friend) at Mr. Loeffler's house in Medfield, Mass.

Casals had his cello with him, and after lunch he played one of the Bach *Suites* (solo) for us alone! It was an unforgettable experience.- And, besides his heavenly playing, his sweet, warm, dear personality was there, just as it is described in the book.- Of course, I heard him play in recitals too. Possibly you did too?- But no, you weren't born yet. I have almost finished the book. Each chapter is wonderful. Besides all the accounts of his life, his concert tours, his work as a conductor and all this- his philosophy of life!- And the chapter on interpretation full of marvelous points,- and you are sweet to say that much of it coincides with my ideas on interpretation.

Ouida, my visit at your charming house in Roslyn Heights was wonderful. You are the same lovely, dear girl you have always been. And your nice boys, and your dear sister,- I was glad to see her too,- and her children. I

hope I may see your good husband this
coming winter when perhaps we all have
lunch together in New York--

Thanks for including the new booklet of
"Blattitudes! They are brilliantly written,
like the other. Please tell him. Your whole
family is unique, all gifted and charming.

My life here is just what I wish it to be
in my "retirement"— I am very happy with
Peggy, my daughter,- your pupil,- her husband and my two grandchildren,- Marlene 3,
Johnny Michael 8, and our nice house and
garden. I teach six former pupils of mine
who live now in this vicinity. I practice
two hours every day. I am doing some great
review work, The *Well Tempered Clavichord*,
both books, forty-eight *Preludes and Fugues*,
and the 32 Beethoven *Sonatas* and the 24
Études of Chopin. And I am composing again,
and I have finished my book "The Art of
Pedaling" which has just been accepted for
publication by G. Schirmer of New York.

Sometime I hope you and Josie and Sam may
be able to come here for a day. And please -
all my love to you, to Josie, and Hester and
their families and to your father and
mother.

Your,

Heinrich Gebhard

P.S.- Your songs are delightful. I hope
the publisher you spoke of will bring out a
lot of them.

Lots of people come here to see us. Henry
Levine and Helen Coates have been here several times. Peggy sends her love to you.

15

I MEET PAUL SIMON

*I look forward to the time when
"successful" will not mean rich.*
William M. Blatt

I hired a fellow from Queens College named Jerry Landis to make demos for about sixteen of my songs. I met him on Wednesdays at Associated Records at 723 7th Avenue, New York City, where the engineers sat in a glassed-in control room. Jerry and I recorded the songs in the adjoining studio where all the instruments were. It was exciting to see how talented he was – able to take a lead sheet and turn it into a record in one-half to one hour of over-dubbing his harmonies and singing the lyrics. I was so impressed that I introduced him to some good friends I knew in the business – Alex and Joan Kramer – who had written *Far Away Places* and *No Man is an Island,* etc.

They were always ready to listen to my songs and to meet young, talented people. They thought Jerry was talented, too, and paid him to make a demo of a song of mine that they liked called *Yesterday's Child,* with lyrics by Selma Praga. However, they never recognized his possibilities or how successful he was to become, so they neglected to sign him up. Eventually, Jerry must have been glad they didn't, as he later became his own publisher.

One night, a few years later, I saw a guy on the Tonight Show who looked a lot like Jerry Landis, but Johnny Carson had introduced him as Paul Simon, and he sang *The Sound of Silence* with Art Garfunkel. I called his mother in Queens to see if it was indeed my friend, Jerry, and sure enough, it was! When he and Garfunkel were singing together as kids, they used the name, "Tom and Jerry"; and that's how he came to use "Jerry Landis." Before this, he had gone to England with Art, as they were not having any success here. In fact, he had complained bitterly to me that he could no longer listen to music on the radio because he was so discouraged. While they were in England, they happened to hear a version of *The Sound of Silence,* which had been part of an unsuccessful album they had recorded for Columbia Records. It turned out that the A&R (Artists and Repertoire) man at Columbia liked that particular song and decided to "soup it up" with echo chamber and rhythm section, and it was released as a single. It became an instant hit, and they headed home on the first plane available.

Of course we all know how many other hits Simon had. There was *Mrs. Robinson* (from "The Graduate," sung by Simon and Garfunkel) which received a Grammy, as did *Bridge Over Troubled Waters.* Also, his albums *Still Crazy After All these Years,* and *Graceland.* Paul tried acting in films for a time with his "One Trick Pony," in which he had the lead. He also had a part in Woody Allen's "Annie Hall." And then there was the "Born at the Right Time Tour," Johannesburg, South Africa, 1991.

I guess if I had an inkling of how important Paul Simon was to become, I wouldn't have complained to him so much when he was late for an appointment, or told him he should sing a bit louder when we were in the studio making my demos. I should have been happy that he spent so much time overdubbing different instruments and extra voice parts. Sometimes I had long phone conversations with him after he made a demo, and when I asked him if he thought I had a hit song, he usually responded positively.

It's amusing to recall the titles of the songs of mine that he recorded; they were so unlike his style. Here are a few of them:
Cross Your Fingers, Light a Candle, Say a Prayer
Yours is the Kiss that Counts
Right Now
Just a Kid

Every Night (When I Turn Out the Light)
I'm Scared
The Third Rail
Spider Web
The Growing Up Years
Too Many Memories
The Beginning of the End
Where There's a Will There's a Way
Wedding Waltz
Where's My Girl? (Paul sings the solo as well as
all parts of the background group).

I often sang with him on some of these demos. He once told me I could be a folk singer, which I felt was quite a compliment, coming from him.

Recently Paul Simon returned to Queens College in New York to receive an Honorary Doctor of Humane Letters Degree, and told graduates that he had not bothered to attend his own graduation in 1963. "I hope you won't take my observations as advice," he said. "Fame is a very dangerous acquisition. Don't waste your time pursuing it. If you do get it, use it to help others. Otherwise it can be poisonous."

He seemed to be a very private person when we were making demos of my songs. I never felt that he was happy, as he rarely smiled. Every song of mine that I gave him to record was taken very seriously. He gave it his all, playing whatever instrument he found in the studio, beside his ever-present guitar. He even played drums and harmonized on several tracks with his own voice. I was convinced this guy was going to go far one day, though no one I introduced him to agreed. I was right of course, and realized it when I saw him accept the first of several Grammy awards on TV.

After Paul Simon's first success, I had to look for other talented people to make my demos. Jack Carroll and Bernie Knee were the ones I chose. The latter was almost as versatile as Paul Simon because he played the guitar very well. My favorite demos that these two talented people made were called *A Blessing in Disguise* and *I Tell My Heart*. Six of my songs that become records are:

Looey, Looey, Wait for a While (lyrics by Roz Frankfort), *Pa, I Passed My Driving Test* (also with Roz), *Too Long Ago, The End of the World for Me,* and *One and Twenty,* adapted from Dvorak's *Slavonic Dance #2 in E minor,* and sung by Tommy Edwards. This was my most successful record, and I had to give up half the profits to some mysterious person. MGM was the record company. The song was #2 in Chile and I made about three thousand dollars. People in the business used to kid me by saying I had a song that was "Hot in Chile." My sister, Jo, adapted the lyric from A. E. Houseman's "When I Was One and Twenty." I had written another lyric for it called, *My Heart Will Go on Dreaming.* ("My heart will go on dreaming though we said goodbye, It won't believe a love like ours could ever die. My heart will go on hoping this is not the end, I know I can't forget you, why should I pretend?") Jo insisted that her adaptation was an inspiration. Evidently the publisher, Larry Taylor (Jim Skip Music), thought so too. Taylor was determined to get a record, and he did. I became a member of BMI as a result.

When I Was One and Twenty (Jo's Lyrics)
(Adapted from A. E. Houseman)

When I was one and twenty
I heard a wise man say,
"Give gold and precious stones,
But not your heart away;

———————————

Give rubies and give pearls,
But keep your fancy free" —
When I was one and twenty
Who could talk to me?

———————————

The heart you give away,
You may want back some day,
But then you'll pay in tears —
In tears you will pay.

———————————

Once I was one and twenty —
Now I'm twenty two,
And what the wise man told me,
Oh, 'tis true, 'tis true.

Now, in his middle fifties, Paul has
had a much greater challenge — his first musical, *The Capeman.*
As he had no experience in the musical form, the project was not
only a risk to the reputation he had gained through the years, but
a tremendous monetary risk as well, with a budget of over eleven
million dollars and a cast of forty three. He hired top theatrical
people to work with him, and said that the reason he did the show
was that he wanted to avoid being remembered just as the guy
who played Central Park.

The plot of *The Capeman* would seem to be a bit weird for
a musical, to say the least. It's a true-life story that had intrigued
Paul for seven years; the tale of a barely literate sixteen year old
Puerto Rican boy named Salvador Agron who belonged to a gang
called the Vampires and murdered two teenagers of a rival gang in
New York City.

Agron reformed himself in prison and miraculously evolved
into a fine writer and poet. I thought that if "The Titanic," a very
tragic story, could become a hit musical on Broadway, as well as a
blockbuster movie, then perhaps *The Capeman* had a chance.

The Capeman had only a short run, but Paul's music from
the show sold very well on CDs.

His personal life, however, is the best it has ever been, as
he is happily married to his third wife, Edie Brickell, a former pop
singer, who has given him a son and a daughter. He has an adult
son, Harper, from his first marriage.

Now, life is definitely putting a smile on the face of the
formerly serious, Paul Simon. He will be performing at Madison
Square Garden with Bob Dylan in New York City among other
places.

****

I received the following letter from Gebhard in response to a valentine in 1959. I hadn't seen him in a long time as he had been living with his daughter Peggy in New Jersey:

Heinrich Gebhard

5 Millar Place

North Arlington, N.J.

February 14, 1959

Dear Ouida,

Thanks for your delightful, deliciously humorous Valentine!

Terribly sweet of you.

Of course, I'll be your Valentine!

The best news of all is about Josie, - Peggy and I are extremely happy that she is home from the hospital and doing well again.- Special greetings to her.

Two weeks ago I was at the big dinner given in honor of "Lenny" (Leonard Bernstein) at the Hotel Astor, and I was at the head table with him and Madam Koussevitzky - and dear Lenny in his after dinner speech said a lot of wonderful things about me, - and also about Helen Coates, and we both had to get up to bow many times.

Here we are all well. - Hope the same for you all.

You have seventeen pupils - Bravo - Good for you!

Lots of love from Peggy and me to you all.

Your, Gebby

P.S. - I am "plunged deeply" in the *Well Tempered Chlavichord*! I am studying all the 48 *Preludes and Fugues*, as I never did it before. Bach - Mighty God!

On July 25th 1959 my birthday gift to Gebby was two books, "Music and Imagination" by Aaron Copland and a book by Pasternack.

Heinrich Gebhard
5 Millar Place
North Arlington, N.J.
August 12, 1959

Dear Ouida,-

Many, many thanks for the two books!

I don't know how many years it is now that you have sent me Christmas and birthday presents. You are incorrigible, the way you spoil me with all these gifts- and especially the unusual books - the great book by Pasternack I have not started to read yet, but "Music and Imagination" I have read three times, and certain paragraphs I have read four and five times.- I admire Aaron Copland tremendously. He is, to me, the deepest thinker among the modern American composers. I have his book, "What to Listen for in Music" and have gone to his lectures at Harvard College and Brandeis. And I have known him for a good many years and have seen a lot of him in Boston and find him (even if not a handsome man!) a charming, warm-hearted man.-

His new book is terrifically interesting and extremely engrossing.- In one way it is a unique view of the history of our music, and of the inner essence of music. His knowledge is tremendous- but judging from this book, his insight into the real roots of the act of composing is revealing and inspiring. His compositions I admire, but only some I love. It is the same with the other Modern American Composers,- Walter Piston, Roger Sessions, Roy Harris, Carter, Ives, Foss, Diamond, Virgil Thomson, etc.-

Copland's sincere and honest appraisal of these, his fellow composers, is very fine. Even what he says about the Americans that came just before them, is very keen in appreciation, - for instance, my beloved great friend, C. Martin Loeffler, who wrote his *Pagan Poem* for me, which I performed sixty-six times with nine great orchestras, - and which is influenced by the French Impressionistic School, but not a copy of Debussy or Ravel.

Copland's appraisal of Bartok, Schoenberg, Alben Berg and Anton Webern is also very keen.- So again, dear Ouida, thank you warmly for the lovely, fine books.--

We have had a nice winter in spite of bad weather. I am having a lovely time with my music. I am at the piano two to three hours per day, working on Bach, Beethoven, Schumann, Chopin, Debussy, Ravel, our glorious piano literature.-

Six of my former pupils come to me once in three weeks for a lesson. I have gone to Carnegie Hall four times this year to see and hear "Lenny" conduct the Philharmonic (once Peggy came with me).

You must have had a grand time taking your sweet children to the Stadium Concert to hear and see Lenny do his great symphony, *The Age of Anxiety*.— He is a genius and I am terribly proud of him.

Peggy and I think of you often and she sends her special love to you,- and also special love to your sweet sister Josie- and we are extremely sorry for her ailments,- and we pray a special prayer for her complete improvement.- With love and best wishes for you all from us all,

Your 'Gebby' -

H.G.

Ouida's sister, Josie -
artist and poet

16

LENNY,
THE CONDUCTOR

Anything can be improved; nothing can be perfected.
William M. Blatt

In 1958, Bernstein was appointed Music Director of the New York Philharmonic. In his first year, the orchestra showed great improvement under Lenny's dedicated guidance, and audiences filled Carnegie Hall and later Avery Fisher Hall.

During his eleven years of conducting the Philharmonic, he recorded a tremendous amount of music with Columbia Records, much of which is available today on Sony CDs. He was also able to fit in several tours of Western Europe, as well as Russia in 1959, when the Philharmonic stayed for almost a month. At each concert, Lenny conducted one American work, usually his own *Age of Anxiety* with Seymour Lipkin playing the piano part. The highlight of the program was Lenny's rendition of the Shostakovich *Fifth Symphony*, which always received shouts of "bis, bis" (encore, encore). The Russians were also very impressed when he conducted from the piano, playing Mozart's *Piano Concerto in G Major* (K453).

In the summer of 1959, when Lenny was conducting the New York Philharmonic outdoors at Lewisohn Stadium, I brought my three kids backstage at intermission. He was delighted to see me and immediately sang the ditty he had made up years before when he came to my performance with orchestra in Jordan Hall, Boston - "Ouida's (Weeda's) going to play with Thiede (Teeda)." My kids were thrilled to hear him do it in person, as they had heard the story many times. It must have been caused by his early memory of being jealous that I played with orchestra before he did, and it stuck with him. Lenny often told me of his exciting experiences abroad when I saw him at Tanglewood. Helen Coates, who also worked with me during the Gebhard years in Boston, recounted stories of Lenny's concerts in her letters. I remember especially the letters from Israel about *Jubilee Games*, a short work that Lenny composed for the fiftieth anniversary of the Israel Philharmonic, which Sid Ramin orchestrated.

Off and on in these hectic years of conducting, Lenny managed to work on *Kaddish*, his *Third Symphony*, which is a prayer for the dead. It had been commissioned by the Kousevitzky Foundation in 1955, when Charles Munch was conducting the Boston Symphony. He finished it in August 1963. The Speaker was to be his wife, Felicia, with a mixed chorus, a boy's choir, and a solo soprano. Lenny was moved to dedicate it to John F. Kennedy.

--- with Lenny at Tanglewood

In 1961, Lenny appointed Seiji Ozawa to be assistant conductor of the New York Philharmonic for two years. Seiji learned how to conduct Mahler with Lenny, who he said always made him feel like an equal. Madame Kousevitzky invited Ozawa to study at Tanglewood with Charles Munch.

Ozawa was born in China, but his family moved back to Japan where he studied piano at an early age with Hideo Seito. His mother was a Christian, so he was brought up listening to western church music. He has said that he is very Japanese, but he eventually came to feel that Boston was his home during his twenty five year tenure as conductor of the Boston Symphony Orchestra.

In addition to Lenny and Munch, Seiji was also greatly influenced by Herbert von Karajan, with whom he studied for about a year. Later, Ozawa often phoned him when he had a question. If Karajan was busy he would hang up immediately, but when he had time, however, he gave Seiji advice on how important it was to listen and watch intently, and to conduct with long lines and phrases. Ozawa felt it took him about ten years for him to get the Boston Symphony to produce the heavier and deeper sound he was seeking.

Roger Nierenberg was a conducting student of Lenny's at Tanglewood. He practiced every night for about two years on my piano, as his own had been damaged. We used to talk music by the hour and I hope I inspired him.

I had the thrill of hearing Roddy conduct the Pro Arte Chorale and Orchestra in Haydn's "The Creation" at Avery Fisher Hall. You can be sure I was very proud of him, as was his mom, Juliet, and his dad, Gerard, the prolific author of books on Body Language and Negotiation, and other business subjects.

In the summer of 1966, a few short months after my son, Billy, was killed in a canoe accident at the age of twenty, I went to hear Lenny conduct a concert at Lincoln Center. I remember that they were playing Stravinsky's *Rite of Spring*, with Igor Stravinsky seated in the hall. The audience gave both the conductor and the composer a standing ovation after an exciting performance.

At intermission, I went backstage where Lenny greeted me warmly with a hug and a kiss, at which point I told him about my recent tragedy. I never expected his reaction. He ignored all the people lined up to see him, took me aside and sat me down while he rubbed my face with both his hands as if to protect me from this crushing blow. He couldn't understand how such a thing could happen and wanted to know the details. His anguish at my terrible loss made me realize what a compassionate person he was!

In 1969, Leonard Bernstein retired and was appointed Laureate Conductor for life of the New York Philharmonic Symphony Orchestra.

Lenny now felt free to conduct other orchestras at home and abroad. A great deal of that conducting was done with the Vienna Philharmonic in Salzburg. In the United States he made one appearance conducting the Metropolitan Opera Orchestra in a Met production of *Carmen*, and he had engagements with many other American orchestras.

Lenny had never conducted *Candide* himself, but he felt this work was as close as he had come to writing an opera. Near the end of his life, in 1989, he was eager to record a concert version of it and he hired some of the top operatic stars to perform. Jerry Hadley was to be Candide, June Anderson was Cunegonde, others were Nicolai Gedda, and Lenny's good friend, Christa Ludwig. His pal and boyhood chum, Adolph Green, was chosen, in an inspired move, to play Dr. Pangloss.

Deutche Grammophon recorded *Candide* in London with the London Symphony Orchestra. In spite of the fact that most of the cast came down with the "Royal Flu" as Lenny called it, the recording was very successful – almost as great as the one Lenny had done with *West Side Story* a few years earlier in 1984. That one was so popular it broke all records for sales.

One of the most dramatic events in Leonard Bernstein's life took place in Berlin on Christmas Day 1989, when Germany's reunification celebration took place. The Berlin Wall came down, and thousands of East and West Berliners surged through the Brandenburg Gate. The people hacked away at the despised wall with any tools available, and Lenny managed to get a piece of it to take home to his family as a keepsake. He conducted the *Ninth Symphony* of Beethoven in the Main Hall in West Berlin and he changed the *Ode to Joy*, which the chorus sings in the last movement to the *Ode to Freedom*.

My friend, Lenny, always seemed to be at the right place at the right time, and what could be more important than this memorable occasion! Throngs of people were there to see him conduct, and he enjoyed it all, but was exhausted by it after his bout with the flu. He had the satisfaction, however, of showing for a short time, what brotherhood around the world could be like, and that made it all worthwhile, because he had always resented that dividing wall in Berlin.

17

HOW TO WRITE A SONG

*So many beautiful songs about love before marriage,
and so few about it after marriage.*
William M. Blatt

Everyone feels at one time or another that he would like to write a song. He feels that his song is sure to be a hit. Let me set you straight about songwriting from one who has written over two hundred songs. It's a very frustrating business, but if you can't control your creative instincts, then go for it, but don't say I didn't warn you.

A song is like a puzzle; an original title is a must. You have to keep your ears open, and when you least expect it, a title appears. I was walking down Broadway one day, when I came to a man who was passing out ads for a show and he said, "Don't Pass Me By."

That phrase became the title for a passionate ballad that I wrote. I used the conventional AABA formula for this song with the title repeated at the end. Briefly, those letters indicate that the first, second and fourth verses have the same melody and rhythm while the third verse is the bridge with a contrasting melody. This is usually the climax of the song. After you write a good lyric with an interesting story, you figure out some great harmonies and then make a lead sheet, a very neat one. But just remember, you can copyright a song but not a title. Most of my titles have been taken, either by coincidence or on purpose, as a result of my showing them to record companies and publishers. Incidentally, the Beatles wrote a song they called *Don't Pass Me By.*

Next comes the expensive part, the demo. In the sixties it cost about fifty dollars just to hire the studio for an hour. Today it would be several times that. In those days I hired a singer who could play the guitar and other instruments and could make an on-the-spot arrangement of the song. The singer I used the most was the afore-mentioned Jerry Landis, who later turned out to be Paul Simon. He not only dubbed-in several instruments but also harmonized with his own voice. He made about sixteen demos of my songs. What a find! Of course, today a CD demo can be made in one session with a complete orchestral background created on a synthesizer.

I had three collaborators (lyricists), though I mostly wrote both words and music to several hundred songs. My second partner, Kay Wells, wrote the words for *Looey, Looey* which Buddy Hackett sang. It was about a poodle, Looey, who was petted and loved by the girls and made this guy jealous of the dog. I found a publisher for it and it became a commercial record. One afternoon I met Buddy at the Roslyn Country Club where he came with his accountant, Wally Sheft, whose boys I taught. I told him I wrote *Looey* and he said "I didn't make a cent on that song!" "Neither did I," I said.

I met Kay when I heard she was a songwriter who had tried out for "Songs for Sale," a TV show in the early 50's emceed by Steve Allen. She won and had a recording done by Brenda Lee but it was just a demo so nothing happened with it. When I met Kay, she was suffering with cancer of the jaw, the same thing that Richard Rodgers had. Kay's father was Billy Williams who developed Baron Munchausen and wrote the material. Kay must have inherited his ability as she had a great flair for writing. We wrote at least a dozen songs together, and when Buddy Hackett recorded our song, *Looey, Looey*, it lifted her spirits considerably. Another of our songs was called *The Twirl* which we did during the "Twist" craze. Unfortunately, Kay's disease progressed too fast and even though we went to the city several times to attend ASCAP meetings, she finally had to curtail her activities because she had difficulty talking and could only drink, as she was unable to chew. She kept up her enthusiasm for life and appreciated her husband and three daughters all the more. I was so impressed with her bravery in coping with her illness, that I encouraged her to write more lyrics, and I was glad to be able to help keep up her spirits.

Another partner I had was not for songwriting but for "Recordings for the Blind", which was done at Temple Sinai. We sat in a small booth where I read the script and Bea Burkett worked the recording machine. Bea confessed to me that she had cancer and didn't have long to live. She had three sons and a fine husband.

Selma Praga was my third collaborator and we met at an ASCAP meeting in the city. She wrote poetic lyrics like *Yesterday's Child* which became a demo sung by my former student, Jon Stroll.

It doesn't always help to know the right people in order to sell a song; it's the material that counts and it has to be outstanding.

I find my strength in music and creativity, and a part of me goes into every song I write. When I wrote *I Tell My Heart*, I found a certain solace which helped me come to terms with the unbearable loss of my younger son, Billy, at the age of twenty. When I played it for some friends of mine, they cried at the end of the song. We must accept change, and when we experience a sudden loss, we shouldn't dwell on it, as death, after all, is a part of life. Of course, it is much harder to accept an accidental death.

I TELL MY HEART
(copyrighted)

I tell my heart to forget you,
But it doesn't seem to hear.
No matter where I go, my love,
I feel you're always near.
I tell my heart to be patient,
I'll find somebody new.
But it keeps repeating, "You're my love,"
It won't believe we're through.
You took my heart and made it sing,
Like a symphony to Spring.
I'll see your face, feel your embrace,
By just remembering.
I tell my heart it's all over,
And it's time to say goodbye.
But no matter what I say or do,
This much I know will be so true.
Whenever my heart thinks of you,
It will break right down and cry.

Last year, Jerry got a call from an Ed Engel, who asked if a Ouida Mintz lived here. When I came to the phone, he said how glad he was to have found me, as he had been saving my demos for years.

I learned that there's another world out there – of people who collect demonstration tapes. I should have bought the master tapes of my demos when I made them, but I neglected to do so, as I felt it was an unnecessary expense. I was wrong.

When I called Associated Records on Seventh Avenue a few years ago to order a copy of one of my demos, I was amazed to find that they no longer existed. Evidently Ed Engel was there at the right time to acquire those master tapes that I should have bought, so they were his - not mine.

We met a few times at my house and he was kind enough to make a few tapes for me from his masters of my songs.

****

Following are Gebhard's last two letters to me. The last book I gave to him was the biography of Artur Schnabel.

```
            Heinrich Gebhard
            5 Millar Place
         North Arlington, NJ


                           August 5, 1961
Dear Ouida,-
    Thank you again for your lovely birthday
wishes, lovely card and lovely letter,- and
thank you for the record of your new song.
    It is very fascinating what you and your
sister have done with the Dvorak, and her line
"the heart you give away you may want back some
day- but then you'll pay in tears, in tears you
will pay!!" are wonderful!
```

Josie is a true poet. She has always had a great gift for poetry all her life.

But I must say something terrible- we cannot use the record. This type of record doesn't go on our machine. Peggy and I feel dreadfully sorry.

Just now I am alone here with Jack (Peggy's husband)- She is in Lancaster, N.H. for two weeks, visiting with an old high school chum of hers. It is a big reunion. The two children (Johnny 10 and Marlene 7) are both with her. They have come by plane, (the kids are very excited about it).

The great excitement for me here now is twofold - I am slowly and most carefully reviewing *Das Wohl Temperierte Klavier* again,- all the 48 *Preludes and Fugues*.

A pupil of mine has just returned from a trip to Germany & brought me Schweitzer's Bach in the German Edition. So I am having a tremendous time reviewing the music and at the same time brushing up on my German. Each week I take one *Prelude and Fugue*. It will take me two years. I feel that I should end my life really knowing Bach.

After all the Beethoven, Schumann, Chopin, Brahms, Debussy, Liszt and modern music I have studied,- I say: The Alpha and Omega of Music is Johann Sebastian Bach. If we don't know Bach well, we don't know music.—

Loads of love to you & your family,

               Your "Gebby"

         Heinrich Gebhard
         5 Millar Place
              August 1, 1962

Dear Ouida,

Thank you deeply for your wonderful birthday present to me, the biography of Artur Schnabel!

You have given me so many wonderful books thru
the years, - but this book touches me especially, as it brings my four years in Vienna
with Leschetizky close to my heart, and close
to Artur Schnabel.

Schnabel and I were great chums. We used to
walk the streets of the great city together,
and go to the opera together. In those years
the opera was at its height in Vienna, - magnificent performances of Mozart and Wagner's
operas, and by order of the good old Emperor
Franz Joseph - cheap seats for young music
students!

We also went together to hear the great
pianists of those years - Busoni, DePachman,
Mme. Essipoff, Emil Sauer, Eugene D'Albert,
Carreno, Rosenthal, etc. Those were great
days. I love to dream of them.

Ouida, dear, - just think, I am now 84
years old! - I cannot believe it! I sleep
well, I enjoy my food, and I play the piano as
I used to. I am very grateful to the dear Lord
in heaven! I practice 2 hours every day. I
review my old concert repertoire: Bach,
Beethoven, Schumann, Brahms, Chopin, Debussy.
- As for Bach, - the older I get I feel that
the *Well Tempered Clavichord* is really the
pianists Bible - the 48 *Preludes and Fugues*. I
play one *Prelude and Fugue* each day for the
benefit of my fingers and my musical soul.

Do you have the book "Conversations with
Casals"? Thru my great friend, C.M. Loeffler I
met him a number of times. He is not only one
of the greatest cellists of the world, but
also a fine pianist.

Here is a quotation from his book: "I have
been told that for many years I have been in
the habit of starting the day at the piano,
playing Bach *Preludes and Fugues*. That is so.

At my house at Salvador my maid, Therese, used to hum many of the themes of *The Well Tempered Clavichord* from having heard me play them so often."

As I think back on my life- of the great happiness I have had in my concert career and my teaching career and my dear beloved class of pupils, of whom you are a big contingent, - again I am ever grateful to the Lord in Heaven. - and I am extremely happy with my beloved family here (retired) - -

Now the exciting thing for me is my book, "The Art of Pedaling", which is being published by Ricordi Co. of New York. I wrote the book five years ago, and dedicated it to the memory of my great master, Theodor Leschetizky. - Lenny (Leonard Bernstein) has written a wonderful Introduction to the book.

Ouida, - with all this happiness, I am delighted that your children are doing so wonderfully well. I am not surprised, with a mother such as you.

Lots of love to you and Samson and to all your family from Peggy and myself.

Your, Gebby

Following is an appreciation of Heinrich Gebhard written by Lenny as an introduction to Gebhard's book, "The Art of Pedaling."

MY TEACHER, HEINRICH GEBHARD
by
Leonard Bernstein

Reading this beautiful book has been in the nature of a recapturing experience for me -the tenderly nostalgic re-experiencing of an old set of emotions. So clearly does the essence of the Gebhard personality emerge in his writing that it transported me almost physically back into his gracious studio in Brookline, Massachusetts, absorbing again the gentle urging, the massive charm, the malice-free wit, and the overwhelming love for music (romantic as a young lover is romantic) that stamped each piano lesson I had with him as a major event. We would sit at two fine old Mason and Hamlins, abreast: I would play, he would play: he would leap up with that light, deer-like energy, and over my shoulder coax my Mason and Hamlin to sigh and sing like his. Anything I did that pleased him was magnified into a miracle by his enthusiasms, my failures were minimized and lovingly corrected. And all was bathed in the glow of wonder, of constant astonishment at the golden streams of Chopin, the subtle might of Beethoven, the fevered imaginings of Schumann, and the cooler images of Debussy. But nothing ever became really cool. Sound, in itself was passion; the disposition of sound into constellations for the piano was life itself. I never once left that studio on my own two feet: I floated out.

In my last year of study with this Delphic fountain, I came upon, and was infatuated with, the *Variations* by Aaron Copland. A new world of music had opened in this work - extreme, prophetic, clangorous, fiercely dissonant, intoxicating. The work was unknown to Heinrich. "Teach it to me," he said "and then, by Jove, I'll teach it back to you." And that is precisely what happened. Obviously Gebhard's greatness as a teacher resided mainly in his greatness as a student. Not long before his death he wrote me that he was in the midst of "reviewing" the works of Bach and The *Ring of the Nibelungen*.

By Jove, that was a great man.

Mr. Gebhard was such an important person in my life because he inspired me to accomplish my goal, and I feel I helped to make his life happier at the same time.

Peggy Gebhard, my teacher's daughter and my former piano student, and I had not been able to see each other often because we lived rather far apart. We had kept in touch by writing a long letter every Christmas to relate what had happened during the year. I was shocked when I received her last letter a few years ago:

Dear Ouida,

It has not been a good year. I had more surgery, radiation and Chemotherapy - but none of it has done any good. It has metastasized to both lungs (I never smoked), liver, and bones - Doctor has said there is nothing more to do - but I say I may have this disease but so far it doesn't have me - he has given me six months, so we are taking another cruise while I'm still up to it.

We are going to San Juan, St. Thomas and an Island off the coast of Haiti - only natives can go there - and since our ship line bought the island, only its passengers can disembark there - no commercialism - only a small native bazaar - loads of empty beaches and mountains - seems like Paradise to me.

Love,

Peggy

Sadly, this marks the end of our long friendship, which started when we were young children.

18

HOW I TEACH

Patience is the one virtue that is rewarded.
William M. Blatt

When I was fourteen years old, I had no real teaching background, but I learned quickly from experience, and my students progressed remarkably well. Now that so many years have passed, if someone gathered all my students together, I believe we would require a large ballroom, as I know I have taught over a thousand. I owe the start of my teaching career to the help I received from my loving parents and uncle, and I am very grateful. Most of my later students came from recommendations, of course.

I have found many new students just by standing in line at a tag sale and conversing with some mothers who were looking for a piano teacher. One person in particular, a Mrs. Stratton, was looking at an upright piano and asked if I would try it out for her to see if it was worth the money. It was very nice sounding and was in good condition. I suggested that she buy it, which she did. In about a month she called me up and said she would like me to teach her daughter, Eve. She did so well in about six months that everyone who heard her play wanted to study with her teacher. That's where I came in. Before I knew it, I was visiting a dozen homes in Great Neck and teaching many of their children. I found that tag sales proved to be good for business.

One day, when I was driving to a lesson, I saw some kids in their driveway across the street with their dad holding up a sign "Sale Here!" I shouted, "What are you selling?" One of the little girls answered by holding a tiny toy rabbit, which I said I couldn't use. "I have some nice rings," she said. Then her dad gave her permission to cross over to my car and I put my hand out so she could try on the rings, which unfortunately didn't fit. I guess I should have bought one anyhow, as she seemed so anxious, and the rings, I'm sure, were inexpensive.

At any rate, the father had now joined his daughter and I told him that I love little kids because I teach them piano. "Really?" he responded. "We've been looking for a good piano teacher. Do you have a card?" I told him I didn't have one with me so I wrote down my name and telephone number for him. This is a rare example of how one can get a new student, but most of my students come from recommendations. It doesn't hurt, I found, to mention that Leonard Bernstein and I studied with the same teacher.

Every teacher should use psychology at lessons. I feel it is most important to put a student in a relaxed frame of mind. In that way, he or she feels free to ask any questions that concern him. For instance, I allowed a student who had a problem concentrating, to talk about anything he wanted, even if it interrupted the lesson, as long as he didn't do it too often. This sets the climate for good communication.

The secret of success is in the repertoire. It should never exceed the student's ability. Building a repertoire, especially if it is memorized, also builds self-esteem. Sometimes I run into a smothering mother who tries to live her life through her child, a mother who wants her son or daughter to be a concert pianist, a distinction that she was never able to reach herself. One such mother was constantly bribing her nine year old and nagging her to practice. When the daughter refused to listen, it was I who was given a lecture about being more strict with her. This is against my philosophy as I would never show anger toward a student. Instead, I try to inspire my students by giving them music I feel they could enjoy and have the ability to master. I also have taught elderly adults who really enjoyed playing as a hobby.

I often teach a piece by rote, that is by my playing two measures at a time and having the student imitate it. I explain that the keyboard is like a design which you can envision away from the piano; that is, the relationship between the black and white keys. It is very important to determine the best fingering by trial and error so that each hand position leads easily to the next. That is called finger memory. People often ask the best way to memorize. I always answer that the more ways the better because it is a combination of many methods: most important are the melody and harmony, which have to be analyzed. The three main chords are the Tonic, Subdominant and Dominant, or the first, fourth and fifth chords of the scale. The chord that is used a good deal is the Dominant Seventh which is G,B,D and F. The Diminished Seventh is a half step less than the Dominant Seventh and is used often for a feeling of mystery. To achieve the diminished it would be G, Bflat, Dflat, E. In other words, there are two piano keys between each note.

My teacher, Gebhard, was noted for the beautiful tone he produced at the piano. He would explain to me that the way to achieve this effect in playing chords slowly was to hold the wrist high and lower it into the keyboard with a relaxed arm as if it were sinking into a pillow. He also warned that one should not lose the very important melodic line of a composition by not letting up on the pressure of the keys and by not using too much pedal when notes are close together. Gebhard also insisted that one should first practice the scale relevant to the piece that is being studied; playing four octaves up and down the keyboard many times. Play the scales hands alone, then together. In addition, the arpeggio or broken chord of that key should be practiced the same way, four octaves hand over hand - for instance, C E G. Gebhard felt that every new piece should be practiced very slowly, correctly, with the right rhythm, fingering, and all mezzo forte (medium loud). He would say, "in slow motion." This was called "fundamental practice" that his teacher, Leschetizky, advocated and everything was to be played with no pedal or expression. My dad could never understand why I practiced so slowly in order to play a piece very fast. I think he finally got the idea when he heard me play at the proper speed in recital.

After a piece was learned, Gebhard had one play a difficult section in a deliberately distorted way which he called, "jerky divisions." This would consist of taking a difficult run, for instance, and playing the notes alternately long and short. Another way is to accent the first note of each measure without changing the rhythm, and yet another is to play the notes long, short, long. A very good example of a piece that lends itself to this kind of practice is the *Étude in F minor* by Chopin, dubbed the *Murmuring Brook* because of its even notes. For any particularly difficult spot, one can invent his own exercise that would apply to it. I don't know why this method works so well, but I can testify that it has helped me in my technique and saved me from practicing irrelevant exercises by Czerny or Hanon, two notorious authors of finger-breaking exercise books. I must admit that most Czerny exercises are very musical, and some are even beautiful. A good friend of mine loves to play them.

When there was a fast arpeggio, or run, Gebhard used a method he called "bluff legato" which meant that the fingers do not actually connect, but to the ear it sounds as if they do. It's almost impossible to connect some rapid passages.

Gebhard taught me to be patient with my students by just watching the way he tirelessly worked with me at my lessons. He always let me play a piece to the end, then he praised what he honestly believed was worth praising – in my case he usually appreciated my interpretation the most, but then he would take one or two measures and go over and over it until he got his ideas across. Some teachers, I've heard, get very angry if a student doesn't catch on right away; and that's a big mistake. All the student remembers is the anger and it accomplishes nothing.

Gebhard was so inspiring that I confided in him as if he were my second father. He even allowed me to bring a boyfriend, that I especially liked, to meet him. When Byron Waksman, who is still one of my good friends, met him, they conversed in German for a half hour, and Gebhard couldn't believe that Byron wasn't a native German. In fact his parents were both Russian. He also approved of another friend, Arthur Knight, who became the famous movie critic. He thought he was very handsome.

What especially appealed to me was how important the interpretation and feeling were to Gebhard, and he spent many hours conveying this to me. One learns from experience that repetition is the best teacher. Most kids hate to repeat anything, so one has to explain how important it is to go over a section or a line at least once. Also, when a student makes a mistake, it's best to let him correct it himself. In that way, the correction will be remembered much better than if you pointed out the correct notes. We call it a "trouble spot." Theory given by itself is pointless, so I teach harmony and scales when it's relevant or when a chord change appears in the music. I was fortunate that I was never forced to play exercises — only scales before the pieces I played. I feel that most students would lose interest (as I would have) if given too many exercises.

When I give a piano lesson, I try to put myself in the frame of mind of each student – for instance, I sweeten the lesson by offering gum. Once, a new student said to me at his first lesson, "I hear you give gum!" Some kids even say, "Can I have my gum now?" if I forget to offer it at the start of a lesson.

It is very important to play a masterpiece for a student as often as possible (even a portion of one can be effective). I remember when my first teacher, Helen Wallace, played part of a Beethoven *Sonata* for me; I was greatly inspired and decided right then to work much harder. I just love to watch the expression on a child's face as it lights up when I play an excerpt from a great masterpiece. It takes a little effort but it can mean a great deal to them.

I was once teaching twin girls who were decidedly at different stages of development. One was able to play difficult music, whereas the other was technically far below her twin's ability, but loved music just as much. At one point when I had them playing duets, Jill, the less advanced one, asked me whose part was more difficult, hers or her sister Jean's. In order for Jill to keep her self-esteem, and though I knew her sister had the more difficult part, I answered, "You have a very important part because you're playing the melody." That satisfied her.

When a teenage boy I was teaching a few years ago was gradually losing his sight, I had him play mostly by rote; in other words, I would play a phrase with one hand and immediately have him imitate it. Sometimes I put my hand on top of his and I pressed the correct fingers down with my own. It worked very well and he learned quite a few pieces. I also had his music enlarged so he could see the notes better.

His family planned to take him to a well known specialist in hopes there would be an operation that would be a miracle for him. I wish I knew what happened to this boy, but when a student drops out after about three years, I hesitate to call because it may appear to the parents that I'm more interested in resuming lessons than in the student's welfare. It makes me rather sad, as I get so involved with each family that it's almost like a little death when they drop out of my life.

19

MY WONDERFUL STUDENTS

Anyone with a good memory can be a good scholar.
William M. Blatt

What a privilege it is to influence the lives of children and young adults. It is so important for a teacher to give his student as much praise as possible. It is very rewarding to know one has changed so many young lives for the better. It gives me a little feeling of immortality, as I know that someday these young people will want their children to study music.

This is part of a letter I received from Linda Kaufman Schroeder: "Dear Ouida, I really have you to thank when I think of my love for music- between my choir that I'm in (and I have been singing for fifteen years), my piano playing, and my passion for listening to all kinds of music, you really were a big inspiration. I try to enhance my kids' lives with music too."

In the 60's and 70's, I taught ten families on Bengyfield Drive in Roslyn. One family told another and my students multiplied. The Ruiz family, from the Philippines, invited me and Sam to a barbecue and it was there that I met the Hamid family who became one of my favorite families. I must say a belated thank you to the Ruiz family, which I did in a way, when I helped them buy a gorgeous Baldwin grand piano at a bargain price before they moved out west to Iowa.

Electa Hamid, a pediatrician and mother of three girls, asked me if I would consider going to Garden City to teach her eldest daughter, Giselle, or "Gigi", as she was known. This young prodigy was truly amazing. She had perfect pitch and could name harmonies and all the notes when I played a chord on the other side of the room. She could memorize a piece by merely listening to it played. Needless to say, she absorbed all my repertoire, except the Beethoven *Third Piano Concerto* and the Caesar Franck *Symphonic Variations*, which I had played with orchestra, but had never taught her. She loved learning music that appealed to her, and would learn it on her own. For instance, her dad, Dr. Delfin Hamad, who was a surgeon and a great lover of music, played a recording of the Rachmaninoff *Piano Concerto #2* every night at bedtime. Before long, Gigi was able to play most of the first movement. She also loves Gershwin and plays the *Rhapsody in Blue*, etc.

The three Hamad sisters were Gigi, Kim and Sandy. Gigi played in the student concerts of APTLI in the Port Washington Library for about ten years in a row, and everyone thought her progress was amazing. Surprisingly, Gigi has not pursued music as her career. Instead she followed her father's path into surgery and has graduated from the Massachusetts Institute of Technology and Johns Hopkins in Baltimore. She is now pursuing a seven year course in plastic surgery.

"Music will always be my first love," Gigi told me recently, and she is never without her piano. She has taken a break from her intensive study of plastic surgery to work in cancer research. Here is her account of the activities she had been pursuing the past two years:

<pre>
                              10 May '97
Dear Mrs. Mintz,
     Happy belated Mother's Day! I was very happy
to receive your letter. I am also glad to have
the time to respond because my relaxing
lifestyle as a researcher is coming to a close
on June 15. The research was sort of hard to
master because I'm sort of a late bloomer with
it. But it has worked out very well in the last
few months.
     I think your newest project of memoirs is a
fantastic idea! I'll have to ask Mom to send
you a picture of the three girls. I look for-
ward to reading it.
     I got a lovely Jack Russell Terrier puppy
last year and she has become the "grand dog" to
</pre>

my parents. They absolutely adore Brittany,
much to my surprise (we begged for a dog for
years & never got one, as you know). She is
very intelligent & exceedingly mischievous and
willful.

I have also been studying dance over the
last few years (flamenco, jazz, salsa, all
sorts of Latin dance) and have really enjoyed
it. I am also learning Spanish on my own
(learned French in high school and college)
because many of my friends speak Spanish here.

Hope you are well. Thanks again for thinking
of me..

Love — Gigi

Kim, the middle daughter, who also graduated from MIT is now
on a scholarship at Berkeley studying to be a research chemist. She specialized in Bach when she was my student and she also studied ballet, as
her sisters did. Here is an excerpt from a recent letter from Kim:

Dear Mrs. Mintz,

Thanks for remembering my graduation from
MIT. Graduate school is very difficult and time
consuming. It could take me six years to get a
PHD, but I'm ready for it. I'm nervous about
moving so far away - I won't have much free
time to fly back either but I think I'll get
used to it.

Although I don't have much time for practicing the piano, I still try to do it as much as
I can. I want you to know that you have been
such an influence on me and my sisters, and I
consider you to be a prominent mentor in my
life. Thank you for teaching me music and how
to appreciate it. Take care and thanks for
everything and wish me luck.

Love and Best Wishes,
Kim

Sandi was always very enthusiastic about Mozart and played a good deal of his music. She has graduated from Brown University in Providence, Rhode Island. Here is an excerpt from Sandi's letter:

```
Dear Mrs. Mintz,
    I hope everything is well with you. I just
graduated from Brown this May. I am not exactly
sure what I will be doing next year. I am
listed at a couple of medical schools. If I
don't get in, I will be going to Bucknell to
get an M.S. in Chemistry.
    I just want to say thank you for the years
of support and instruction you've given me
because it has really made a difference in my
life. Thank you for having the patience to give
me an appreciation for music.
                              Love, Sandi
```

Julia Lee was one of my favorite students. I found a Kawai baby grand piano for her, which she loved. This is a letter she wrote when she was in high school:

```
Dear Mrs. Mintz,
    Hi! How are you? I'm doing fine. Eleventh
grade is harder than I thought, but with a
little struggling I think I can handle it.  I
just want to tell you that I haven't forgotten
about Mrs. Mintz, or my Baby Grand. In fact,
every time I pass the Baby I think of you and
become so sad 'cause I miss my lessons so
much!! But, never fear; I know that after this
difficult first 2 months of school (PSAT's), I
shall once again begin my piano lessons. I hope
you'll be ready to teach me 'cause this year
I'm gonna be an avid student.

                         Love Always
                            Julia
```

Another Philippine student, Donna Visaya, studied with me at age five. I can still remember our first meeting. Her dad, Rolly, picked her up from a nap and brought her in for her first lesson. We talked in baby terms, like the note F is for frog, E is for elephant, etc. She studied with me for ten years and her progress was remarkable. She played at the Port Washington Library student recital (Beethoven *Pathetique Sonata*). Her younger brother, R.J., also plays. They live in California now. Her dad is a banker who frequently works in Africa. Before they left, I helped them get a grand piano — a Baldwin that belonged to Morton Estrin, the concert pianist. Donna is now majoring in music at college, teaches piano and sings in clubs. She played the Grieg *Piano Concerto* with orchestra and is in her late twenties.

Here is a letter from Donna Visaya, one of the few students I have had who is making music her career:

```
Dear Mrs. Mintz
     I am writing from school - San Louis Obispo-
midway between San Francisco and L.A. Sorry I
haven't written, but know that I think of you
often. I really do!
     I just changed my major last quarter from
political science to music! I'm really happy
with this. Am currently working on Ravel's
Sonatine (I'm trying to master it for a recital
in May) & Brahms' Rhapsody in D minor. I look
forward to talking more with you about my music
and college, etc.
          FOR A WONDERFUL PIANO TEACHER

               To sow a dream and see it
               Spread and grow,
               To light a lamp and watch
               Its brightness gleam.
               This is the gift that is
               divine, I know, to give a
               child a dream.
               Thank you for being
               Part of my dream.
               Music is more of a reality
               every day.
                    Love and peace, Donna
```

I taught Donna's friends, Jenny and Jeanette Arcillas for years. It's been over a dozen years now and Jenny is out of college and practicing physical therapy. I'm not sure what Jeanette is doing.

Ronnie Sternin Silver was one of my first students when we moved to Long Island over forty years ago. Here is part of a letter she wrote to me after her four children had grown up:

Dear Mrs. Mintz,

I must confess I think of you quite often- weekly in fact when I take our ten year old son to his piano lesson. His teacher is warm and caring, and very patient- just as I remember you.

We have four children- Leslie a high school sophomore who loves the dance- Amy, A freshman at Leheigh, an aspiring writer- Gregg, who loves tennis and music, and Danny who is seven and very energetic.

I will think of you again this week when Gregg goes to his lesson, but no matter how he feels about his teacher, she is not as good as mine was. Thank you for all your patience so long ago, I am glad I learned piano!

Fondly,
Ronnie

Saundra Simonée is a very unique student of mine. She and her daughter, Shatura, who are African-Americans, have studied with me for about five years. Besides teaching them piano, I coach Saundra in her singing career, which she takes very seriously and claims, half jokingly, that she is a diva in the making. Her soprano voice has an unusual quality, and can be very powerful. Because she keeps her crimson nails at least an inch long, I find it difficult to teach her piano, as it's almost impossible to get a decent technique when the fingers cannot fit easily between the keys, but she has learned to play a few pieces.

I really do admire Saundra as she is the single working mother of two beautiful kids: Shatura, 12, and a boy, Sterling, four years old. Besides holding a full-time job, she has a prominent position in her church choir. Saundra has tremendous faith in God, and feels that He will make all her dreams come true.

Recently she realized the beginning of her dream when she sang the *Star Spangled Banner* in the main auditorium of Tilles Center on Long Island for a high school graduation. She sang beautifully and looked radiant in her long black gown.

Another of my students is 15-year old Frankie Sanchez who is very talented but had the difficulty of learning piano for several years on a small electric keyboard. He saved the money that he earned from doing various jobs and eventually he was able to buy a good piano, which his folks desperately wanted for him. I encouraged them to wait until I could find one at a private sale, as I had found at least fifteen pianos for various students that way in the past — mostly grand pianos. Recently, at a tag sale, I spotted a Baldwin Acrasonic for $850 and I put a bid on it. The next day they said it was still for sale so I offered to buy it and immediately gave them a deposit. A few minutes later, the lady of the house came up from the basement and said she had just sold it. It seemed so unfair that I refused to take the deposit back. She forced it into my hand and said the owner of the piano had the final say (I'm sure she got more money). When I came home and told my son, Jerry, about it, he was so enraged that he went to the house and said he was representing Mrs. Mintz and wanted to ask them some questions. He took out a pad of paper. They said, "How could you represent that woman?" Jerry answered, "Is she wrong to help a very talented boy get a piano?" At any rate, he gave them a few worried moments even though he knew he couldn't get the piano for Frankie. My wonderful tuner, Joseph Gattie, saved the day when I asked him if he could find a piano for me. Sure enough, he called me back a few days later and said he had a piano in great condition that belonged to a woman who was moving; it was also a Baldwin Acrasonic. Frankie got his piano after experiencing that big letdown, and now all is well. He has improved so much since he's had it and we're working on his music reading ability as well as his classical repertoire. Last year he received "Outstanding" (A+) at NYSMA (New York School Music Association,) and this year he won an award in musical achievement and drama at The Wheatley School in Old Westbury. He also loves opera and musicals, and plays excerpts from them by ear. It's a wonderful feeling when you have influenced a child's life. After all, if Leonard Bernstein's Aunt Clara hadn't stored her old upright piano in his house, the world would have missed one of the greatest musicians who ever lived. She must have been very gratified.

Frankie is now playing piano for his high school musical. He called me to say they are putting on Cole Porter's *Anything Goes* this year. He's not only the pianist for it, but he also acts and sings in the show. Last week I heard some girls from his school sing ballads on a Temple Sinai program. One of them is the tall and attractive daughter of Howard Stern, of Radio-TV notoriety. When I told them I was Frankie's piano teacher, they got all excited, and one of them exclaimed, "Oh, we just love Frankie. He's such a genius. When I called Frank to tell him what the girls said about him, he said, with pride, "Now you've met my entourage." Quite a change from the boy I knew who had so little self esteem, and who is now King of the Hill. I believe Frankie will accomplish his goal in music, because he is very creative. Time will tell.

Stephanie Kovol is one of my prodigies who always gets an "Outstanding" (A+) at NYSMA, loves playing piano for audiences, but she had a painful experience in auditioning for the annual APTLI concert in Port Washington, which turned her against performing for auditions or contests. I hate contests. When I watch the Van Cliburn contestants, I feel so sorry for those marvelous young pianists who have dedicated their lives to perfecting their craft, and in a few moments become losers when they are eliminated by the judges. You can imagine the disappointment of those who don't make it. It makes me very sad to watch it.

However, I want to talk about auditions on a smaller scale, in which I have entered some of my students, in this case, at APTLI. I find it rare these days to have students who are able to give much time to practicing because they have so many distractions including sports, dramatics, debating, band, orchestra, etc. Also, the computer seems to have taken over a lot of their spare time, and my serious students get very little sleep because they have to do homework well into the night hours.

Now, back to the subject of auditions. In the following situation, I feel that two out of the three judges failed to see the whole picture. My straight-A student, Stephanie Kovol, who was then a beautiful fourteen year old brunette, had learned the difficult last movement, the *Rondo a la Turka*, of the *A-Major Sonata* of Mozart. I had never taught this piece before, so I take the blame for the fact that the version I gave her to study had eliminated the tremolo in the octave passages at the end. I knew APTLI had a rule that simplified versions of pieces were not to be used in the student recital, but I felt that, since she had mastered this difficult piece, she could have learned the original ending had she been given the chance. It was an unfeeling decision by the judges to eliminate the piece altogether. After all, these kids were all strictly amateurs, and in Steffi's case, the omission happened through no fault of her own. One judge showed some compassion for Steffi's feelings and said, "Let her play it at the concert this once, but we won't allow it next time." But the other two judges were adamant, with the result that she was allowed to play only a short Chopin *Prelude*. Incidentally, when I gave Steffi the original music of the Mozart *Sonata*, she learned the ending very quickly.

The final result was that Steffi was so hurt by this experience that she refused to try out for our student recital ever again. So what have we gained? We should be more sensitive to the feelings of young people.

In Frankie Sanchez's audition, he played a Clementi *Sonata* so fast that someone jokingly said that it should be in the Guinness Book of Records. Of course, Frankie was nervous and I assured the judges that I would definitely get him to slow down in the two weeks he had before the concert. They refused to take a chance, which I felt was another unfeeling incident, not only for Frankie but toward me for their lack of confidence in my ability to slow him down. Result: Frankie says he will no longer audition for the student recital. Was it worth it to not take into consideration the feelings of a young sensitive pianist?

One of my favorite families was the Sheldon Rabin Family — the most caring family I've ever met. My granddaughter, Jeni, had met them at one of my recitals and after they saw her (I have to admit she was adorable — about seven or eight at the time), they would give me gifts for her at the various Jewish holidays. If I came to their house in Great Neck to teach three kids and one of them couldn't be there for the lesson, Carol insisted on paying for all three. They were quite religious and they built a sukka every year in their backyard. It has fruits, vegetables and leaves attached to the sticks that hold it up. When I came to give them lessons, they asked me if I would like to participate in the candle lighting ceremony and sing the appropriate songs. Because I am a reform Jew, I wasn't brought up with these traditions. It's almost like a different religion, but I enjoyed the opportunity to learn these customs. They even called their daughter, Laura, and she sang with them by phone from Northwestern College.

Julia Lee, a talented student of mine, whom I mentioned earlier, invited me and a guest to her sister's wedding, and then to hers a few years later. Her sister's wedding was a Chinese-style wedding as the bride and groom were both Chinese. She wore a white dress for the ceremony and changed into red, as that color signifies happiness according to the Chinese tradition. The wedding banquet consisted of 15 courses, including jelly fish which I managed to taste—I was told by those at my table that it was a delicacy. Ugh! Julia's wedding was different from her sister's as her husband, David Cowan, was not Chinese. But it was a beautiful wedding.

Jon Stroll was one of my first students on Long Island over thirty years ago, and he was outstanding at eight years of age. His mom and dad, Judy and Milton, were still good friends of mine and came to see me after my son, Bill, died several years later. Jon had become interested in popular music even though he had studied classical music while at Columbia University. I had given him my copies of Billboard when he was a kid, and he offered to make some demos for me. He surprised me with the results, as I didn't know he could play several instruments as well as he did.

Today he is a successful producer, director, and composer, and lives in California. On the TV Series "Robo Cop" he was the musical director and principal composer of its twenty two one-hour episodes, and he was nominated in 1995 for the "Golden Reel Award" – outstanding music composition. He was also nominated for his musical direction of "The Raccoons", an award-winning animated series, originally produced for Canadian Broadcasting Corporation and the Disney Channel. Jon's songs have been recorded by well-known singers, such as Ronnie Milsap, Brenda Lee, Petula Clark, and Tony Orlando. He has also composed and arranged music for many TV commercials, as well as composing and conducting his own music with the Toronto, the Denver, and the Baltimore Symphony Orchestras.

Jon had a good friend in elementary school, Leonard Lehrman (more about him in the appendix), who was also very musical and is a composer-pianist in the classical field. Jonny and Lenny were so competitive in school that their teacher decided it was necessary to do something about their jealous conflicts, as they were getting out of hand. He sat them down and gave them a long lecture and a writing assignment on the meaning of humility. Since I have seen them both lately, I have heard them admit in different ways that it was the most important lesson they could have learned in their youth, and they've never forgotten it.

It was very rewarding when a former student, son of Martin and Rita Kroll, whom I taught when he was six or seven, called on the phone many years later and I heard this deep voice saying, "Mrs. Mintz, I didn't appreciate you enough when I was a kid, and I'd like to take some lessons this summer if you have the time." He spent that summer studying several pieces that he had always wanted to learn, and by the end of August he had accomplished what he wanted and felt very satisfied. I still can't get over the feeling I had while teaching him, of looking up at this tall, handsome fellow and realizing that he was the same little seven year old I had taught many years before. He is now Dr. Spencer Kroll, married, and the father of two children. His younger brothers also studied piano with me: Jonathan is now a lawyer, Evan is a Rabbi, and music will always be an important part of their lives. It's experiences like this that make teaching worthwhile.

The same thing happened with another student, Michael Rabin, who called to say, years later, he'd like some lessons so that he could learn the first movement of the *Moonlight Sonata* before he graduated from High School. I was happy to oblige because his family was one of my absolute favorites.

The mother of one of my students even went to the trouble of making a "gingerbread house" at least one foot high made of cookies which she gave to Jeni in appreciation for my teaching of her high school age son. I took a picture of my delighted granddaughter standing on a chair next to the cookie house, and presented it to the builder. She was very pleased.

Jenifer with gingerbread cake

When I think about these warm, compassionate people with whom I spent so many years in their homes teaching their children, I get a sad feeling of loss. I particularly remember Dr. Ruiz who took care of my finger when I slammed the car door on it, Dr. Hamad who prescribed medicine for my sore throat, Dr. Rabin whose wife, Carol, noticed that I had a pink eye and asked her husband to look at it. Then there was Dr. Gade, the Director of St. Barnabas Hospital, who put an ace bandage on my hand after I had tripped and fallen in my bedroom. They made me feel as if I were part of their families and that I had made a difference in their children's lives. I try to keep in touch with them as much as I can, and when I have lunch with some of the mothers, I'm able to keep up to date on how their children are progressing.

At my annual student recital, in my house, I invite the parents and friends to be an audience. At one recital, a young girl had just finished playing her piece and the audience applauded enthusiastically. Her father then stood up and announced, "I'm glad you liked my daughter's performance, and I want you to know I figure that piece cost me about seven hundred and fifty dollars!" He sat down and the crowd fell over themselves laughing.

I am still in touch with Mary Finnerty who is a singer and had a trio. I taught her kids, Randi, Robby and Richelle, who are now productive adults. Their dad is Raymond, a charming man, and their four poodles' names all start with "R".

One of my ten year old students, who strongly resembles Robin Williams and has a similar sense of humor to boot, once greeted me by saying, "I'm not really here; I'm just a figment of your imagination" because he probably hadn't practiced for his lesson. When another boy saw his mother paying me for his lesson, he quipped, "Mom, do you really pay Mrs. Mintz to torture me?"

Sometimes a little incident happens that can brighten up your day, like the following: Once when I was on the way home from teaching, I stopped for a red light and another car pulled alongside mine. I thought he was going to ask for directions, but instead he called out, "Why don't you smile, you're too serious for such a nice day!"

And then there was the very young student who, when asked to describe J.S. Bach, said, "J.S. Bach had twenty children, and in his spare time he practiced on the 'spinster' in the attic."

Student recital in Ouida's studio

The Kroll boys
(left) Jonathan, now a lawyer
(center) Evan, now a rabbi
(right) Spencer, now a doctor

Star students, Kim, Gigi and Sandi Hamad

--- at recent reunion with the Hamad family

--- with Jon Stroll

---with Jenny Arcillus, R. J. and Donna Visaya, and Jeanette Arcillus

--- with Donna

--- with Visaya family in California

--- with Aron Frey

--- with Frankie Sanchez

--- with Steffi Kovol

Ouida - a happy piano teacher

Julia Lee Cowing with husband, David,
and dog, Prelude

--- With Saundra and Shatura Simonée
Baby Sterling is hiding

The Rabin Family
Parents: Carol and Dr. Sheldon Rabin
Children: Harris, Brian, Laura, and Michael

Jordan Hall in Boston, Massachusetts
where many of the greatest artists have performed,
and to which all young artists aspire

20

SOME OF MY DAD'S WIT AND WISDOM

When Henry Thoreau was quite elderly he was asked
by a friend, "Have you made your peace with God?"
He answered, "I don't recall having any quarrel with him."

My dad was very introspective and was always questioning what life was all about. Whenever he made an observation he would jot down his thoughts, even if it was in the middle of the night. These thoughts became epigrams, some serious, some witty, and many were philosophical. He decided to publish them in three booklets of epigrams.

They were titled, "'I Always Say,' Attempts to be Right and not Trite.", "'Blattitudes,' Poor Things but My Own.", and "'Inklings,' One Man's Oservations."

His epigrams appeared daily on the masthead of the Boston Post for many years.

I spoke to Howard Fast when he lectured on Long Island and told him that my dad never missed him when he appeared in Boston; even in the worst winter weather Dad managed to get to his lecture.

Howard Fast, now in his eighties, is one of the best selling novelists of the twentieth century, having written fifty novels. He claims that he never has writer's block. His latest novel is, "An Independent Woman," which his companion, Mimi Dennis, put on the computer. His books have been translated into eighty two languages. Some of his most famous titles were, "Freedom Road," "Citizen Tom Paine," and "Spartacus." Around the time he wrote these, he was imprisoned for refusing to give

Ouida's dad, William M. Blatt

Mom, Lucy Blatt

the names of Communist sympathizers to the House Un-American Activities Committee. Although he was once a member of this country's Communist Party, he feels that our Constitution is a miracle and the greatest social experiment of our time. "This happened nowhere else on earth," he said, "The Chinese couldn't do it! The Russians couldn't do it! We did it!" Fast believes that democratic socialism will come someday, as the disparity between the wealthy and the poor must end.

I gave him a copy of my dad's "Inklings," and a few weeks later he responded with this letter:

```
                              November 19, 1979
Dear Ouida Mintz,
    Thank you for your very kind and warm let-
ter. I have been reading your father's booklet
with great interest.  I find it all the more
fascinating because it was published by the
Haldeman-Julius Company. They play a fascinat-
ing role in the history of American letters and
also in the history of the American radical
movement.
There was a time in the past when literally
hundreds of thousands of mine workers and tim-
ber workers in the West carried Haldeman-Julius
Bluebooks in their pockets. It's a fascinating
story and it might be a project for you to work
on. I think your father would have enjoyed the
notion.

                         Sincerely,
                         Howard Fast
```

My father sent one of the booklets to Heinrich Gebhard and received this reply:

```
                    Heinrich Gebhard
                    33 Manchester Road
                    Brookline, Mass.


Dear Mr. Blatt,
    Excuse this late acknowledgment of your
booklet, "Inklings" which you so kindly sent
me. I have been away a week in N.Y. and only
now got to reading your delightful epigrams.
    I think the whole collection wonderful -
brilliant in the highest degree. To me you have
always been a man of the keenest mind. What
powers of observation you have! I think in this
book you are a combination of Socrates,
Aristophanes, Moliere, Rabelais and Mark Twain,
all in one!
    Many Thanks for your "Inklings" which I
shall use as my daily bible! Warmest greetings
to you and all your dear family.

                    Sincerely yours,
                    Heinrich Gebhard
```

Owen D. Young was a colleague of my father's at Boston University Law School. During his long career he served in important appointed positions under five presidents. He also acted as Chairman of the Board of General Electric and Radio Corporation of America as well as Chairman of the Federal Reserve Bank of New York during a long career in the world of business. Here are his reactions to some of the epigrams:

```
Washington Oaks - St. Augustine, Florida

Dear Bill:
    Thank you for sending me "I Always Say." I
am reading it with care and it teaches me much.
    I am grateful to you for your accumulation
of philosophy and your capacity  "to say."
    Many thanks for your thoughtful remembrance.
                            Sincerely yours,
                              Owen D. Young
```

I met Ruth Slenczynska, who had been the most famous of twentieth century child piano prodigies, when she played in Roslyn. I have followed her career since she made her debut in Jordan Hall, Boston. When I saw her come out onto the enormous stage, I thought sure she was going to walk right under the piano, she was so tiny. One of the pieces she played was Chopin's *Winter Wind* etude, which is a technical challenge to a pianist of any age. Her little fingers played every note; not quite up to tempo, but with a great deal of feeling for someone so young. I understand that her father forced her to practice several hours a day from a very early age. Because of this cruel exploitation, she had a nervous breakdown as a teenager and was unable to concertize for several years. When she celebrated her fiftieth anniversary of performing on the concert stage, she received great reviews. I gave her one of my father's epigram books and she wrote the following note in response:

```
                              Dec. 13, 1962
Dear Mrs. Mintz,
    I am chuckling over your father's charming
little booklet and thank you for presenting it
to me. It was especially thoughtful of you
because now I have a tangible souvenir of a
conversation with a colleague on music..
    Many thanks and happy holidays.
                        Ruth Slenczynska
```

Here are examples of the epigrams, culled from the booklets:

There are people who won't lie
  but like to see how close they can come to it.

One of the worst faults is telling people their faults.

The United States has two hundred million odd people.

We should holler when we give compliments
  and whisper when we scold - thus fooling the neighbors.

The prisons are full of people who wanted more freedom
  than was good for them.

A woman wants to look beautiful; a man just wants to look
  normal.

A man marries mostly to have someone to talk to,
  but it usually works out the other way. He has to listen to her.

Nothing like telling the truth to improve your memory.

Politeness consists of not telling people what you think of them.

You can't appeal to little children by appealing to conscience;
  talk to them as one gangster to another.

As for money, what good is it unless you spend it.

I have lost many friends by death and some by wealth.

Take a lesson from the snake; don't rattle unless you intend to strike.

Telling your wife's age should be grounds for divorce.

The truth is the best lie.

A lie is often a shortcut, but it's usually a dead end.

I like the pensive girl rather than the expensive.

Law is the science of reducing friction among people.

Making money is sordid and vulgar but it's a lot of fun.

People who think they are out of this world ought to be.

Everyone has a right to be a little crazy.

Marriage to most people is a form of entertainment.

The professional criminal's idea is to live at the expense of the public and he usually winds up that way, in prison.

The world needs a new casting director.

A decent married woman doesn't want strange men to make love to her, but she wants them to want to.

People usually work hard for sentimental reasons; they love money.

It is good to have a relative for a physician; he cures you as soon as he can.

When an immovable object meets an irresistible force, they get married.

Marriage is a school of diplomacy.

No woman ever forgives anyone who guesses her right age.

Age saves, youth spends, each the rule of sense offends.

Travel is an excuse for writing one sentence on a colored postcard instead of the letter you owe.

The following are various essays and poems, some humorous, others serious, written by my father at different times of his life.

THE AMERICAN WAY OF LIFE.
by Willam M. Blatt

A lot of people are telling you in the papers, on the radio, TV and in magazines that this or that is or is not "The American way of Life." Be careful. There is an American Way of Life, but it's not always what the speaker or writer says it is. At best it's a vague description, and when an argument or an appeal gets very vague or very general, you ought to be on your guard. Crimes are committed in the name of liberty, of democracy, of rugged individualism, of the Constitution, of patriotism, of religion and of almost every other broad term in the dictionary.

By "The American Way of Life" some people mean that we ought to leave everything in this country just as it is. We couldn't if we wanted to and we shouldn't if we could. Even cemeteries change, because change is the law of life. But some people who have plenty of money and good social position don't want any change because they've got what they want. They are sitting on the top of the heap, on the heads of the others and they feel comfortable. They call themselves conservatives, but they are not. Conservatism is "holding on to that which is good" to use St. Paul's phrase. It isn't holding on to everything. Conservatism is the brake on the wheel of progress. A brake is all right too. It comes in handy when you are going too fast. But to keep the brakes on all the time is bad.

What is the American Way of Life? Is there one? Is there a common denominator for the North, the East, the West, the South, the rich, the poor, the white, the black, the Protestant, the Catholic, the Jew, the agnostic, the ignorant hill-billies, the monastic research student, the artist, the business man, the Democrat, the Republican? This is a big country with huge groups of people who differ widely on many things. What have they in common?

Well, language, for one thing. And language is important because it means that we draw our ideas, our ideals, and our expressions from people who write and speak English. That means that we shall always be more influenced by Shakespeare and Lincoln and Burns and Shaw and Longfellow than by Marx or Tolstoi or even Goethe.

What else? The history of the country we live in. And that means the struggle for political independence, for union, for material comforts, and for wealth, individual personal wealth, selfish competitive wealth. Not the pleasantest thought but that's one of the things America stands for throughout the rest of the world. The country of millionaires, the country where every child looks forward to being enormously rich. Of course he can look forward to being President, but he is seldom serious about that. There can be only one President at a time but there can be many thousands of very rich men and he can be one of them. That, friends, is one of the most characteristic features of the American Way of Life. Is it a good one? I don't think it is. And I believe that lots of people in this country don't think it is. Security is a natural and proper objective, freedom from want, as the President puts it, but a million dollars? The power to hire and fire, the ability to light cigars with hundred dollar bills and to have three or four homes you never live in, that ambition is becoming more and more associated with criminal conduct. And if that's what a speaker or writer means by the American Way of Life, he's growing more wrong all the time.

We are coming to emphasize certain other national ideals with which the name of America is associated in Europe and Asia - the love of peace, the lack of desire to take land by force, the willingness to see virtues in all kinds of people, the insistance on fair play, the protection of weak peoples, the hatred of bullies and tyrants, and the quantities of humor, sympathy, generosity, modesty, yes modesty, for although the American traveler is represented as doing a lot of bragging, the psychologists have taught us that is only an inferiority complex and that in reality we have always worshipped Italian art, English magnificence, French styles and manners, and German scholarship.

We've recovered from the inferiority complex but we've kept our modesty. Let us also keep our kindness, our courage, our gentleness and let these be the American Way of Life.

MY CREED

To love what I have,
To long for no richer,
To use as a salve
The joys of the morning.
To turn off my thought
When self-pity enters,
To know peace is bought
with minutes and hours.
To welcome sound sleep
And the sounder the better,
No matter how deep
Or how long it endures,
To learn that alone
I can meet troubles bravely,
That fame is a bone
For curs to contend for.
To realize all
Will be gone and forgotten
Whatever befall.

FUNERALS ARE FUN

by William Blatt

Funerals are really fun. You have the pleasant knowledge that this funeral is not your own. If it is, you don't know it. Of course, you feel sorry for the person who died on the general principal that death is an incomprehensible, shocking, unnatural tragedy anyway, and if you really liked the deceased you have a painful sense of loss, but just as you can enjoy a joke while you have a toothache, so you can take pleasure in meeting old friends, listening to the sermon and the music (that's what they are for, of course) and reflecting on what's going to happen now, and on how much the dear departed left and who's going to get what. More often than not, the taking off of the late lamented was a considerable relief to all concerned. He or she was probably a nuisance as practically all old people are. They are tired, uncomfortable, disillusioned, disappointed, frustrated, resentful and ugly, notwithstanding all the songs and poetry. Everybody at the funeral tries to look sad, but very few do. And on the way home they tell funny stories and when they get home they have a nice lunch and soon the corpse is just a corpse and is forgotten until something that he said or did is brought to mind and then a stab of regret strikes you. But it passes quickly and soon you are concerned with your own problems. And this is not selfish or callous, for everyone has a right to treat death with contempt. Indeed, that is the only way to treat it, and because you and all of us must experience it, so each of us may properly regard it calmly in others and in ourselves.

LEGAL ETHICS

I'm tired, Mother, past belief,
I've tried a case all day.
They said my client was a thief
And wished him sent away.
They said he stole a watch and chain,
I told them they were wrong;
I tried the case with might and main,
My conscience made me strong.
I riddled the evidence,
I proved beyond a doubt
My fine young client's innocence.
The jury let him out.
His grateful tears did flow and flow,
His joy was almost pain,
He had no money, Mother, so
I took the watch and chain.

WHY, INDEED

Why should there be
Life in the deepest sea,
Where all is bleak and black and cold,
And cruel, silent, joyless, old?

———————

Why should there be
The tiny dots of life we see
Only by magnifying glass?
They love, but think not, die and pass.

———————

Why should there be
Beasts whose ferocity
Drives them to tear and rend
And serve no useful end?

———————

Why creatures of the lightless sea?
Why bugs that near infinity?
Why beasts that murder cruelly,
Why you?—Why me?

POST MORTEM

Green grows the grass above my grave,
Laughing and gay my relatives,
Me I no longer am a slave
To wonder drugs and sedatives.
Gone are my problems, one and all,
No pain, no fears, I've had my hell,
My friendly bores no longer call,
I am asleep and all is well.
The books I wrote you never see,
My feats and I are all forgot,
The universe is over me,
Fate checks my name,
"He was – is not!"

March 27, 1957   William Blatt (80 years)

GOODNIGHT SWEET PRINCE;

MY CLEVER DAD SHUFFLES OFF

THIS MORTAL COIL

One can get used to any prospect, even dying.
William M. Blatt

Here are two of many postcards from my dad when he was ill:

Oct. 22, 1957

Dear Pie,

Time for a postcard. Wish it could be a long letter but I'm not up to it. Visitors keep coming but I excuse myself and go to bed.

I like that lyric of yours very much. You have a perfect ear for rhyme and meter as well as for music, and you get it down to simple ideas and one syllable words without becoming inane. Can't see why you don't get a break. Well, after all, I am now convinced that the only thing that really matters is pain. I think it was Shaw who said that a toothache is worse than a broken heart. Keep well and have lotsa fun.

Love,
Dad

Dear Pie,

The visit was a big success. Holding you in my arms was oxygen, but when you went a lot of the pain came back and other miserable symptoms.

```
    Jerry has discovered a cure for leukemia and
lots of other things. I used to at his age.
Billy is quiet but friendly, pleasant and hand-
some.
    The nurse came yesterday and did a good job.
So did I.  Did you read about Jack Benny? He
was held up by a man who said, "Your money or
your life." Jack said nothing for a long while.
The man asked, "Well?" Jack said, "I'm thinking
it over."
    I get tired very easily so must close. Love
to all of you, and if I controlled the blessing
department, you'd have lots of them.
                                          Dad

P.S. - "The Last Angry Man" starts very well.
```

When my dad was operated on for stomach cancer, he asked the doctor when it was over if it was malignant. He was told that he had adhesions from an old operation. My dad said, "I'm glad you didn't tell me the truth, because I really don't want to know if I do have cancer." Eventually he did learn that he had cancer when he was given chemotherapy. Unfortunately, he had to beg my mother to give him sleeping pills to put him out of his misery. But her hands were tied and she had to refuse. There should be another way.

Eddie Rose was a lifelong friend of my dad's whom I vividly recall playing symphonies superbly on the harmonica when he entertained his guests. Here is the heartfelt poem he wrote in memory of his good friend:

WILLIAM M. BLATT

In Memoriam

So like a dazzling light that fades,
A glowing fire that dies,
A brilliant star that disappears
Forever from the skies;
So went our dear friend Billy Blatt
Beloved by one and all,

Forever gone, oh mournful thought,
Beyond - beyond recall.
His soul was like a diamond gem,
Each facet bright and clear.
His heart was warm with tender love,
His friendship was sincere;
For he was fair and just and good,
His candor wore no veil
 And black was black and white was white,
His truth was not for sale;
A poet and a scholar he,
Well versed in legal writ,
And one recalls the banquet halls
That sparkled with his wit.
A loving husband, too, was Bill,
And Dad of daughters three,
A wealth he prized above all else,
He loved them tenderly.
He worshiped not the golden calf,
He did not yearn for fame,
But he made countless numbers laugh,
And honored was his name;
A man of letters and of art,
So much he leaves behind.
The memories of dear Billy Blatt
Will stir the heart and mind;
Farewell, farewell, dear friend, dear friend,
Farewell, forever more!
A part of me departs with thee
And leaves this earthly shore.
For I shall miss your hand and heart,
Your voice and smiling face,
A friend like you, so dear, so true
None other can replace

M. Edward Rose

21

LOSS: MY BELOVED SISTER, JO, AND ADORED SON, BILL

Make your own light and it will always be day.
William M. Blatt

Everyone knows that eventually our parents get old and die, but when my adored sister, Josie, told me she had a serious blood disease, I could hardly believe it. Sam gave up his business in Worcester, Massachusetts, partly because he knew that my dream was to live near Josie on Long Island. After living here only two years, and being with my wonderful sister, I was faced with losing her from aplastic anemia. Knowing how much she meant to me, she wouldn't let me visit her unless she felt pretty well, as she didn't want me to be depressed. What a caring person! Whenever she bought something for her daughter, Ellen, like a coat, she got one for my Lisa. When we were kids, she helped me with my homework, even drew cartoons for me.

Why someone so caring and thoughtful of others had the misfortune to undergo two serious operations and so much pain, I'll never understand.

Even though she had asked me not to visit her, I decided to ignore her wishes one day. It must have been ESP because when I went to the hospital she looked as if she were near the end - so pale and unable to speak to me. I said, "I just want to say how much I love you." She seemed to respond with a blink of her eyes. I kissed her hand, and then walked slowly out of the room. She succumbed that night. It was Christmas eve and only a year or so after our dad died in 1958. She was 45. I have often thought her disease was partly due to a broken heart as she was so close to her father.

So many children who have lost a parent at a young age have unanswered questions, and it leaves a vacuum in their lives. Since Josie, for instance, died when her children were quite young, it was lucky that I had carefully saved all of the postcards and letters which she had written to me. This correspondence brought her closer to her children by revealing much of their mother's charming personality.

Here is a selection of Jo's poetry written from her earliest years to her latest:

TO AN ANGEL

(Written by Josie Blatt after the death of
her Grandmother.)

I never guessed, I never dreamed,
It never for a moment seemed
That you could go,
To think the angels had it planned,
Were waiting up in Heaven- and-
I didn't know!

I thought I saw a little sky,
A glimpse of Heaven in your eye,
A bit of blue;
but, oh, I didn't see it clear,
I didn't think you meant it, dear,
I never knew.

'Twas often that I wondered why
you lingered at that last good-bye,
You held me so,
How could I dream; how could I guess,
You meant it for a last caress,
How could I know.

O, all the things I didn't say,
The things that e're you went away,
I didn't do,
The little gifts, the trickling tears,
The kind embraces, tender fears,
That I will treasure all these years,
I never knew!

Jo Blatt, circa 11 years

FRIENDS

I have sat up long hours with Night,
Gripping his black hand in my own,
Watching him make the stars less bright,
Whittle the hours to a bone.

Silent we sit as aged men
Beneath the friendly village tree,
Who knowing they will meet again
Wear not each other's company.
Always in just the same old way,
He waits at my brief slumber's end,
And nods to me as if to say,
"Are You awake? Hello, my friend."

No longer do I bid him go
Who find him when I look for rest
Or shun his waiting presence - no,
He is my friend, my welcome guest.

And stepping softly hand in hand
We walk his watch, at every bell
He turns the hour glass of sand,
And smiling, whispers, "All is well."

Jo Blatt, circa

THE COMING OF THE NIGHT

It was morn: I had awakened
    When the mist had ceased to fall
The outer world was dismal for
    There was no light at all.

When far above the misty hills
    I saw a lantern away
And God appeared behind it
    And He guided in the Day.

Then the shadows took their places
    And the birds began to sing
And what a world of Happiness
    These guests did seem to bring.

And the people threw their bedding off
    And all the world was gay
While God up in the Heavens
    With his lantern led the way.

And I saw this lantern slowly move
    Across the spotless sky
To where the dusky wood cuts off
    The view from every eye.

And day and God and lantern
    Slowly sank away from sight
While the hooting of an owlet
    Told the coming of the night.

Jo Blatt, circa 11 years

This sonnet was read at Josie's funeral. It seemed very appropriate.

DOUBLE SONNET TO A FORGET-ME-NOT

O azure flower, bit of Heaven's blue,
How often I have lingered by the way,
And watched your color brighten day by day.
A little bit of happiness it seems,
And tucked within it all, a heart of gold,-
All blessed by God's own angels, I am told,
One needs no more to suit an artist's dreams..
You surely should be where all people pass,
And shining where their eyes would quickest fall,
Where we could watch thy colors brighter grow,
All shaded by a poplar and a wall,
And yet, I guess, perhaps 'twere better so.
I have watched thy color paler grow,
And seen thy petals slowly drop away
As one who weakens at the end of day,-
For Father Time must reap if he would sow.-
I saw thy golden heart in splendor shine,
I saw thy petals wither as they fell,
O lovely flower, do I wish thee well,
I feel your sunshine slipping from my heart,
God must take your worth from out the field;
O, golden treasure, must we truly part?
Yes, to his power even thou must yield,-
And, then again, perhaps 'twere better so.

Jo Blatt, circa 15 years

SONNET TO A WAVE

I wonder if each weary wave that throws
Itself upon the long and lonely beach
Curses the God that made it, when it knows
Its life to be no longer than its reach.
I wonder if each frothy wave that leaps
Headlong upon the new undampened land,
And then, when it can run no longer, creeps,
As if on little legs along the sand,

'Til, at its height, it rushes down to meet
The next, and started on its backward slide,
Exhausted, sinks into eternity --
I wonder if it knows that its retreat
Has swelled the power of a mighty tide,
The heartbeat of an everlasting sea.

Jo Blatt, circa 15 years

IT SOMETIMES HAPPENS

You meet a guy at a summer dance,
And it seems to be a real romance.
He likes your smile, and you like his jokes,
And he asks you up to meet his folks.
You fall in love with his charming mother,
And make real friends with his kid brother.
His dad's so nice, he's like your own,
And you meet and love his sister, Joan.
What happens after all this stuff?
You find you don't like him enough.

Jo Pall

ODE TO AN OVARY OVERLY EXCITED
OR
GIRLS SHOULD GET MARRIED EARLY

1.
'Tho girls over twenty
May exercise plenty
and use up their energy walking,
'Tis vainly expended
For nature intended,
it seems, something further than talking.

2.

If somehow they miss
That connubial bliss
And live for a love unrequited,
They face the event
And the savage intent
Of an ovary over-excited.

3.

And nothing will save them
Except what God gave them—
The power of Love's consumation.
A tardy fruition
Makes worse the condition
For ovaries need relaxation.

4.

Then should they just marry
Some Tom, Dick or Harry
To humor this ovary "Hitler,"
And thusly condone
The imperative tone
That the bigger employs to the "littler?"

5.

Would Shakespeare have done it?
Would Browning have done it?
Or Byron, or Kipling, or Shelley?
Have married in haste
To avoid being faced
With a difficult pain in the belly?

6.

No! such misdirection
From my "middle section"
Is something I feel I'm above.
'Tho others may bend to
I'll never descend to
A simple Ovarian love.

7.

Bring on your phenomenal
Distress abdominal
I will not alter a peg
I'll put my request in
For love and Progestin
Hurray for a shot in the leg!

Jo Blatt, Age 24

(As published in the Journal of the American Medical Association)

YOUR LAWN

You soak the seed until you're sodden,
Post signs forbidding it be trodden,
Weed out the weeds and seed the patches,
That look like they'd been scalped by Natchez.
You pull out crab-grass 'til you're crabby,
And feel as old as Hammurabi.
You look at verdant lawns with malice,
Your hands are raw, your thumb's a callous.
Your leisure time goes down the drain,
You get obsessive about rain,
Your back is bent wherever you go
You're something out of Victor Hugo
You're getting nervous, losing weight,
And then, at last, you see your fate.
A battle to the Death is on, --
It's now between you and the lawn;
It may take six months or a hundred,
It won't get green until you're under it.

Jo Pall

TENTH ANNIVERSARY

Your habit of wearing blue with green,
Since we were married, I've learned your ways,
Your practice of walking around in a daze,
Of keeping your mail in a soup tureen.

Those little things I have come to know,
How you like to sleep with the sheet at an angle,
The way you stop when the lights say "Go,"
Your fondness for letting one shoelace dangle.
I'm looking back over all those years,
And I'm not just saying this to be formal,
I've learned to cherish your little ways,
And I'd rather have you than someone normal.

Jo Pall

ADJUSTMENTS TO GRAY HAIR

Your woe's begun
When there's just one.

Next step is when
There's nine or ten.

But you don't frown,-
It's mostly brown.

Third stage you say,
"I'm still not gray."

When overnight
You find you're white,

Why be appalled?
You could be bald.

Jo Pall

Josie, the middle sister in the Blatt family, was a most charming, sweet and caring person. She had high cheek bones and adorable dimples. Everyone who had any contact with her was captivated. It was such a privilege to be her sister, and just knowing that she was in this world made me happy. She wrote the lyrics to a song titled, "As Long as I Know You're Somewhere," and several others.

She was always worried that she hadn't been a good mother, especially when she found that she had a serious disease. Of course she had been a devoted mother and very conscientious. She was able to put herself in another's place and know exactly what each person needed, especially at birthday time. When my dad was bedridden in his 80's, she came all the way from New York to Boston with heavy sound equipment to record his thoughts on Shakespeare, as she knew it would cheer him up.

Anyone who had ever come in contact with this dear sister of mine, whether through her artistic career of painting, or her husband's extensive filter business, felt they had been touched by an angel who had

Ouida
watercolor by sister, Jo

Ouida and Jo
in their early teens

magical powers. Some said she was too good for this world. For instance, she would treat the lowliest worker at Pall Corporation in the same manner as directors of the company. Many people have told me that they had never met anyone so caring. Also, she often told me how worried she was about my son, Bill. How prophetic she was! As he was also an artist, and couldn't stop painting, she felt even closer to him, and once pronounced him a genius, which amazed me. She felt I didn't appreciate his work, and we'll never know whether he could have become a fine artist.

Josie had such great charm that it is hard to describe. She had many admirers before she was married. The following love letter from a very special boyfriend she knew as a teenager gives you some idea:

```
            10:30 Sunday night
    Josie, sweetheart,
        It was the moon...a rather golden
    affair hanging plump and lopsided right
    over the shaggy silhouette of
    trees...that told me that I really had to
    talk to you tonight or else I'd toss and
    turn until my poor bed was churned into a
    sheet and blanket omelette!
        I just want to thank you, my dar-
    ling, for perhaps the loveliest weekend I
    have ever had. We had swell fun, and you
    are such perfect company. I liked having
    you around,and hope I can, for a long
    time to come, be able to look down into
    clear, honest and merry blue eyes and see
    in them a warmth and depth that means, "I
    love you." That's what I saw last night,
    and that's what made me so happy the sky
    seemed small and crowding and cramping my
    style.
        The weekend started with stormy
    clouds...and still heavier thunderheads
    glowering on the horizon. But when the
    sun burst through, it all dissolved and
    left me wondering if the clouds weren't
    missed after all to be sent running by
    the first warmth of a rising sun.
        Inside me there is something spin-
    ning madly...a gay and airy feeling that
    is entirely senseless.But I hope it stays
```

there.I could really start telling you so
many things about yourself...how I could
sit for hours and just watch the thoughts
flicker across your face...your mouth
tense with the ghost of a smile...or part
with the wonderment of a child's. But
you'd probably end up with an incredulous
look on your face and a "Really!" in your
mouth...and I wouldn't be quite sure if
your eyes were laughing or not!

On the sightless windows across the
street I can see reflected a silver
sheet...that's the moon, now risen higher in
the sky and no longer the moon you love.So I'm
glad it's only a reflection and indistinguish-
able from the reflection of the corner street
light.

Good night now, beloved. A kiss for each
sleepy eye.A kiss for your nose...and a kiss
for each lip. One for the thin straight upper
one. And for the full red pouting bottom one.

I love you, Jonas

THE WORST TRAGEDY OF MY LIFE

The young die good.
William M. Blatt

It is many years since I had the most traumatic experience of my
life — the day I learned that my healthy, adored, sweet, creative son, Bill,
had lost his life in a senseless canoe accident while on an annual college
outing. It happened on the evening of May 6, 1966 on the tremendous
Lake George in northern New York, on a school outing. My son and a
lovely girl named Barbara, who were finishing their freshman year at
New Paltz College, were in one of seven canoes on the way to Bolton
Landing when their canoe capsized that cold, windy night in the early
spring. It wasn't till the next morning that the lifeless bodies of these two
beautiful grown up children (20 years) were discovered adrift in the friend-
less lake – Barbara, floating in a useless life jacket, and my son wedged
inside the canoe. We assumed he had climbed back in after losing Bar-

bara in the darkness, and the numbing cold prevented him from looking further; but we will never know exactly what happened.

I feel compelled to write about this in order to prevent other tragedies which bring such heart-break to so many devoted families, simply because of the complacency on the part of these inexperienced young people who enjoy taking chances. I can still remember Bill's good friend, Joe, who was in the same outing saying, "It was a challenge to go at night." Another friend, Joyce, tried to console me by saying, "He had twenty beautiful years." Of course it only made me feel worse. Why in the world didn't anybody think of sending out a launch with a searchlight when they realized Billy and Barbara were missing? I'll never understand this sin of omission as long as I live.

I would not have wanted to be in Sam's shoes, as he had visited Bill the afternoon of the canoe trip and never saw the danger of the cold water. Ironically, three weeks earlier, on his 20th birthday, Bill said to me, "Mom, these twenty years have been the most important years of my life." He was sitting on the oil burner in the kitchen. This was his favorite place, and he loved watching me work from his warm perch.

I realize there are many families who have lost a child through war or accident, but after having gone through the process of adjustment to a terrible loss, I believe I have become a stronger and more understanding person. It has made me want to reach out to others who have had misfortune, and share the philosophy which one has to develop in order to keep from falling apart. You get so tired of being miserable.

It is hard to accept that I had to give him up because of a senseless accident that could have been avoided if there were more safety precautions, such as a launch with a spotlight to escort them. It could have prevented the loss of my precious work of art; for, after all, isn't that what a child is? You protect it, nurture it, and treasure it. You gaze upon it in wonder — a God-given miracle — only to have it snatched away in a moment. You feel more than robbed. It's so unthinkable because you have never given any thought to this possibility. Just when the bud begins to flower, it is destroyed.

Bill was branching out in all directions. Suddenly the world was opening up for him. He had been a lonely boy in high school, although he had a very good friend in Ricky Miller. Billy felt hemmed in by the pressures of getting high marks in order to get into a good college. He was accepted at Shimer College in Illinois which was the one his big brother,

Jerry, thought he should attend. However, at the last minute, he was accepted at New Paltz, which was closer to home and less expensive, as it is a state college. His dad made the decision that he go there, and though Bill was very disappointed, he agreed to try it for a year.

When he was at college, he became suddenly aware that he had the opportunity to try his wings. He was happier after making close friends, some of whom were insecure and looked to him for help, which he was glad to give them. Bill tried out for the college play in his freshman year, "School for Scandal," and landed a fair-sized part (Moses). Of course we came to see him in it and were very impressed with his mastery of the part, as he had no prior experience. We went backstage to congratulate him.

Bill was a tennis counselor one summer, and enjoyed working with the children. However, they took advantage of his good nature and dumped a pail of water on him one night. He told me he kept it quiet as he didn't want to be fired for not being in control of his group. He loved kids in spite of this experience.

Billy was a prolific abstract painter and won a prize for one of his oils — a painting of rooftops. The judges thought it was a watercolor, and he never corrected them, as he thought he might not have won the prize if he told them. "That was nice," he'd say in a falsetto voice for "nice." That painting is now hanging in a prominent place on a wall of Temple Sinai in Roslyn Heights with a plaque saying, "In loving memory, William Michael Mintz."

Our rabbi, Aaron Petuchowski made it possible. When I told him about my dream of having it on a wall and asked if he could do it, he said it would be an honor. I was thrilled at his reaction because I know that a board usually has to give its approval. Of course he knew that the history of my family is connected to Temple Sinai. Bill's Bar Mitzvah took place there in 1959, and seven years later, his funeral.

Bill taught me by his youthful enthusiasm how beautiful and exciting life could be. He said, "What good is being alive if you can't look forward to something interesting." He was never bored. What a privilege it was to have had the joy of bringing a beautiful life into the world and being able to nurture his love for music and art. Thank goodness he was able to live his short life to the fullest; at least that's some consolation.

We're only transients in a temporary world and nothing can take away those precious years we've spent with our loved ones. You have to be grateful for what you have had and what you have now, and learn to live with your joys and sorrows. Think of the positive. We have an obligation to enjoy life and to realize that life is a privilege if you're in good health. Billy loved life most of the time, although he admitted the absurdity of it and the "meaninglessness," as he called it.

Poor Sam had to go to Albany with Manny, the father of Barbara, who wanted to sue the state for negligence. They should have provided a launch to rescue them, as it was obvious they were missing. Since there was no jury, the judge, who was retiring, concluded, after many sessions, that these kids were old enough to know this was a dangerous trip, and so we lost the case. Gair and Gair, one of the biggest negligence law firms, had wanted to try to win a case against the state which they had never been able to do. It didn't work even though they appealed. The judge wanted to leave the bench with a clean State record.

I have to confess that I was bitter toward Sam for not sensing the danger of a canoe trip on Lake George in early May. I would have tried to stop Bill from going, but I know in my heart he still would have gone. Sam admitted that he never realized that the cold can kill. I understand, now that my husband is gone, that it wasn't his fault, but he was Billy's only hope. If he had been convinced of the danger, he would have insisted that he not go. He asked Bill if he was going to wear a bathing suit and Bill responded, "Dad, it's too cold for a bathing suit." That was his clue, but his father neglected to respond. Oh well, life is a struggle — but it is precious. Enjoy it while you can.

I grew up with a mother and especially a sister who were always conscious of the danger in things. Jo used to call me and say, "Don't drive today – it's slippery out." I would have been outraged at the thought of his going in a canoe. The fact that it was a canoe and not a big boat (rowboat) makes me feel that there was too much complacency. Their lives depended on the cooperation of the weather and although it seemed calm on land, it is always windy on the water. One gust of wind took their lives.

I was miserable, but I knew I had to cope with it somehow. Either I could go up and start to recover, or go down into the depths of despair. Fortunately, I had a husband and two other children to think of, and I had to help them adjust to the tragedy also. Jerry, Bill's older brother, was in Ohio getting his Masters in Education at Antioch College when he was called about Bill's tragedy and was told to take the next plane home. You can imagine the shock he felt about losing his brother, who idolized him, and who, a month before he died, had even flown out to Ohio to visit him. When Billy got home, I remember his telling me how hard it was for him to leave Ohio, as he was fascinated with the work Jerry was doing in organizing a recreation center for children in his work-study program. Ever since Jerry's flight home to attend Bill's funeral he has hated to fly, and now takes a train whenever he can.

Lisa, Bill's younger sister, was very close to him and had a hard time adjusting to the loss of her brother. Every now and then she would let out a scream and then curl into bed in her misery. I used to think of Bill as the middle of the sandwich, which held the friendship of his brother and sister together. Music was very important to all three of them. Jerry and Bill collected classical records of Brahms, Prokofiev (Billy's favorite), Ravel, etc., and Lisa and Bill played duets on the guitar and clarinet respectively.

They had a favorite song, *Try to Remember* from the show, *The Fantastics*. It was hard for us to learn to live our lives without him, as Bill had such a unique personality, and enthusiasm for life in all its aspects.

He had a crush on Lisa's best friend, Shelly Hershcopf, who later became a fine pianist and songwriter. She created her own style of music called "Clazz," a combination of classical music and jazz. She is known on her CDs as Shelly Nan.

Lisa recalls the evening she and Bill looked out the upstairs window in his room and watched the first star appear. They agreed to recall that magical moment for the rest of their lives, and they realized it would be easy, as it happened to be November tenth, Mother's birthday.

Sam had a very difficult time of it. I had never seen him cry until he experienced the trauma of losing his younger son. I remember seeing a tear trickle down his cheek as he blurted out, "This will make it easier to die!" He was so proud of Bill's accomplishments, and admired his sweet disposition.

TOO LATE FOR TEARS
(by a heart-broken mother)

It's too late for tears
But my eyes aren't dry;
Remembering you
Makes me cry and cry.

The people we loved,
The music we played,
The dreams we had
Are beginning to fade.

I feel so lost and helpless,
But then,
Remembering brings you back again.

It's too late for tears,
And yet I cry.

For one who has loved
There is no goodbye.

Bill's mom, Ouida

Bill at twenty, the year he died

The following poem expresses a heartbroken younger sister's grief over the tragic loss of her brother.

TO MY BROTHER

Five years ago today, you left me all alone.
You left me in my sheltered world.
I wanted you to come home on my birthday,
All you said was that you would try.
The day came when I was in a play.
I looked out at the audience but you were not there.
At the cast party everyone lit matches
And wished me happy birthday and many returns;
It was nice but I wanted to see you.
Even though you were my brother,
I felt we were better friends than many.
You confided in me like I was an older sister,
You had four years more on me.
I always listened even if you were in pain.
When we were young, I was a terrible tease.
Now I am twenty-one and one week.
All I can do is sit and remember the day,
I was sixteen and you were but twenty.
You came home a week too late;
I was not mad at that, but you came home in a box.
You went boating in the middle of the night.
I could not cry because it did not seem real.
Now it is just five years ago
When you were lost to the cold, rippling tides.

Lisa

LISA'S CAREER IN SOCIAL WORK

When my daughter, Lisa, shared her room, which had twin beds, with her grandmother, Lucy, she learned about caring for the elderly, as she became very involved in her "nana's" welfare. This must have influenced her decision to become a social worker, and she later graduated from the New York Institute of Technology in Behavioral Science.

Lisa also loves working with little children, as did her brother, Bill, and she was a camp counselor for a few summers, specializing in arts and crafts. After her marriage to her second husband, Leigh Harris, who is the chief accountant for his family's business, Pam Narrow Fabrics, she worked with the disabled and mentally retarded. I always admired her patience and understanding in dealing with these people. Many of them became very attached to her and greeted her when she arrived in the morning with hugs and kisses.

Before Jenifer, her daughter, was born, Lisa worked at the Nassau Medical Center on Long Island, where she advised teenagers on how to avoid pregnancy. Most of these girls had become mothers already and wanted advice on how to prevent any additional pregnancies. This was a challenging job which she enjoyed very much. After Jen became a teenager, her mother became a substitute teacher in the public schools.

At college, Billy had become very close to the family of his English professor, who was so devastated by the tragedy, that it took him a long time to write to us. In the letter that he finally wrote, he enclosed some of Billy's best writing, including the following poem:

Untitled
by William Mintz

The track is long, lonely, and lurky
That leads out of sight,
Far into the fantasy of future dreams;
Into lonely laughter of children
Into sights yet to be seen by future eyes,
Eyes which have been blinded too often
By blaring brightness harshly obliterating,
Obliterating those gleaming dancing eyes,
Obliterating supple gentle movements
Found in chimerical laughing children.

We look back along the track,
Eyes meet in murky blur of days elapsed,
Days never more to be had but in dreams.
Days blackened out, blurred and blasted
By present moments of blind perpetual gyrations,
Present moments to be absorbed presently,
Present moments that guide those yet to come,
All to come down there where those rails collide,
And all we can do is watch and wait and ride.

Because of Billy's untimely loss, He never got to see what would have been his only niece, in other words - his sister's daughter.

MY GRANDDAUGHTER, JENIFER

Jenifer was the cutest little baby grandchild. She fit very nicely in a doll's crib I bought at a tag sale. I had no idea then that we would have a big hand in growing her up. I hasten to add that she was the best thing that ever happened to my husband, Sam, and me because she helped to heal the large emptiness we felt after our Bill's death in 1966. Jen was born in 1979 to my daughter, Lisa, and Harley Goldman. Their lives had been pretty hectic during the years before they became parents. Harley and his partner had big dreams for the water-saver they manufactured in Taiwan, and in which he managed to get us involved. Unfortunately, their dreams (and ours) went down the toilet — literally and figuratively. Their invention was intended to diminish water expended when the toilet was flushed. They had bragged about the yachts they would buy, and I was always skeptical. Since they had financial problems and we had two bedrooms and a bath upstairs, we invited Lisa, Harley and Jeni to live in our house for two years. While Jeni's parents went to work (he became a manager in the biomedical department of Pall Corporation through Sam's recommendation), I dressed Jeni, my granddaughter, fed her, and walked her to The Temple Sinai nursery school next door.

Ouida with her one and only grandchild, Jenifer, one year old

Jerry with his good friend, Nellie Dick, one hundred years old,
a pioneering teacher in alternative education

Jenifer gave Sam some of his happiest hours as she grew up. She would sit in the crook of his arm in the den recliner while he read story after story to her. Her vocabulary grew so fast that we were amazed one day when she watched a plane take off at an airport and exclaimed, "That's incredible!" She was two years old. Sam did the food shopping with her as I was busy giving piano lessons. She would go up and down the aisles in Waldbaum's and call "Grandpa" at the top of her lungs. Once a shopper saw her bump into Sam coming down an aisle and said, "So that's Grandpa!" He loved to tell the story about when they took the usual route to get the newspaper and she spotted some colorful confections behind a glass case. She asked, "Grandpa, don't we need some candy?" With her mop of golden curls she resembled Shirley Temple, and people urged us to have her audition for TV shows in the city. Lisa signed Jeni up with a manager who thought she had great potential. The only trouble was that when they called her up for an audition, no one in the family wanted to go all the way to the city and then look for a parking place. A few times, Jerry volunteered, although Jeni learned everyone's part and was a real natural. The answer is you have to live in the city so you can be in the right place at the right time. Jerry, Jeni's adoring uncle, took her along whenever he had a group of kids going to Colorado, Montana, California, etc. The first time she saw Colorado, she was so overwhelmed by its beauty that she vowed to go back there to live some day. She has now graduated from high school, is going to college there, and lives with her dad and boyfriend, Jonathan. It is hard on her mom and all of us who love her not to see her more often, but she is twenty years old and has made up her own mind.

Under Jerry's guidance, Jeni wrote about her experiences in a book called, "My Life as a Traveling Homeschooler" when she accompanied him on a trip across the country. She was only eleven and swears she wrote every word. It sold quite well.

It's such a privilege to be alive. As Lenny Bernstein said in his song, *I'm So Lucky to be Me*, I'm in love, someone loves me, I'm healthy and very active, and enjoy being creative. I'm not sure I understand what life is all about but I want to make the most of the time I have left here on earth. My dad once said to me that if you attain only one accomplishment that is recognized, consider yourself lucky. I try to help people who are in need of encouragement. I enjoy inspiring the young students I teach; I have already been rewarded by seeing how much music has meant to those who come back to visit me when they reach adulthood to renew our friendship.

It's most important to give children a good environment from the start. I feel sure that neglected children with absent or abusive mothers and fathers may easily go wrong when they are older, and I believe that accounts for the many young people who fill our prisons.

I try to see the good in everyone, even those I'm not particularly fond of, as I find there is no one who is all bad. Love is the basis of a happy life; don't take people for granted; tell those you love how you feel. I try not to let little problems upset me since I have experienced some big tragedies and I realize how insignificant small annoyances can be; they only make you tense and unhappy, and who wants to feel like that.

I hate to see people getting older because that means that I must be getting older too, but I do know it's better than the alternative. For instance, when my friend, Ray, and I went to Israel in December of 1996 I was reunited with relatives in Tel Aviv, Netanya and Haifa I hadn't seen for thirty years, when I went there with Sam right after the Six Day War. It was such a shock to see how much they have aged since then, but that's life; living in Israel under the hot sun tends to bring on those aging freckles and wrinkles. Very few Israelis wear makeup I noticed. That's a mistake, as I think any cream would tend to protect the skin from the ravages of the sun.

I like to call friends who are ill and almost bed-ridden. It shows them they are not forgotten and it makes me feel how lucky I am not to be in the same boat. I also get the satisfaction which comes from giving a little cheer to good friends. Life is inevitably a tragedy as it can never end happily. Enjoy every day and make the most of it – create, love, give somebody a compliment, listen to a great Mozart *Concerto*. I hate to waste the empty space of time, so I keep music playing on the radio all day long, except when I practice, of course. No matter what I'm doing, I love to have the music of the masters in my life.

I love to do several things at once — read the NY Times and Newsday, listen to classical music, which unfortunately is hard to find on the radio these days. Also, I know I annoy some people because I'm a slave to TV. That box was my friend and therapist when I lost my son so suddenly. It was the only thing that took my mind off the tragedy and the horror that Bill and Barbara must have gone through when they froze to death. I also like to work on my biography in spurts. I do it best in bed, and I write in longhand.

Jen and Ouida

Jen

Ouida with Billy's painting, "Rooftops",
hanging in Temple Sinai, Roslyn Heights

I want to influence my one beautiful granddaughter, Jenifer, who brought such pleasure to me and my husband when the tragedy of losing our wonderful son, Bill, made us feel that life wasn't worth living. She changed our lives and lifted our spirits when she was born. Now that she's twenty, I want to set an example rather than give her lectures which kids always dislike. I must try to encourage her with praise instead of criticizing her. I'm grateful that I kept her from smoking, as most of her peers do, even though I had to bribe her to stop. I also explained that smoking could bring on a horrible disease and shorten her life. I want to show how much I love her and trust her judgment. Jerry's feeling is that the more responsibility you give to young people, the better judgment they will have.

Now that she has moved to Colorado and is getting top marks at college, I don't see her very often but she does stay in touch. When she told me she wants to study to be a vet for large animals at a zoo, I expressed my concern at the danger. She answered, "I enjoy working with animals, as they don't talk back." I retorted, "Maybe not, but they could eat you up!" I trust she will have a happy loving life surrounded by beautiful music and good friends.

Even though I'm not a religious person, I'm convinced that there's something very mysterious at work that cannot be explained. Some people might call it "God" but whatever it is, it's a puzzlement (remember "The King and I?"). Almost everything that happens in life seems to be a coincidence, and one thing I can't comprehend is how my husband, Sam, happened to visit his son at New Paltz on the very same day Billy was to die in the canoe accident; Sam had never visited Billy before, while he was in college. I don't know if it is relevant, but Sam happened to be driving home from a business trip and his route brought him near Billy's dormitory. Early May can be quite cold in New York State, and on a road near New Paltz, his car hit an icy stretch which made the car spin around so fast that he expected to slam into a tree. Fortunately it stopped safely. He told me about this years later because he felt that his own moment of peril might have been a sign from above. To me, Sam committed a sin of omission in not warning Billy of the danger of extreme cold, and by not objecting to his taking the trip when it was too cold to go to Bolton Landing in a canoe.

People who lose a child feel that they must talk to someone else who has undergone a similar tragedy. After I started to deal with Bill's death, I called Kate and Marvin Korobow whose daughter, Marsha, had just graduated from Roslyn High School with honors and had been accepted at Radcliffe. She was driving her Cadillac on Northern Boulevard, when a drunken driver jumped the divider and went into the side of her car, killing her instantly. Her mom and I talked over the phone, consoling each other, and later got to talk some more in person. I'm convinced that talking to a sympathetic friend can sometimes be more effective than consulting a psychologist who has never experienced the loss of a child. Subsequently, I taught piano to Marcia's younger sister, Amy, who was having a difficult time adjusting to her only sister's sudden death, and was being helped by a therapist. I feel I also helped her as she came to discover how much music meant to her. Also, I think I understood what she was going through, since I had had to deal with my own daughter's loss of her brother.

Years later, I was glad to hear that Amy had become a doctor, and is happily married with two kids of her own by now. I forgot to mention that Amy has an older brother, Jerry, who is a lawyer and a fine musician. I've lost touch with their mom, Kate, but I know we helped each other at the time that we most needed an understanding friend. I'm still very close to Trudy, however, as we became like sisters after our children were killed in the same canoe accident.

Recently, I read the tragic story of a family from Australia, the Greenes, who were sightseeing in Italy. They were driving down a strange road when their seven year old son, Nicholas, was fatally wounded in a drive-by shooting. Luckily, their six year old daughter, also sitting in the car, was spared. In the midst of their anguish, the Greenes did something very heroic: they decided, when approached with the idea by the hospital staff, to donate their young son's organs to seven people who were desperately in need. This generous deed was very much appreciated as it was seldom done in Italy, since the Catholic Church doesn't approve of organ donation.

After losing a child, many couples break up, but the Greenes supported each other knowing that their son's organs had given a new life to seven other human beings. The father said that the people who responded to this event strengthened his view of decency in the world. Incidentally, the Greene family was blessed a year later with twin boys, after the tragic loss of Nicholas.

Some of us are lucky enough to sail through life without experiencing any real tragedies except the usual loss of our grandparents and parents at an advanced age. However, I happened to meet and become very fond of an elderly widow whose later life reads like a Shakespearean tragedy. Rose Kramer was a member of my Temple Sinai and Hadassah, and many people adored her as I did. She was only about five feet tall, stocky, and had a most ingratiating smile. The aprons she made by hand and on the sewing machine were unique and beautiful; they made marvelous gifts for birthdays, baby presents, and holidays, and people clamored to buy them, especially since they knew all the profits went to Hadassah and subsequently to Israel. Rose also sang in the temple choir and a dedicated friend, Renée Greenbaum, faithfully drove her to and from rehearsals for years.

Soon after we met, she experienced too many losses for one person to endure, but managed to survive and cope with her sad lot. First, since she lost her husband early in her marriage, she lived in the lovely home of her only daughter and did all the family cooking for several years. Then her world suddenly turned upside down. The oldest of her three grandchildren died in a fire; his apartment's metal door was too hot to open and he couldn't escape. A few months later, his younger brother couldn't take the loss and committed suicide in the garage. Rose's son-in-law was the only one who died of natural causes shortly after in the hospital. About a year later, after Rose and her daughter, Fredda, had moved from the house to an apartment, this daughter lost her life when she crashed into the side of a local bank.

All Rose's many friends gathered around her after each tragedy to comfort her. It was a privilege to know this brave woman who was grateful to have one granddaughter, Steffi, left and so many friends who continued to look after her. I drove her to different places until she had to live in a nursing home, where she had many visitors. I used to trim her hair and cut her nails. She died peacefully at the age of eighty nine.

We all learned a lesson from Rose Kramer, the survivor; instead of complaining about the tragedies life handed her, she continued to live in a positive way and even formed a group of older people at the temple, arranging rides for them so they could attend some of the lunches and festivities there. They called it, "The Rose Club."

When I was in third grade at Runkle School, we were given an assignment to memorize something about the Civil War. I chose the following letter of sympathy from President Abraham

Lincoln to a Mrs. Bixby regarding her loss. I have never seen the letter since those many years ago, and I recall it for you here.

Dear Mrs. Bixby,

I have been shown in the files of the War Department that you are the mother of five sons who have died gloriously on the field of battle. I feel how weak and fruitless must be any words of mine which should attempt to beguile you from the grief of a loss so overwhelming. But I cannot refrain from tendering to you the consolation that may be found in the thanks of the Republic they died to save.

I pray that our heavenly father may assuage your anguish and leave you only the cherished memory of the loved and lost, and the solemn pride that must be yours to have laid so costly a sacrifice upon the altar of freedom.

Yours very sincerely and respectfully,

Abraham Lincoln

I realized, after being miserable for many months, that I must change my attitude, if only for my remaining children's sake. They also had to adjust to losing a sibling. Barbara's mother, Trudy, and I used to talk on the phone for hours, which made this most horrible tragedy of a lifetime – losing two loving and talented children at the start of such promising lives – a little easier to take. Trudy and I became like sisters, and even our children became close.

Incidentally, Carol Shanker is the older sister of JoElla and is a fine artist who lives in Huntington, New York, with her husband, Steven, an attorney, and their three daughters.

JoElla had been very disillusioned with men, as she once had an unpleasant experience on a blind date, and so was understandably cautious and avoided dating new people after that. However, one evening while teaching the father of my former student, Bob, who should walk into the room but Bob himself, all grown up, a handsome six-foot man! A light went off in my brain and I pictured JoElla and Bob as a future couple. I told Bob that I would like to introduce him to a pretty young woman whose family I knew very well. He answered that he was going with somebody at the moment, but his parents told me that they would love to have him meet someone else. The situation required persistence on my part, but he finally agreed to call her. When I told JoElla about Bob and what a handsome, sensitive person he was, she agreed to go out on a date if I arranged for him to call her. when JoElla opened the door to greet Bob for the first time, she was pleasantly surprised. Later, she told me he had the look of a male model, and felt he was really attractive. He must have liked what he saw, as they dated steadily for the next two years, during which time they became a close couple, and made plans to marry. About then, Bob told me he'd like to take some piano lessons again. I knew he had continued to play the piano while he was growing up. But he told me he would like to work on some more advanced music. I obliged by driving to his apartment once a week for several months. He increased his repertoire with some classics, but mostly songs from musicals, plus Gershwin. Frankly, I think it was his way of showing me his appreciation for introducing him to JoElla, though he was too shy to actually mention it.

Their wedding was in a charming setting at Bob's parents' house in our community in Roslyn Heights. His mother said jokingly to me when we came in, "This is all your fault, you know." They now have three lovely children, a boy and two girls, Joshua, Samantha, and Alyson.

January 17, 1998 was the joyous occasion of Joshua Brandon Jacoff's Bar Mitzvah on his thirteenth birthday. The custom is to call up members of the family to light a candle in honor of Josh's special birthday when he became a "man." I was so proud to hear my name called. It was a most satisfying moment when Josh's dad, Robert, who was my student so long ago, escorted me to the front table to light a candle and to have a picture taken. That meant I was considered one of the family, and it was then I knew that I was really appreciated.

As a result of the common tragedy between JoElla's family and mine, I was able to bring a new generation of life into the world. I told this story to Joshua a year ago and he was fascinated - which shows the happy result of a little romantic idea I had in my brain.

I realize now that one person's idea can make a difference. I feel I changed Jerry's life with one angiogram, which prevented a heart attack at the very least. Also, the idea of introducing JoElla to Bob Jacoff made a happy change in both their lives. Though we lost JoElla's sister, Barbara, and my son, Billy, we now have added three new lives to this crazy world -- all because of one idea which, in a way, was the result of the tragedy.

22

TRIP TO EUROPE AND ISRAEL
WITH SAM

Truth speaks in whispers not in shouts.
William M. Blatt

Sam wanted to take my mind off of our tragedy, but I couldn't stop crying off and on until he called a halt to it with his "tough love" attitude. It hurt him very much to see me cry. Since we had been married 25 years, it seemed like a good idea to travel abroad. Sam was able to take four weeks off from his job with Pall Corporation.

In 1979, we took the most memorable vacation of our lives by Eurail Pass – six weeks through the greatest cities in Europe, carrying one bag each. Mine had tiny wheels so I could drag it along. We were in London, Paris, Strasbourg, Nice, Switzerland, Austria (Salzburg and Vienna), Holland, Venice, Cannes, and Monaco.

Lisa and Jerry were our guests in London and Paris. Jerry never liked flying because of the trauma he felt when he had to fly home from Ohio for his brother Bill's funeral. He wasn't too keen on going to Europe with us on Freddie Laker's plane. To say the least, he was upset when we first got on the plane to London, and before we even took off, they announced there was engine trouble and we were told there would be a long delay. In fact, it turned out we tried to sleep in Kennedy Airport and finally were driven by bus to a nearby hotel. Jerry recorded the whole episode on his tape recorder. We left after breakfast the next morning.

In London, we visited the magnificent Tate and British museums, and after a few days of trying to avoid the British cuisine, we all sailed to France, then on by rail to Paris, where we visited the Louvre with all its many treasures, also the impressionistic pastel paintings at the Jeux de Paumes, as well as the live artists and their paintings on the bohemian Montmartre.

After our family had experienced all this beauty, we said farewell to Jerry and Lisa, who returned to London and traveled by Britrail Pass to Wales (Summerhill, a famous alternative school). They had a fantastic time. Sam and I continued on by Eurail Pass to Switzerland and stopped off at Lausanne and Morge, where Rubenstein, the pianist, lived. We visited a nephew there. Then on to Lugano, Zurich, Bern and Geneva. We spent a day in each city. It was so wonderful to hop on a train and be able to arrive anywhere we desired in an hour or two – like being in fairyland.

Next we took a five hour train trip to Salzburg in Austria, and without any reservations, stayed at the lovely Wolf Dietrich Hotel. The next day we saw the unique dwarf statues and lovely flowers at the Mirabel Gardens. Then on to Edelweiss, made famous by the "Sound of Music." We entrained for Linz, where Mozart composed his symphony dedicated to that lovely city, and then continued down the Danube to the one and only Vienna, where we stayed in a pension for three nights. The artistic carvings on the buildings of the city were something to behold, and concerts were around every corner.

Having had our fill of culture, we took a nine hour train trip through the most breathtaking scenery I've ever come across. I never thought the Alps would be even better than I had imagined them to be after reading "Heidi" as a child.

Next we went to Venice where one has to take a boat to get across the street. It's very picturesque.

Gondoliers, with the Bridge of Sighs in the background

In Nice we went to a quaint outdoor restaurant where we were seated next to a couple who couldn't speak English, but we managed to find out that they were celebrating a belated honeymoon, which they hadn't been able to afford for several years.

In Monaco, we went on a tour of the Palace where Princess Grace was married. In Monte Carlo I gambled on the one-armed bandit and won twenty dollars in the machine, but found out later that if I had turned in the receipt for another twenty dollars that was with the cash, I would have collected a total of forty dollars. C'est la vie! Sam played blackjack, which I don't understand, but he was an expert at it.

Next stop was Shacthausen where the impressive Reins Falls, the largest in Europe, is located.

Ouida at Reins Falls

We took our next train to Offenberg through the Black Forest and a hundred tunnels. We were lucky enough to get a friendly conductor who acted as our personal guide, pointing out five hundred year old houses with low roofs as we chugged through the mountains and around the bends.

238

Back in France, we visited Strasbourg and climbed the three hundred and thirty six steps to the tower of the Cathedral and took pictures. I saw a signature carved in stone up there in 1832.

Ouida on tower of the Strasbourg Cathedral

The next morning we took the train to Brussels, Belgium, where we dined on the famous Brussels' mussels. We visited Antwerp, where Rubens lived, and Amsterdam, where we saw great paintings by Van Gogh, Jan Steen and Vermeer in the Rijks Museum. Amsterdam was the only city in which we had difficulty finding a place to stay; we found a rather run down rooming house with a very narrow staircase that we had to walk up and down sideways. It was lucky one day, while we were trudging across streets to look around, that I was trailing behind Sam dragging my small bag on tiny wheels. In the distance I saw a car speeding like a bat out of Hell toward us as we were starting to cross the road. That car would certainly have run Sam down if I didn't scream "STOP" at the top of my lungs! He stopped just in time before the car whizzed by.

We finished the trip sailing back to the White Cliffs of Dover, then on to London where we took off for Israel, where we spent the last two weeks of our trip. We visited with several relatives of Sam's there.

During our stay at the Dan Hotel in Jerusalem, I spotted Danny Kaye in the dining room. I couldn't resist going over to his table. He was alone so I bent down to get a better look, and asked, hopefully, "Danny?" He had a dead-pan expression, so I quickly announced, "I studied violin with Harry Ellis Dickson," remembering that Dickson had given Danny lessons in conducting a few years before. His face lit up; I knew music was one of his passions. He put out his hand and smiled. I happened to have a booklet of my dad's epigrams in my bag, so I quickly fished it out. I asked if he would like to have it, as I thought it would give him a few laughs. He said, "Yes, thank you" and suggested I write my name on it, which I did. I hope he used them.

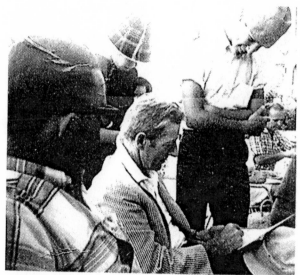

Danny Kaye signs autographs for Israeli soldiers

Sam's older sister, Mary, had moved to Avichael, Natanya, in Israel with her husband, Aaron Herr, when they were married in the thirties. He was a real pioneer, as he had fought as a member of the Jewish Legion in the twenties, and had bought a good sized piece of land there. Mary's family (Sam was her youngest brother) was very unhappy when her husband was insistent that they settle in Israel. The family only saw her when they made expensive trips there.

Mary and Aaron had two sons and a daughter whom Sam and I visited much later. Mary had died several years before. When they first came to Israel, it was called Palestine. She and her husband had an orange grove on their land which has been passed on to their son, Alvin (Sonny), his wife, Eva, and daughter, Shula. Sonny worked as a travel director. Shula and her husband, Arik Rimmerman, and daughter, Netta, came to New York about 1978 so that Arik could study for a Ph.D. at Adelphi University. We found them an apartment near Lisa and her husband Harley's place and helped them get settled. Sam found a suitable car for them and I took them to tag sales to find furniture that they would need only for two years, as they would be returning to Israel. We shopped around at various garage sales and I finally spotted what looked like a perfectly adequate mahogany desk which had a few scratches, but cost only ten dollars. Arik thought it was just what he needed and, sure enough, he was so right - it enabled him to get his degree, and he was even at the top of his class. Subsequently, he became successful as an authority on head trauma and preventative medicine. Arik comes to the USA very often now to give lectures. All of his trips are paid for by either the Israeli government or from grants. He has fought in all the Israeli wars. Recently in New Orleans he was named Man of the Year by the American Mental Retardation International Foundation. Jerry went to Israel in the summer of 1993 by invitation to help with the alternative schools, and again in 1996. He stayed with Arik and Shula some of the time. (Pictures of these Israeli relatives, taken when I visited Israel a few years later, may be found at the end of Chapter Twenty Seven).

Amiram Rigai is a fine Israeli pianist who moved to the United States to pursue his career. Scott Joplin and Louis Gottchalk were his specialties and he recorded much of their music. He liked to do a rehearsal program at the home of Ruth Davis in the Country Club before his concerts. After one of these, he spoke to the small audience and I thought I'd ask him what part of Israel he was from. He answered, "Avichael." Sam and I were amazed at the coincidence, as Avichael is such a small town, you don't need an address, only a name on a letter. When I asked him if he knew the Herr family, he exclaimed, Of course! I grew up with them!" and, glancing at Sam, he said, "You look just like Marky!" (Mary's son and Sam's nephew, who had been his childhood friend.) He was going to give concerts there the following summer and he said he'd give our love to the relatives. What a small world!

23

LUCY IN THE BIG CITY

All the world's a stage,
And all the men and women merely players
Shakespeare, *As You Like It,*

After my dad died, I talked Mom into moving from Boston to New York City which was her dream, as she could then work on selling his plays and having them produced on Broadway. In the course of this adventure, she met many prominent people and would charm them into reading his plays. (There were 35 of them but she concentrated on one or two.) I remember conversations she had with Henry Fonda, Robert Preston, and others. Mom lived at the Whitby, right in the theatre district on 45th Street and invited many friends, male and female, to visit her. It was a big worry for us as some of them stayed over and slept on the couch. Mom was so grateful that Jo and I convinced her to move to New York that she was fond of saying, "It's wonderful! All I have to do is put on my fancy bathrobe, go across the street to the theater and see a play!" I remember so well when my mother, the former actress, caught me looking grumpy one day. She mentioned the well-known song, "Put On a Happy Face," and said, "Not only will it put you in a better mood, but people around you will perk up and smile back. It's a contagious reaction." She illustrated by first showing me her downcast expression, and then in a split second she lit up the room with a delightful smile. "Which did you like better," she asked. Of course there was no doubt about the answer – the happy face!

When she walked around the city, she would often go to Paley Park and meet people. Her eyes were so bad that she had to go with the crowd when she crossed the streets in order to be safe. One of her favorite haunts was the famous Takashimaya Gift Shop where she got to know the sales people, often invited them to her apartment, and tutored them in English.

My mother and I were often joined by a long time family friend, Rabbi Abraham Nowak, whom we called "Buddy" (so called because he was a soldier in the first World War) on regular Wednesday luncheon and matinée expeditions. Buddy was a widower and connected with Kingsbridge Hospital in the Bronx. Years before, he had been a very important rabbi with a congregation in Cincinnati. My sister, Jo, often sent him theater tickets, which encouraged his interest in the theater. When my mother first came to New York, she thought that he might have a romantic interest in her since he had encouraged her to move to the city. However, he had been too much in love with his late wife, Ann, and had no interest in remarrying.

When I was a little child, "Buddy" gave me an unusual toy which I still have and display in a prominent place in my den. It's a goofy looking boy-doll, made of metal and wood. His arms and legs come apart and are connected to the body by ball joints. It was lots of fun to pull apart and put together again. It may be a valuable antique toy today.

Young Ellen Pall with Rabbi "Buddy" Nowak

"Buddy" wrote many uplifting short sermons which he called his "Prescriptions for Living." He gave them out to patients in the hospital and in so doing enabled them to face their problems in a more positive way. Here is an excerpt from his "Prescriptions:"

LIFE'S ADJUSTMENTS

Life can be described as a series of inevitable adjustments. On how well we make them depends on our health in all its aspects.

Fortunately, most of us are able to make the major adjustments of life without much strain and tension. They are the natural and normal processes of growth. The difficulty arises when some shocking and sudden event comes and jars our life — upsetting our plans, dashing our hopes and puncturing our dreams – some accident, some illness or sorrow. The event becomes a crisis.

There are three possible ways in which we can face a crisis. One – we can be overwhelmed by it; two – we can be embittered by it; three – we can cooperate with it. The last attitude is, of course, the only sensible one. It is of paramount importance that we learn as soon as possible to accept the realities of life, however hard, and to realize that there are certain situations in life which we cannot escape and over which we have no control.

It is the better part of health to bow before the inevitable than to meet it head on. Just as a tree, when it does not give with the gale, snaps and splinters, so with man, when he does not bend to the storms of life, he collapses and breaks down. To survive, we ourselves must be adjustable; we must have spiritual resiliency. This depends on our faith in God and our belief in His providence. It will not banish the eventualities that make life's inevitable adjustments necessary. But it does give the inner qualities of life that enable us to adjust to them, and not be broken by them.

Since life's adjustments can make or mar our health and happiness, it is well that we remember these simple rules: do not fight the inevitable. Accept it. And having accepted it, face the future with new hope and fortitude.

A couple my mom met were working on a musical and told her they needed a lyricist. Of course, she got me involved and I wrote the words for about 20 songs. The musical was called *Castle on the Dee* and was set in Scotland. The show didn't go anywhere, but it was an interesting experience. However, if I had known how difficult it would be to work with these people, I would never have undertaken this project. They thought I should be grateful that they allowed me to be the lyricist for this "marvelous composer" whom I had the privilege to work with, and that should be enough payment. Many years later, I wonder why Sam and I took that long trip to Brooklyn so many times for meetings with them. Now I think I know why; they were always talking about their musical eventually getting to Broadway, and it seemed to be such an opportunity that we kept pursuing that pot of gold. You have to have faith in yourself if you're going to get anywhere in life, I guess.

My mom was a unique person. She loved life and people so much that when she was over 80, she said to me, "I'd love to live to be 100." Of course, at that time, she was healthy and had all her faculties and most of her charms. Unfortunately, her eyesight was failing because her best eye had a bad cataract. The ophthalmologist was hesitant to operate as she had very little vision in her other weak eye and she would have no good eye left to fall back on if the operation was unsuccessful. Mom started to get small strokes when she moved to Scharf Manor and she began to fail in many ways. She had been there for a year and a half, and during that time she had a beautiful friendship with an older man, Mr. Coleman. They took walks every day and even did a little shopping. Every baby they saw provided a moment of wonderment, and the lovely gardens fascinated them.

My son, Jerry spent a day with my mother when she lived in New York City. Here was his report:

A VISIT WITH NANA
by
Jerry Mintz (age seventeen)

Lucy Romberg Blatt is a grandmother, mine to be exact. She is the most unusual person I know today.

I telephoned her New York City apartment to ask if I could visit. A bright, alive voice answered the phone. "Hello," she said, and in that one word there was no doubting the fact that this was the charming voice of upper Boston society. We talked for a while, and I happened to mention that my cousin, her niece, had taken an apartment in Greenwich Village. "That's wonderful," she said, "a girl was raped there just the other day."

Of course, the two statements were not meant to be connected in that way. What she really meant was that she was glad my cousin would not be roaming the streets at night looking for an apartment. Nevertheless, the effect was disconcerting. This was just another of what my grandfather called, "Lucyisms." The classical Lucyism took place quite a few years ago. Lucy wanted to go to a Boston Symphony Orchestra concert, and she wanted to order tickets over the phone. She couldn't remember the number, so she called information. "Information," she asked, "could you tell me the year that Columbus discovered America?" This, it turned out, was the number she wanted and thought she'd make it easier for the operator. Needless to say, it didn't.

It may surprise you to note that out of all this confusion emerged a wonderfully real person, whose strange logic somehow became fused with a unique living philosophy.

The next weekend I went to her apartment in a neat little hotel called The Whitby on 45th street in the heart of the theatre district. I took the elevator to the fourth floor and found the apartment. After warm greetings, I walked in and looked around. Her place was very compact but completely adequate; there was a living room with a tiny kitchen and one bedroom, in the corner of which was a large pile of manuscripts which turned out to be my grandfather's plays. "Nana" told me that her big dream was to have one of these plays produced. She spent much of her time seeing theatrical producers and going backstage to present copies of the plays to well known actors. The play she was most determined to have produced was called "Strictly Kosher," a comedy about intermarriage.

I recognized much of the furniture from that which I had seen in her former house in Boston. I hadn't even a chance to sit down when I was handed a small booklet entitled, "Money is God in Action." From then on things happened in rapid succession. I tried to take notes on everything, but it was soon obvious that that was impossible. At any rate, she first lectured to me upon the subject of the booklet, then handed me her coat, and instructed me upon the proper way to help a lady put her coat on. After that, she looked for her rubbers and found them, seemingly using some mathematical formula in the process. Since Nana had always had bad eyesight, she had a place for everything to make things easier. Unfortunately, when she visits us in Roslyn Heights, she also puts our things in their proper places, but we can never find them.

After putting on her rubbers, checking to make sure that she had her keys, and reminding me to set the clock ahead an hour because daylight savings time was just over, we were off - I still didn't know where we were going. It turned out to be a most marvelous cafeteria on the eleventh floor of the old Times building in the center of Times Square. She explained how she found it. Seems that in the process of taking one of her destitute friends out to dinner, she had happened upon this "divine cafeteria.." I have to admit the food was very good.

We started walking back from the Times building. Her hotel was convenient to all the places of entertainment in and around the theater district. As we walked, almost everyone we passed seemed to know her. I can't say she wasn't conscious of this. She asked me, "How old do I look?" My honest guess was about fifty-five. "Fifty or so," I said.

There started a little psychological battle which goes on with many of the people she knows. How old is she really? I don't know. And what does she look like? Well, it really is amazing. Her hair is naturally black with a few tinges of gray. When it is down it is very long.

She is fairly tall, with very good posture, average build. Her teeth are her own, and you have never seen such a disarming smile. It is of the Mona Lisa variety. Indeed, it is easy to believe that she was the prettiest girl in Boston, as my grandfather always said.

After we bought lunch, we went into her background. She was born in Kharkov, the Ukraine. Her parents were "old fashioned," her own description. Her father played the violin and loved music. I inherited his violin and treasure it, not only because it belonged to my great grandfather, but because it has a beautiful, rich tone. The only thing she remembers about the Ukraine was that her family had a cherry orchard. The family emigrated to this country when she was three years old. On the boat, she and her sister contracted the measles and were not allowed to go ashore at Ellis Island. They were kept aboard the ship until they recuperated, and were then allowed to rejoin the family.

They came to Boston and settled down in the slums. I'm still not sure which slums. My mother said she thought they were in the West End. When I asked my grandmother, she first said the North End, then said, "You'd better change that to the South end. It was a better part of town." Details, I found out, never mattered much to her.

In the Ukraine her father had been wealthy; he owned a brewery there. In this country he had to start at the bottom. He had to learn English. He first worked in the upholstery business. Later he owned a hardware store, and then a grocery store.

Lucy went to grammar school and then Girl's High School, both on the West side. One of the turning points in her life happened when she was fourteen years old. She belonged to an organization called "Saloons Must Go," and she won a prize speaking in a contest sponsored by that group. It might have ended right there if her sister, Lena, had not decided to send an article about it to one of the Boston papers. The next day, a man knocked on the door and introduced himself as Albert Murdock. He told her that he was interested in helping deserving young girls who wished to go to college. Since Lucy hated mathematics, she hadn't been eager to go to college, but, with her father's permission, Murdock sent Lucy to the very exclusive Leland Powers School of the Spoken Word. There, she perfected her speaking voice and was trained for speech and acting. She always wanted to go on the stage, but first she got a job teaching speech to the "greenhorns," the Russian immigrants.

During this time she gave speaking recitals in many places. One of them was the recitation of "Enoch Arden," a 144 page story by Tennyson, set to music by Richard Strauss. She memorized not only the words but had to know cues from the musical accompaniment. Lucy worked on this at the Leland Powers School and gave a recital to a large audience. My grandfather was in that audience, and that is where he first met Lucy. After the performance he talked to her and she signed up for a Shakespeare course he was giving at the time. His name was William M. Blatt. He was a fairly well known lawyer who had come to hate the law at that time, and aspired to be a playwright.

We'll let Mr. Blatt, her husband, tell some of what happened in his own words:

In 1911, I married Lucy Romberg, whom I had known for a couple of years as a slim, beautiful girl, much younger than I, a graduate of Leland Powers School, with a lovely voice and a remarkable ability to enunciate well and speak good, cultured English. For a girl reared in a slum, she had an unbelievable ability to get along with all kinds of people including some of the Mayflower crowd, who made a pet of her. I thought of her as a kid, a rather bewildered one, but she used to call at my office for advice, and I liked her in an off-hand way. She moved to New York, got a job with a stock company as a character actress which she held for two weeks, and then went to work for the National Cloak and Suit Company. What her duties were I don't know, but she was fired when, after two weeks, she asked for a raise. I happened to go to New York just then to attend a wedding. I decided to call on a girl I knew and I thought I might as well see Lucy too, so I wrote her and made an appointment with her at noon, and one with the other girl at two o'clock. I arrived ten minutes after she had been fired and took her to lunch. After that we went to a club she belonged to and I suddenly found myself asking her to marry me. She stalled a little but made another date with me for the evening. I forgot all about the other girl, met Lucy, took her to another restaurant and clinched the proposal She was broke. I gave her a blank check to pay expenses which she lost and never found. I wrote her a long letter on my arrival in Boston to which she sent me a belated reply telling about the check. I sent her another for carfare and she arrived in March. We were married April second in her home with no one present but the immediate families and an old boyfriend who played the wedding march. We went to Quebec on our honeymoon and stayed at the famous Chateau Frontenac.

It was a strange marriage. My grandmother was at least six inches taller than my grandfather. He thought that she was an intellectual, serious type. "She wasn't, but she was good fun," he said later.

William Blatt was considered the best reference judge in Massachusetts at one time and he taught law in five colleges. At Boston University, he had 150 students, the largest for a non-examination elective course in B.U. history. He received an Honorary Literature Degree from Calvin Coolidge College, became president of The Law Society of Massachusetts, and was one of the founders of the New Century Club, and was in "Who's Who in America."

As my grandfather's career grew, Lucy took on the new position of hostess to his new acquaintances, which included many "bluebloods," the Beacon Hill crowd. Among them were Henry Wadsworth Longfellow Dana, the grandson of the poet, whom she took to the Yiddish Theatre. And there was Isaak Goldberg, a close friend of George Gershwin, and the painter, Charles Prendergast, as well as many others. The entertainment at the gatherings of these people was often the marionettes which my mother and her sisters manipulated as my grandmother narrated, and guests (often frustrated actors) spoke the parts of my grandfather's plays.

Some of my mother's friends at the time included Lenny Bernstein, Mike Wallace, Arthur Rosenheimer, Jr. (well-known as Arthur Knight, the film critic), and Byron Waksman (who has been research director of Multiple Sclerosis in New York and a professor of Microbiology at Yale), the son of Selman Waksman, the discoverer of streptomycin and a Nobel Prize winner.

During all this time, Lucy was a first-rate home economist. She managed to acquire mother's helpers and later, maids at practically no expense. They now had three children, all girls. The oldest was Hester, the next Josephine, and the third was my mother, Pauline Louise (Ouida). My grandfather died in 1958 and just two years later, Josie died of a rare blood disease. Such blows can be enough to destroy any person, but Lucy's philosophy sustained her. Not many could have held up under the strain of such tragedy.

Last year, Lucy moved to her present apartment in New York.. She tried to start all over again in a completely new environment. My grandfather had been careful that Lucy would have enough money in the event of his death.

She told me she has joined a local actors' guild. "We just listen in on them, but I'll tell you something: I'd go on the stage in a minute if I had the courage."

I'm sure it won't surprise you now if I tell you that she has a few admirers. One man in his early sixties asks her to marry him every time he sees her. He barely earns a living now, however, so Lucy wouldn't even think of it. Another man, about the same age, is quite wealthy and, like my grandfather, is mentioned in Who's Who in America, Charles Fonk.. Now he is assistant to Robert Moses in planning the New York World's Fair. She showed me some of his beautiful letters.

Speak of the young at heart! She still gives reading recitals. The next one will be at Mount Sinai Hospital. She will read poetry to music. She also got someone at the United Nations to put on the added final act of "The Merchant of Venice," my grandfather's play-let in the style of Shakespeare.

We left the cafeteria after one of the best meals I've had in a long time. We walked up Broadway toward her apartment. We passed a man who was walking on an artificial leg. She looked at him and said to me, "I don't know why I worry. See how lucky we are. I love life so much!" And she does.

Lucy gave me a first impression of complete and utter confu-sion. But it seems that she somehow comes out on top. My grand-father summed it up pretty well when he said, "It took me years to realize some of her best points. She is jolly and good natured, a lover of all the arts and none of the sciences, patient, adaptable, loyal, energetic, and a lot of other good things. After a long while, I noticed that, while she never seemed to understand any of the problems of life, she could solve them as well as I could, some-times a lot better."

Lucy took me by the Hotel Manhattan. She wanted to see the fish display in the window. One large red fish was resting along the side of the tank.

"Look," she said, "It's sleeping. I didn't know fish slept. And its eyes – they're open. Won't the water get in?"

My mom enjoyed living in the heart of New York City in her beloved theater district. I used to come in every Wednesday morning to see song publishers and record companies. Then, Mom and I had lunch at Lindy's where the actors and comedians hung out. It was fun to see Milton Berle or Alan King eating corned beef sandwiches at a nearby table. After lunch we would go to a matinée - a play or a musical. Mom always got the cheapest balcony seats beforehand, and during the performance, I'd scan the orchestra to see if there were any empty seats. I usually spotted a couple, and I'd lead her downstairs to them at intermission. Since she had poor eyesight, it was a real treat for her to sit in the third or fourth row and get a good close-up of the actors. Under the bright lights you could see the spray come out of their mouths as they spoke.

One day I got a call from the manager of the Whitby Hotel where Mom was staying. He told me that she had collapsed on the sidewalk and that a kind stranger had walked her back to the hotel. That meant that Sam and I had to find a senior home for her, which we finally did in Long Beach, Long Island. Scharf Manor was an ideal place for her as it was right on the boardwalk, where there was no traffic to worry about. It didn't take long before mother found a very nice male companion. They used to take walks every day to get away from the retirement home atmosphere. My mother lived there quite happily for two years, and I came to visit her every two weeks. At the end of her stay she began to have small strokes. It was time to bring her to my house to live.

When mother came to live with us at age 83, she couldn't understand why she was not on her own any longer, as she had never wanted to be a burden to anyone. She was usually quite lucid, but I could tell her mind was deteriorating as time went along. She sometimes would ask, "Why am I living here in your house?" Before long, I could tell she was getting more strokes and she would ask, with a puzzled look, "Are you really my daughter?" We took short walks, only around the block, because she tired easily. A doctor had told me that I should give her a pill for her blood pressure, which I did - only once. She went into a semi-coma that night and I told my brother-in-law, Dr. Morris Shapiro, about it. We decided she couldn't take the medication. Eventually she stayed in bed longer and longer, but once in a while she used to joke with Sam by saying, "Good night, Jimmy." He would answer, "Good night, Irene." Sometimes she used to come in my room to watch television. One day I came in to find her standing next to the bed and wearing Sam's shoes which she found on the floor. She looked a little sheepish about it as she couldn't figure out why she had put them on. It was both humorous and pathetic at the same time. I was worried if I had to leave her with a stranger when I had to teach piano, as she was likely to wander off somewhere; she had to be watched constantly. Finally, she was bedridden, and even though my sister, Hester, and her doctor husband thought she should be in a nursing home, I refused to consider it. She was so sweet, loving, and uncomplaining, it was a privilege to care for her myself. I was her private nurse. When she lost the ability to swallow, I had to feed her each liquid spoonful of strained babyfood and let it drop down her throat. She would say to me, "You do everything for me. Do you know how much I love you." You can imagine how I felt about her. She never lost her sweetness and loving personality.

After six months of gradual deterioration, she went into a coma. Dr. Paley, our family doctor, was called to examine her. He was surprised that I was still caring for her, so I called my brother-in-law, Dr. Morris, and he arranged for an ambulance to bring her to Schenectady. The family watched as she was carried out on a stretcher. It was traumatic for Jerry and Lisa as they had been so close to her. I went in the ambulance and held her hand. They gave her oxygen to revive her now and then, as it was a hot day and the bus air-conditioning system was not functioning.

Morrie took care of her for a week at his hospital, and she passed away quietly at the age of eighty four when Hester was visiting her. I feel I had helped ease her out of this world.

24

OTHER FAMILY MEMBERS

The old folks who hang on serve a purpose;
they make middle-aged people around them feel young.
William M. Blatt

Sam and I took many trips to Worcester and Boston. When my mom and dad lived in Brookline and then Brighton, I was the one who kept in contact with them the most and brought our three kids to visit. Sam's mom was in a Boston Hospital for eight years and his sisters, Nessie and Fay, lived in Worcester with their husbands, Nathan and Eli ; Sam's older brothers, Myer and Nelson Mintz also lived in Worcester with their wives, Bessie and Esther. At that time his two other sisters, Janet and Molly, lived in New York City with their husbands, George and Al.

The youngest of Josie's three children is Ellen Jane who fortunately inherited the writing genes of her grandfather and mother. I'm so proud of Ellen, as her mother would be, since Josie was an unfulfilled writer who never received recognition.

David Pall fully supported his beautiful daughter, Ellen Jane, until she had graduated from the University of California at Santa Barbara. After that, she started writing historical romances set in the English Regency period. She figured it would be a solid commercial beginning for her writing career and she wanted to be independent. It worked, so she kept writing them under the name, Fiona Hill. After writing eight such books (some titles: "The Autumn Rose," "Love in a Major Key") she decided to write a contemporary novel under her own name - one without the restrictions that historical novels impose. This contemporary novel was titled "Back East." It got good reviews and helped to provide credentials when Ellen started as a journalist soon afterward. She first

Photo: Jill Levine – New York

The Dicker family,
Richard, Ellen and Ben

Ellen Pall playing with her son, Ben

wrote short pieces for the Village Voice and the New Yorker, then began writing longer articles for the New York Times Book Review, Arts and Leisure Section, and the Times Sunday Magazine. A decade after "Back East" came out, she published another novel, "Among the Ginzburgs" which got fine reviews in the New York Times, The New Yorker, the Forward, and Newsday. Ellen has prepared the screen play for a film version of that book.

Steffi, Ellen's older sister, was delighted when Ellen told her that she was planning to marry Richard Dicker, as Steffi had met him and felt that their personalities were very compatible. When I was unable to come up with an appropriate wedding gift, Steffi suggested something that she thought would mean a lot to Ellen. This was a beautiful self-portrait of Josie that her husband, David Pall, had given me after Josie died and he had remarried. I kept that portrait on the wall beside my bed, and treasured it for many years - it was the first thing I saw every morning when I woke up. The sun shone right on her face, which seemed to be smiling down at me and saying, "Good morning Ouida, I'm here. I love you!" Because I felt that Ellen, who lost her mother at the awfully young age of six, deserved it more than I did, I was willing to sacrifice this cherished possession, and I know that Josie would have wished it for her.

Richard Dicker, Ellen's husband, was born in April of 1951 and grew up in New York City, the younger of two sons. He went to P.S. 6, Horace Mann high school, and then to the University of Michigan. After years as a grass-roots labor organizer in Detroit, he returned to school and obtained a law degree at New York University School of Law. He spent six months in the legal office of Amnesty International in London, then joined the staff of Human Rights Watch in New York. There he has worked on behalf of political dissidents in Kenya and China, and is working to gain the release of activists who were imprisoned for their democratic views, especially those who were in the Tiananmen Square uprising in 1989. He led a campaign to prevent the Chinese from holding the Olympics in the year 2,000, and has written reports on accountability for war crimes in Namibia and on labor rights in South Korea. He is currently working toward the establishment of a permanent international Nuremburg war crimes tribunal. Richard spends much of his time speaking with corporate executives, writers, lawyers, doctors, scientists, and teachers, encouraging them to raise human rights concerns with colleagues in repressive countries, such as Rwanda, in hopes of altering the human rights practices of offending governments.

Richard says, "One of the most interesting aspects of traveling is meeting people and being invited to their homes for dinner, be it in China or Africa. But you don't always know what to expect. I wind up eating a lot of foods that I would not normally eat at home." Squirrel is the oddest food he has eaten. "After that, I decided it was better not to ask," he says.

He is also a very nice man with a great sense of humor who loves his wife (whom he met at the New School when both took a class on Latin-American politics) and their dear son, Ben, who is the joy of their life.

STEPHANIE PALL

Here is a letter my beloved niece, Stephanie, wrote to me after her sister's wedding:

```
Dear Aunt,
    How good of you to generously present Ellen
with the portrait of our mother (and to let her
know I'd suggested it, too) - a very noble act
which Ellen (and I) will always appreciate.
    I am sure she will not receive a gift (wed-
ding or otherwise) she would value more than
this! She said you'd also sent some other very
lovely paintings as well.
    I continue to have my "ups and downs" - you
have been one of my greatest consolations in my
illness, always supportive, always remembering
I might need time to reply to letters, sympa-
thetic but not overbearing or overprotectively
concerned... just right, and a rarity. It seems
most people either act as though I'm making up
an illness or go to the opposite extreme and
tell me what I should do - equally distressing
- but you're terrific.
    Hope you have a great time at Tanglewood -
maybe get to see Lenny -
                    Much love from Steffi.
```

Steffi with Mom, Jo

Jo, on patio

Stephanie was the oldest of Jo's three children. She had a short life (45 years) but very eventful one — in fact her life would make a great soap opera. She and I saw each other often when she lived in Huntington. Later, when she moved to Maine, we wrote to each other constantly. She was a charming, artistic and very musical girl. I had taught her piano when she was a teenager and she played several instruments including the recorder, flute and harpsichord. Even when she was in Mount Sinai Hospital suffering with Crohn's disease, she asked me to buy her a special recorder for her birthday present so she could play it in the hospital.

Since Steffi, Bill, and Ellen lost their mom when they were so young, I was able to give them an idea of what her personality was like as I had fortunately saved all the post cards and letters she had written and I keep finding more as I go through some old boxes in the attic. Some are even love letters from one or two old boyfriends of hers. Stephanie married shortly after she lost her mom and her dad had remarried. She was just eighteen and wanted to be independent. Bob was a nice Jewish engineer, but she hardly knew him and was in a rush to get married. It lasted six years and everyone thought they were very happy. Steffi helped him financially and he got his Master's which enabled him to get a position at Grumman Aircraft. He also played clarinet and Steffi played flute, recorder and harpsichord which would seem to make them compatible. However, they announced their breakup. Steffi complained he wasn't exciting enough for her, and they divorced.

Her second husband was Ron, who was a policeman turned architect. Friends tried to talk Steffi out of marrying him, as he wasn't really her type. He was a good deal older than she; Steffi may have been looking for a father figure. Steffi didn't get to see her own dad as much as she would have liked; he was very busy becoming David Pall of Pall Corporation. They had a beautiful house in Huntington, which I visited a few times. It might have been a combination of things that caused Steffi to get Crohn's disease. Stress could have been one of them. She was in and out of hospitals and had at least two operations. Incidentally, Josie knew Dr. Burrill Crohn, and she and I knew his son, Dr. Woody Crohn. Jo illustrated the elder Dr. C's book.

When Steffi, was very ill in Mount Sinai Hospital having a colostomy, Ellen often came to visit her and was inspired to write the following poem:

FLOTILLA

(for Steffi)

A broken mast, she half sits
Green eyes, suddenly close-together
Blink slowly through unmeaning brine.
Two plastic tubes vine down
Anchoring a hand mottled like a map;
They are always here these days
Those two trim sacks, hanging
She turns her head, smiles dreamily, listening,
Skin as fine as the sheets beneath her
Veins that will not drink, drowning.

Look up!
We are slipping away,
All, slipping away forever,
Like flames on dark water
Like boats on dark water.

Ron was very helpful and stuck by her, but eventually they were divorced. Then Steffi moved to Maine and married Freddie, husband number three. He was in Public Health and had some hobbies - ham radio operator, for instance. That was fine with Steffi as she pursued her music when he was busy. They seemed to be happy for a few years. He had two kids from a previous marriage and she got along well with them. Now comes the big surprise: Freddie informed Steffi that he would rather be Freda! That was the end of the marriage.

Number four husband was "Super Dave" as Steffi called him. She finally hit it right. Incidentally, Steffi had a very charming, bubbly personality. We kept in touch by mail as she rarely traveled, because she was rather weak due to her illness. Super Dave took very good care of Steffi, but as luck would have it, he became a cancer victim and lived only a year longer. Steffi was devastated. Her dad enabled her to have nurses around the clock for him. She read to him every night before he died. Steffi met a math teacher after that, but she died (at 45) before they were to marry.

These poems were written by Steffi when she was struggling with Lupus (Latin for wolf):

RAVAGE

The wolf is not at the door–
The wolf is in the door,
Reclining comfortably at my fireside
In my favorite chair,
Devouring the fruits of happiness
Which like a dowry I laid by
For sunny days to come.

I woke one night to find this
Uninvited bridegroom at my side
And I, wings clipped, metamorphosed
Into his carrion prey.
Sated, the beast sleeps;
It is said he will re-awake
And feed and sleep and wake again.
I watch the darkness for signs.

He stirs! Scraps of wing flutter
From his chops, now powdered delicately
With their pastel remains.
There remains for me
(what is left) a state of siege,
The ravening jaws always in reach.
They say this is to be expected
They are wrong: I was not told.

ARRIVAL

All of my life has tended toward this moment;
Oh, God, let me die now content
If I cannot maintain this feeling whole.
For me to have this kind of peace of mind,
For me to have this quietude of soul,
That was my goal.

Steffi's funeral was performed exactly as she had wanted it, and her younger sister, Ellen, saw to it that it was followed to the letter. Most people don't like to plan something like that, but Steffi was unique. She knew, having been in ill health from her early twenties, that her life would be cut short, so she arranged to have one of her favorite pieces of Bach to be played. The selection went on for about fifteen minutes and many members of the party became restless wondering when it would end. After it was over, members of her family came forward to tell anecdotes of her life. It was then that her dad broke down and was unable to finish reading a poem of hers which described the pain she experienced during her final illness. Her second husband, Ron, also was there and we spoke to him afterward. They had remained friends and he had even designed a bungalow outside her home in Maine. After family and friends had spoken, Steffi pulled off her final surprise: it was announced that there would be no trip to the cemetery - she had been cremated!

Her father, Dr. David Pall, is the founder of the Pall Corporation, an international company based on Long Island which manufactures filters for the health, food and beverage, aircraft, electronics, energy, chemical and petrochemical industries. His Leukocyte Depletion Filter removes white blood cells from blood used for transfusions and patients safety. He feels that this filter is the most important of his over one hundred inventions. It has grown more rapidly than any other of his products and is now in use in many thousands of hospitals all over the world. Dr. Pall received a National Medal of Technology from President Bush for his combining of filtration research and engineering technology. Pall's filters were used in the Desert Storm operation to protect helicopters and tanks from the sand. Dr. Pall married his wife, Helen, after my sister died of aplastic anemia at the age of 45. Helen's two daughters, Jane and Abigail, were adopted by their stepfather. In 1997, his only son, Bill, died of a mysterious muscle disease. He had been a successful art dealer in New York City and left his wife, Olivia, and two children, Alexander Jo and Caitlin, as well as his sister, Ellen Pall, her husband, Richard Dicker, and their son, Benjamin. Helen, David's second wife has since died. She was very active in the art field, and was beloved by her family.

Photo: Josef A. Schneider – New York

The Pall family, Bill, Jo, Ellen,
David, and Steffi in early days

--- with Helen Pall,
David's second wife

Every Christmas Jo Pall created an original card describing the activities of family members in the past year. All their friends looked forward to them because they were always very original. Here is an example:

David Pall with his grandchildren, Caitlin and Alexander
Jo, with their mother, Olivia

David Pall's grandson, Ben,
with his mother, Ellen

$\mathbf{M}$y sister Hester's husband, Dr. Morris Shapiro, was a very prominent cardiologist in Schenectady, N.Y. before he retired a few years ago, and is much beloved by his friends and former patients as well as those in the medical profession. He had a very colorful career as a Captain in the U.S. Army during the second World War. As a result of his fighting in North Africa when he was wounded, he received the Purple Heart for bravery and two silver stars, and achieved the rank of Major. For a time he was personal physician to General Eisenhower as well as to Marlene Dietrich when she entertained the troops in Italy. Hester and Morris were invited to the wedding of John Eisenhower, the president's son, after the war ended.

Recently, Hester was honored by her Congregation Gates of Heaven when she was given the Distinguished Service Award, the first time it was ever given. At this temple she also chaired the adult education committee and was a member of the board of trustees for over twenty years. She developed a Sunday night lecture series in which Roman Vishniac, a physician and photographer appeared. He had taken pictures of Polish Jews before they were sent to be executed during the Holocaust, as he wanted them to be remembered by future generations. During the showing of the photos, a man in the audience who recognized his picture as a boy being held by the Nazis, stood up and rushed into Vishniac's arms saying, "That's my picture!" It was such a powerful experience that Vishniac had to call his wife before he could settle down.

Hester also worked in television, writing and producing a series on education and the arts. She also wrote a newspaper column, "Bookbound," which appeared in the Schenectady *Gazette* from 1969 to 1975, and taught courses in Jewish-American fiction, poetry and drama. When Ray and I go to visit them each summer, they take us out to dinner where we are overwhelmed when their friends and his former patients gather around us to show how much they appreciate their kindness and generosity.

Hester and Morris's daughter, Susan, lives in Swamscott, Mass. with her husband, Dr. Edward Bayard, who is a prominent psychiatrist there. Susan became a research chemist and worked for Dr. Land who invented the camera that develops photos on the spot. As the mother of two children, Jeff and Lucy, Susan has conducted a school for tutoring young children. She received her B.A. degree in chemistry from Syra-

266

Wedding picture of Hester and
Captain Morris Shapiro

Hester and year-old Susan, who didn't
meet her soldier Dad until she was two

Dr. and Mrs. Morris Shapiro

Rochelle and Bill Shapiro

Dr. and Mrs. Edward Bayard with
Lucy at Jeff's Bar Mitzvah

Top - Lucy Bayard, daughter of Susan Bayard on right.
Below is Sarah Shapiro, daughter of Bill and Rochelle
Shapiro

Dr. Morris Shapiro with grandson Jeff Bayard

Hester and Morris Shapiro, with
Ouida and Samson Mintz

Credenza, with paintings by
Ouida's family

cuse University, and her M.A. degree in science from the University Of California at Berkeley, and has taught science at Boston University. Her husband, Edward, received his B.A. degree *cum laude* in Russian language from Harvard University. He received his M.D. degree from Harvard Medical School and interned at the University of Rochester and the Strong Memorial Hospital.

My sister Hester's son, Bill Shapiro, works for the Schenectady School System as a counselor for elementary school children. Bill and his wife, Rochelle, have a lovely daughter, Sarah, who attends Hobart College in New York, and Rochelle works with the deaf. When Bill was a teenager, I recall taking him backstage to meet his idol, Henry Mancini, after he played at a concert in Saratoga. He was so thrilled to meet him and asked what he planned to do next. Mancini floored him when he said, "Right now I intend to go back to my hotel room, take a shower, and go to bed!"

I am also proud of my nephew, Alan L. Mintz, who is professor of Hebrew literature at Brandeis University in Massachusetts. He is the son of Sam's brother, Nelson, and his wife, Esther. Leonard, Alan's brother, is in the jewelry business. At Columbia University, Alan earned his doctorate in English literature. "He is the author of, "Hurban: Responses to Catastrophe in Hebrew Literature," (Columbia University Press, 1984). He wrote the book partly because of the preoccupation American Jews have with the Holocaust. He said, "I felt that American Jewry was becoming so Holocaust-centered that they were taking the Holocaust out of history." Mintz noted dryly that, in close to 4,000 years of history, "Jews, unfortunately, have much experience in dealing with catastrophe."

His book explores the literature of catastrophe. He begins, for example, with the destruction of the first temple by the Babylonian army in 586 B.C. The state was crushed forever, the spirit devastated, the religious life ravaged. But Mintz shows, in the Book of Lamentations, that the people found a way to respond and recover.

The response to the Crusaders in eleventh century Europe was to slaughter their own families and commit ritual suicide rather than convert to Christianity. The events are recorded brutally in synagogue poetry.

M̲y sister-in-law, Julia Sternfield, had a daughter, Freda Bright Reaser, who became well-know as the writer, Freda Bright. Here is a letter I received from Freda recently:

```
Dear Ouida,

    Excuse the delay in answering your note, but
I just returned from a summer in Mexico.
    I'm delighted to hear you are working on a
book about Leonard B. + other interesting
people. Am flattered to be numbered among them.
    It should be fun reading about your recol-
lections of Bernstein and also of Slonimsky. I
wasn't aware that you knew him. His book, "Mu-
sic in America Since 1900", was my bible when I
was in college. I never did read "Perfect
Pitch," though I remember that the reviews were
terrific. He must have had a wealth of wonder-
ful stories to tell, as he was, I believe, one-
hundred something when he died. Perhaps I'll
get around to reading it yet.
    Anyhow, for what it's worth in your own
project, you're welcome to whatever you care to
excerpt from the following bio:
    I studied piano at B.U. College of Music
with Jules Wolffers, then went to Paris to work
with Marcel Ciampi at the Conservatoire. Upon
returning to the States, I discovered that New
York was swarming with would-be concert pia-
nists, and as I didn't want to teach, I decided
to join the "real" world.
    My first job was at RCA Victor, during the
Presley years, where I was editor in charge of
Pop record jackets. So much for a background in
serious music! From there I went to BBDO Adver-
tising, writing magazine and newspaper promo-
tion, before becoming a specialist in motion
```

picture advertising.

I worked in the movie business both in London and in New York, developing print campaigns, TV commercials and trailers for at least 200 feature films. In 1980, I wrote my first novel "Options," which was quickly picked up for publication.

Subsequent books have been "Futures," "Decisions," "Infidelities," "Singular Women," "Consuming Passions," "Parting Shots," and "Masques." My books have been translated into thirteen languages. Scenes set in Boston figure somewhere in almost all of them.

I hope that gives you what you need, Ouida. Feel free to edit or rewrite. No, I'm not working on any new novel at present. Eight is enough, and besides, the publishing climate (at least for mid-list writers) is very chilly at present. I do a little book-doctoring, speech-writing etc., but mostly I goof off, enjoy occasional traveling, play on my lovely Hamburg Steinway (my current project is to learn all the Chopin Mazurkas) and enjoy the luxury of being unemployed. There's a lot to be said for it.

I hope Jerry's book did well. It struck as something that would be a staple item, as are the best reference books. And good luck with your book, too. I look forward to seeing it in print.

Best regards,

Freda

A VERY CLEVER BOSTONIAN

My favorite cousin on my mother's side, Esther Byer Milner, from the Chestnut Hill section of Boston, sent me an obituary of a second cousin of ours, Joan R. Needleman, who died in '97. I believe this woman could have made the Guinness Book of Records as the person with the most degrees and varied accomplishments. I knew her in our younger days when she was Joan Rines, and remember her as being a quite attractive brunette. She became Mrs. Robert Needleman and had a daughter, Lucy, and a son, Barry. Her dad, David Rines, was a lawyer. Her mom was Lucy Sandberg Rines, who provided a place in their home for my mom's family when they came from the Ukraine to Ellis Island.

She held degrees in physics from Smith and Radcliffe Colleges, a law degree and a doctorate in Math Education from Boston University.

Joan later earned a pilot's license, and as if that wasn't enough, she studied computer science, electrical engineering, public administration, several foreign languages, creative writing, and was active in Brookline politics.

I think she should be in the Guinness Book of Records, don't you?

Niece Rachel Vincent, who lives
in Florida with her husband and
three children

25

OTHER TRIPS AND CRUISES

The best part of any trip is coming home.
William M. Blatt

Another trip we enjoyed was to the Orient — Taiwan, Hong Kong, Japan, and Hawaii for a week on the way home. Hong Kong was the most outstanding, though very crowded. However, it was very alive and colorful.

In Hong Kong, Sam and I visited Ocean Park which has one of the most impressive aquariums in the world. On the way there we became friendly with a few Chinese students. We took pictures of them, and a charming young girl named Wyning from Kowloon, Hong Kong took our address. We had no idea why until we received a beautiful red and gold Christmas card a few months later signed, "Your friend Wyning from Kowloon."

There was a lot of poverty in Taiwan, but it had an interesting museum; we saw many religious people lighting candles and praying. There was so much uniformity in Japan. In the heat of the summer, we saw large groups of men dressed properly in suits and ties walking out of factories. The children, who were darling, were all dressed alike in their neat school uniforms. Sam took pictures of me posing with them.

Since I taught piano during the cooler months of the year, we could only get away during the summer, and our Oriental trip turned out to be an extremely hot one. I remember almost passing out in the Tokyo subway, but a little fan I carried in my bag kept me breathing and saved the day.

We were surprised to run into Sam's niece and nephew from the States who happened to be staying in the same hotel. We were delighted to join them for dinner, which turned out to be very expensive, although the shrimp tempura we had was absolutely delicious. We enjoyed walking through neat Japanese gardens the next day.

The department stores were very impressive in Tokyo, although I was surprised at the simple toilets that one could not sit down on. The young women working the elevators were as pretty as models.

- with Chinese students. Wyning is second from right

Ouida in Hong Kong

Ouida with schoolkids in Tokyo

--- with more kids and parasols

Hawaii was so very lush and comfortable that we decided to stay there another week. We had a very attractive suite in our hotel, with our own kitchen, but we were interested to see the other magnificent hotels along the coast, so we walked along the beach and strolled through the lobbies of most of the monster establishments we found nearby and were impressed by the sort of excess that seems to attract tourists.

We found macadamia nuts everywhere in Hawaii. They replaced peanuts on the bars of the island, and were found, either whole or chopped-up, in almost every dish we ate during our stay there. We couldn't complain, the meals were delicious, especially the seafood.

Milton and Paula Gershenson went to Spain with Sam and me in 1986. We stayed at Torremolinos, a charming town and former fishing village on the Costa del Sol. A few years later, Ray and I went to Spain with them and often joined them for lunch at quaint little bistros.

Milton Gershenson was a longtime teacher of prospective judges and professor at Brooklyn Law School. His wife, Paula, a fine linguist, used her Spanish to help Latino patients in hospitals communicate with their doctors. Paula had a very dramatic start in life. She was born in Moscow, but during the Bolshevic Revolution had to flee with her family to Paris, where she spent her childhood. During World War II, she was part of the Lyon underground, and frequently had to move from town to town. On one occasion she escaped the Gestapo by using false documents given to her by a sympathetic French woman.

Milton's sister, Bea Leader, lived in the house behind us years ago. Her older son, Harold, was studying for his degree in research medicine about 1964. At this time Helen Pall's daughter, Jane, was graduating from Roslyn High School and Helen thought she should be meeting some eligible young men, so she asked me if I knew any interesting candidates. Naturally, I thought of Harold, and he dated her subsequently, but it didn't work out, so she met and married his best friend, Fred Block, also a doctor. We were invited to the wedding, which took place in the garden of the Pall estate. Harold Leader acted as best man. Jane and Fred subsequently had a son and two daughters, Steven, Catherine and Elizabeth. I felt rewarded that I had started the ball rolling. Jane is presently an executive at Pall Corporation.

Ouida and Ray in Torremolinos, Spain

Ouida, with Paula and Milton Gershenson

Ray, with Paula and Milton Gershenson
in Spain

Ray, Milton and Paula
at Bajondillo Hotel

When I see my elderly relatives and what they are going through, I know they are not enjoying their "golden years." My deceased husband's older brother, Nelson, at eighty eight was so heroic. His mind was very alert in his last months and he explained to me exactly what was happening to him. He reminded me that thirty years ago he had one of the first heart bypass operations. This worked very well for many years, but then the transplanted arteries got pretty well clogged and he would have been a candidate for another bypass if he were younger. He got frequent strong angina pains which made it necessary for him to go to the hospital for oxygen treatment.

Ray and I happened to arrive at his condo where his wife, Esther, and he lived in Worcester, Mass. As we walked toward the building, we saw him being wheeled out to a small ambulance which stood near a large hook and ladder fire truck. As his stretcher was slid into the ambulance, he waved weakly and said, "I'll be alright." The four of us had planned to have lunch together that day. Instead we took Esther to a restaurant near the hospital while Nelson was being taken care of. This was the fifth time he had been hospitalized in a couple of months, and he was getting tired of it. He hated the idea that a fire engine would come every time, clanging its bell. Esther explained that the fire engine had some resuscitating equipment that the ambulance lacked. Nelson loved going to their house in Florida where it's nice and warm, but the doctors said that he shouldn't go unless he could stay out of the hospital for at least a month. He didn't kid himself; he knew that his heart muscle died a little more each time he got a severe pain.

Nelson had his last episode and died in 1998. He is greatly missed.

26

LOSING SAM, AND SAVING A LIFE

Many of the acts you do that you don't get paid for make you richer.
William M. Blatt

My dear husband, Sam, had a heart attack one morning in 1975 and almost died—he should have awakened me to say he felt sick, but I went into the den when I realized he wasn't in bed. He said, "I have constriction here," pointing to his chest. I immediately called our local doctor, who said to take him to North Shore Hospital. I did, but the doctor was not there to meet us—poor Sam had to walk into the Emergency Room when I left him off, though he was having a massive heart attack. He managed to survive it and lived 12 more years, during which he retired (my idea), and played tennis, golf, bridge and poker to his heart's content. We went out to lunch on rainy days and even went to the Costa del Sol in Spain two winters.

We all should learn from experience. We never know when the information we stored up in our brains can help someone else and may even save a life. I feel instincts help also.

The facts are these: I lost a husband because of a tennis game he shouldn't have played. After having many tests at North Shore Hospital, at my urging, Sam was told at a doctor's conference that he shouldn't play tennis until he had an angiogram as they suspected he had a blocked artery. His good friend, Milton, called one Sunday, and asked him to play in a doubles game. Sam was always agreeable to any games Milton organized and he just threw reason to the wind and said "OK," completely disregarding the doctors' warning. Well, you can guess the rest.

They won the game, I heard later from Milton, but it proved deadly. Sam drove home from the tennis court which is only five minutes from our home, picked up the newspaper on the driveway, and opened the front door. Lisa and Jeni, fortunately, were living with us at the time. I was teaching my Sunday students in Great Neck. Sam said to Lisa, "I'm exhausted," and lay down on the living room sofa. He told Lisa he was not in pain, so she got a washcloth and wiped the perspiration from his face. When she realized it was more serious than she thought at first, she called 911. They came in about ten minutes but couldn't revive him, and he was taken to Winthrop University Hospital where he was pronounced dead. Lisa called me at a lesson I was giving and said to come to the hospital, but wouldn't give me any information except to say her dad was there. When I arrived in a distraught condition, Lisa met me outside the hospital. I asked her what his condition was and she answered, "He's resting now." Of course, she was trying to soften the blow but it wasn't the right thing to say because it made me think that he was still alive. It resulted in a greater shock when I was told he was gone forever. I insisted on going in the room to see his body even though the nurse tried to discourage me; his face was purple and swollen. I had had the non-experience of not seeing my son's body, which would have helped me to realize that he was actually dead. One tends not to be realistic when the truth is too difficult to take. Just to pat Sam's hand and realize that he was actually gone when he didn't respond helped me overcome my disbelief.

A couple of years after Sam died, we had to go to the funeral of Sam's niece's husband, Dr. Harold Finn. He had been on a trip around the world with his wife, Judy. About a day or so after they arrived home, he was asked by his doctor friends to resume their usual tennis game. Just like Sam, he obliged willingly, though he didn't realize he was still tired from the trip. Of course, the tennis game did him in and the doctors were unable to resuscitate him though they wasted no time in trying to do so.

While we were at the burial ground, Lisa and Jerry convinced me that we should visit Billy's stone, which was at the same place in Pinelawn. It was the first time we had been there as we had put off the reality for many years. I guess it was good for us to put a few pebbles (a Jewish ritual) on Bill's and my beloved sister Jo's stone right near his. Someday I'll be near them and we'll have a reunion, I guess.

Also, after the deaths of Sam and Harold, as a result of the extra effort it takes to play a competitive game of tennis, I decided that it was a must for Jerry to have a stress test as he's also an active tennis player. I suggested he enroll in the North Shore clinic. The fact that Jerry is a natural hypochondriac made him agree, and he took my advice. It was in January 1944 that his tests showed a 95% blocked artery, and as a result he has done all the things that might have saved his dad's life - had an angiogram that resulted in a balloon angioplasty, and then undertook a dietary regimen with vitamins and minerals under the supervision of a homeopathic cardiologist.

When Jerry went to have the angioplasty, something interesting happened; he was accompanied by a friend who insisted on being there to hold his hand and make sure things were going as they should. Herein lies a story. Years ago when Jerry organized a science-oriented 4H club in Vermont, a thirteen year old boy, named Antoni Jurkiewitz, was a member. Toni was the very bright son of a Polish immigrant, who was introduced to the world of medicine and research by Jerry during the attempt of the 4H group to find a cure for cancer utilizing bee venom.

He met Jerry again after a few years, during which he had been in a lot of trouble as a dropout. He explained to Jerry that he remembered his teaching and decided to make something of his life.

After many years of hard work, he became a surgeon at North Shore Hospital, and later practiced at Queens Hospital. He confessed to Jerry that if it were not for the inspiration he received from his work with the 4H club, he never would have become a doctor, and that is why he insisted on being present at Jerry's balloon angioplasty.

Now Jerry could go on with his work – he has done "The Handbook of Alternative Education," published by Macmillan, in two versions:, a hardcover book which is to be found in libraries across the country, and a paperback entitled, "The Almanac of Education Choices," on sale in bookstores. The newsletter that Jerry puts out quarterly is called "The Education Revolution," and is the publication of his A.E.R.O. (Alternative Education Resource Organization).

Jerry had his own alternative Shaker Mountain School in Burlington, Vermont, for seventeen years, as well as a house on Lake Champlain especially for runaway teenagers. Madelin Colbert, a former Shaker Mountain student, ran it twenty four hours a day for several years and, I'm sure, helped save many young lives. Many of these children became students of the Shaker Mountain School and continued their education.

In the past few years, Jerry has made many trips around the world to advise educators on how to run alternative schools. In the Ukraine, he has been very helpful to the S.T.O.R.K. School by securing grants that help keep them functioning in a difficult environment. Unfortunately, much of the last grant had to go for a new furnace to heat the schoolrooms. Jerry received a letter saying they would have had to close down the school if it couldn't be heated. They blessed him for making it possible for the school to continue.

--- with son, Jerry Mintz

27

PERSONAL ADS

If music be the food of love, play on —
Shakespeare, *Twelfth Night*

Another life which I was determined to change was my daughter, Lisa's. She had been married to Harley Goldman, and they had several happy years together, topped off by the birth of their beautiful daughter, and my only grandchild, Jenifer. But then, with the downfall of a business venture with a partner, their marriage went downhill and ended in divorce. Well, since Newsday's "Getting Personal" seemed to be the place to find a husband (or partner) for my daughter, I decided (with Lisa's approval) to do some letter writing. I averaged about six letters a week for a couple of years. I dashed off answers to all the ads that seemed compatible with Lisa. She had been engaged to the wrong guy — she met him at a dance. He had no idea of how to deal with Jeni and really scared her with his outbursts. Sam was worried for her. Then there was a guy who said he wanted to marry Lisa, but did nothing about his divorce. Lisa started dating again and was having an exciting social life. When things started to slow down, she reminded me to keep writing. Sometimes I wrote two answers to the same guy if he put two ads in the paper at different times. That was true for the guy she finally married, Leigh Harris. They had a lovely wedding, as it was his first, and his folks wanted to invite all their friends. Leigh is a very good stepfather as he's very patient with Jeni and he knows when he shouldn't interfere. He and Lisa have a lot in common. They love the theater and dining out, and Lisa works very hard to keep him happy, and vice versa.

Lisa and her husband, Leigh Harris

I MEET RAY

How silvery sweet sound lover's tongues by night,
Like softest music to attending ears.
Shakespeare: *Romeo and Juliet*

Since I got in the habit of looking over the Newsday ads, I happened to see a rare ad that was written by an older man who was looking for someone interested in the arts. It seemed worth a try and I dashed off a note. I happened to have a Roslyn News article about my friendship with Leonard Bernstein, who had just died in the fall of 1990. I cut out the picture of me as a student (it said so under the picture) and enclosed some of the article with the note. When Ray put his ad in Newsday and mentioned his age (73), I thought maybe he was too old, but as it turned out he was a young 73 and that's what made the difference. Men usually age faster than women, but Ray was definitely full of vigor.

When I answered his ad, I said I was "60+," though he hadn't asked for an age. Believe me, if I had even said 65+, I probably would never have had the chance to meet him, as I would have been put in the "throw away pile." After we met and eventually fell in love, he agreed that that might have been so, as he had 50 letters to choose from. In fact, I didn't tell Ray my exact age, but then he found out accidentally almost three years later when he saw my date of birth on a document. I was afraid, even when we were so committed to each other, that it would make a difference to him that we were near the same age. It was quite a relief to find that it didn't faze him in the least. Also, the fact that I was Jewish seemed to be a plus for him, even though he was not.

Everyone wonders why I have such a hangup about age. I have good reason. Unfortunately, the number of years one has lived seems to be too important these days, out of all proportion. My mom must have realized that as she instilled it in her children, so we were cautioned never to tell her age. In fact, she told us not to dare mention it in her obituary! Mother never looked or acted her age, so I can understand it. She was girlish, in fact, into her 70's and even 80's. So much for the matter of age.

Ray and I have a wonderful lifestyle, as we have the best of both worlds. We're together usually twice a week — on weekends and Wednesday nights. We used to talk about getting married and even looked into condos in Connecticut and New Jersey where Ray's son, Sandy, lives near Princeton. They were all very beautiful, modern places, but the more we thought about moving, the more we didn't want to give up our way of life. Ray's son, Russell, who is single, told his dad that if he moved, he, Russell, wouldn't be able to pursue his hobby which is taking care of the gardening, painting, etc. of the house he grew up in and enjoyed so much. Russell, who works for HBO, keeps Ray's house in perfect condition. When we go away on a trip we often come home to find one or two rooms freshly painted. Right now he is in the process of painting the outside of the house. He's doing a meticulous job and has changed the color from white to grey.

I also love the house in which my kids grew up, even though it's not as neat as Ray's. Besides, my son has his office for Alternative Educa tion there, and he's good company. I enjoy my time in bed where I write, watch TV, listen to music and sleep off and on. It's real cozy, I take messages for Jerry when he's away or when he's busy doing his radio shows.

Ray would never have put that ad in the paper if he didn't have a good friend named Dorothy who suggested it. She felt that since she thought of him only as a friend, he should find someone that he could have a closer relationship with, and that a personals ad might be a good way to do it. Ray called about seven people of the fifty responses he got. I was number three on his agenda. He said later that he liked my early picture, and the fact that he had worked with Lenny Bernstein as the film editor of the TV special of Bernstein's New York Philharmonic trip to Japan, gave us something in common. They received an Emmy for the show.

When Edward Raymond Sandiford called me, I liked his soft, modulated voice immediately. We talked a bit about composers we liked, and that convinced me I would let him meet me at my house. At 1:00 in the afternoon of February 6, 1991, just when I was expecting him, I was startled by a loud noise like two cars colliding. I looked out the window and saw the cars and decided I'd better go outside to investigate. I thought to myself that my date may be a decrepit old man who doesn't know how to drive. Sure enough, there had been a collision. Ray was standing there looking at the side of the Cadillac that had been severely damaged when it came over the hill and swerved into the front of his car. Ray didn't look in the least decrepit; in fact he is tall and distinguished looking, and you might say our friendship started off with a bang. I put my arm in his as I felt badly for him. After the police came and the details were straightened out, we found we had many interests in common, mainly music. I played the piano for Ray and we were off to a good start.

Ray, who is responsible for putting all this writing on his computer and editing it at the same time, is my significant other. As long as I can listen to beautiful music at night when I lie awake – sometimes for hours – hearing rarely played music, some by lesser-known composers and some by the masters, I am content. Most of this music is found on WQXR and sometimes on WNYC-FM, both in New York City.

Incidentally, Ray was the film editor of the successful Bilko Show with Phil Silvers in the fifties. I guess, because he had to make a living from TV, he definitely has an aversion to most commercial TV. It's about the only thing we don't see eye to eye on, especially since I enjoy watching some TV, which I can do while listening to music and reading, all at the same time.

Bob Rippen and wife, Ruth, with Ouida and Ray

Bob Rippen (Army nickname, Rip) and Ray (Sandy) served in the same Signal Corps unit during World War II. They were both launched into the television era after the war. Rip, among many other assignments, directed the "Howdy Doody Show" on NBC, while Ray edited the Phil Silvers "Bilko Show" on CBS.

Rip retired from Rutgers University in New Jersey as director of their Audio-Visual department. Ray retired from the world of industrial films and TV commercials with few regrets.

I get along very well with Ray's four adult children, their spouses, friends, and five grandchildren. Thank goodness he shares my passion for music and art, and he even recognizes some chamber music that I can't identify. I've been teaching him piano since we met and he plays for my annual student recitals in June. He even does my taxes on the computer. I also admire Ray's liberal political ideas. To top it all off, he is a gourmet cook, makes most of our delicious meals, and even bakes his own bread. In return, I supply him with his favorite nut munchies that I bake every week, which he loves to dunk in tea. I also give him my special haircuts which save him the trouble of going to the barber. So far, no complaints. Oh yes, we love to play Scrabble, and always bring a set on every trip we take.

Here's the way Ray described his hunt for companionship:

GETTING PERSONAL

by
Ray Sandiford

After three years of widowhood, without any satisfactory female companionship, I finally decided that I would throw myself into the field of personal-ad dating, and so I ran an ad in Newsday, our Long Island daily. It was short, and pointed out my main retirement interests: the arts, travel, hiking, and good food and conversation. I didn't expect many responses, considering my age, but was amazed when I received fifty variably perfumed letters. Many of these were admirable accounts of the writer's life story and aspirations.

I started off by having lunch with a few of the local Suffolk County candidates and found them all pleasant, some quite attractive, but I didn't feel any spark. So on to a slightly more distant group. One letter was from Ouida, in Nassau County, and contained a picture of a very pretty teenage girl. The message was on notepaper that showed a cat on the top of the page whose bushy tail curled down the side of the sheet with the inscription, "This is my tale." Ouida said, "I'm a merry widow — pretty, blonde, 5 feet 5 inches, a former concert pianist and current teacher, as well as a published songwriter, (60+). I am looking for a sensitive, congenial companion to have fun with. It's not much fun doing things alone after having had a close, happy marriage."

Amen to that, I said to myself.

"I also like long walks, good conversation, movies. dining out, hugs, and kids (I have an adorable granddaughter)."

Fun and hugs, I mused. Looks promising if she turns out to like me, and the fact that she's fond of kids is a good sign. Then again, I know she was a pretty teenager.

I dialed Ouida's number.

The phone rang twice. "Hello." A sweet feminine voice.

"Is this Ouida?"

"Yes it is."

"This is that widower who ran the ad in Newsday last week."

"Oh yes, I'm very glad to hear from you. Mmmm, your ad showed a number of interests that agree with mine, and in very few words too I might say."

"Thanks," I said, recognizing an appreciation of real economy.

"Well, I must tell you that music has been my great interest, and when you listed 'the arts' I hope you were including good music."

"You can be sure of that, Ouida. Actually, I'm the kind of guy who searches the weekly radio listings to find renditions of seldom-heard Haydn symphonies so that I can tape them. Do you know that of his 104 works in the big form, only a few are well known?"

"Yes I do, and every once in a while I hear a terrific one for the first time."

"I'm getting a pretty good collection," I said. "But I want to ask you if we could meet tomorrow afternoon, say around one p.m. Can you suggest an appropriate place?"

"Any friend of Haydn's is a friend of mine; why don't you come to my place?" She gave me the address.

At midday I made a sandwich and downed it with a small glass of white French wine. Thus fortified, I headed for Ouida's house. The address she had given was on Roslyn Road in Roslyn Heights on the North Shore. As I drove in the slow lane of the four-lane road, I was annoyed to find that few homes had visible house numbers. Suddenly I spotted the number on the left side of the road out of the corner of my eye on a small sign staked at the end of a driveway. I slowed and came to a stop at the curb past Snapdragon Lane, a small street. Looking around, I saw that I had barely passed her driveway and that if I backed into that street, I'd be able to move almost straight across the highway to enter it. From the street I looked to the right and left along the highway; it was empty of traffic except for one pickup truck approaching from the left which I waited to let pass. Now I saw that nobody was approaching from either direction; the highway was empty. Slowly I moved across the road, concentrating on the driveway.

Just as I was about to reach my destination, all hell broke loose. The crash and jolt all drivers fear inundated me; another car had smashed into me at high speed. "Oh shit!" I said in the classic response.

When things settled down I saw that here was a medium-sized Cadillac lodged next to my right front bumper, its left fender smashed in. After shaking myself and disengaging the seatbelt, I got out of the car. Rubberneckers slowed to survey the crash; the other driver stood shaking his fists in the air, cursing and jumping up and down, an expression of rage I had seen at other accident sites.

Ouida appeared at her front door and walked toward the crowd on her lawn. I saw her and smiled; she responded with a smile of sympathy. Not the young girl of the picture, I thought, but certainly a very attractive woman; the same lovely oval face, but the hair had changed from dark to blonde. Ouida had a sweetness about her that reminded me of my late wife, Terry.

"What a way to meet!" I said as she approached.

"I was afraid you might have been hurt," she said and took my arm in a warm, motherly way.

Both cars were drivable, and when the formalities were concluded I pulled into Ouida's driveway.

Seated on the couch in her living room, the centerpiece of which was a fine grand piano, we sipped wine as I commented about the many mementos on tables, on the piano, on window sills – miniature pianos, busts of composers, and small classic statues.

"My students have given me these over the years." she said, and walked to the piano. "Would you like to hear me play?"

"Certainly." I said.

She played a bravura Chopin prelude which I found very exciting, as well as part of a Beethoven sonata. I applauded her fine playing.

Returning to the couch, she asked, "By the way are you feeling hungry? I just got back from teaching and I'm famished. Can I make something for both of us?"

I said, "Why don't we go out to a restaurant? I had something a while ago but I'll have dessert while you eat."

"Fine, let's go".

We drove to a ristorante just down the road where Ouida eased her hunger with a roast beef and onion hero while I munched on the piece she cut off for me, and a beer.

Ouida suggested that we go to the Nassau County Museum of Fine Arts where there was a show of Czech paintings done during the Cold War. "Later we could take a nice walk around the grounds," she said.

The Czech paintings were colorful and well done, but each was a grotesque. As we viewed canvas after canvas, we came to realize that these bizarre paintings expressed the extreme anguish of human beings caught in a totalitarian society.

Ouida said. "I suppose that you would have to have lived through it to really understand these works."

"I hope that we can understand them well enough, anyway," I said.

At the parking lot we examined the damage to my car.

"It's hard to believe that the only thing smashed on this car is the directional signal lamp, but there it is. The other driver did me a big favor when he swerved to hit the front of my car. The bumper took the full blast. If he had hit me amidships, who knows what might have happened," I said.

Ouida took my arm in hers again. "Don't talk like that, I wouldn't want you to get hurt." She held my arm closer and we walked to the museum.

"I don't like to admit it", I said, "but if I had noticed the hill that the other car came roaring over, this accident wouldn't have happened."

Outside the museum we sat down on a bench and talked about our families and friends, and when we got up to walk around the grounds, Ouida took my arm in hers again. As we approached the parking lot, I took her hand in mine.

"There is a good pianist playing in Great Neck next Sunday," she said. "Would you like to go?"

"Sure," I said. I felt that I had come to feel closer to Ouida in this short time than I had felt to anyone since the day I met my late wife.

We enjoyed the recital in Great Neck, and met weekly for a while during which time I decided that there wasn't much sense in pursuing the Newsday quest since I was becoming very fond of Ouida, and had begun to hope that we could become closer.

I phoned her one day to ask if she would like to see a new movie that was playing nearby.

"Alright," she said, "we could go Sunday evening. There's a concert in the afternoon and we'll have an opportunity to spend some time together."

"Speaking of that," I said, feeling suddenly bold, "I've been hoping that you and I will find an opportunity to get to know each other a whole lot better before very long."

"Well," said Ouida in her sweetest voice, "if you feel that way, be sure to bring your toothbrush when you come next time!"

To sum up my first impressions about Ray: he was tall, slim, with an elegant profile, much like one I had seen of Ravel, one of my favorite composers. We've been so compatible for more than eight years. We both love Mozart's twenty seven piano concerti – in particular the last ones from number twenty on. They're mostly all miraculous works of art, especially the slow movements which combine pathos and simplicity with a certain sophistication. His melodies with variations are captivating and constantly continue to amaze me, no matter how many times I hear them.

There's a radio program on WNYC in New York called St. Paul Sunday, which used to air at 6 a.m. I had heard a Mozart Rondo that I was teaching to Sandi Hamad who specialized in Mozart. This was one of Mozart's most original works and I mentioned it to Ray. Unbelievably, he announced, "Oh, I recorded that piece last week. Do you want it?" I couldn't imagine that he would listen to such an early show — it amazed me so soon in our relationship.

Ray and Ouida

The three generations – Lisa, Jenifer, and Nana,
with Ray Sandiford

Ray's children: Raymond, Jane, Roberta, and Russell

Ray's grandchildren:

Jeffrey and Amanda

Caroline

Steven

Teresa

Shortly after we met, Ray's car was being worked on in a garage so he was unable to visit me in Roslyn Heights. He suggested that I come to his place in Huntington for dinner and a movie, which I did. The winter weather became very nasty that day, and by the time we came back from the movie, we were in a full-blown blizzard. I would have been happy to be put up overnight, but Ray was too much of a gentleman, so he waved me on into the snowy night, and I've never let him forget it.

It is now the ninth anniversary of our meeting and we are more devoted than ever. During the years we have spent traveling back and forth between Cold Spring Harbor and Roslyn Heights, we have had several interesting trips. The first was a Caribbean cruise for ten days. We were seated at meals with a group of newlyweds and honeymooners for no apparent reason, and when they asked if we were on our honeymoon, I answered, "sure," as it seemed like that to me anyhow and we wanted to fit in. We celebrated our third anniversary by spending a week in Mexico - Ixtapa, which was built strictly for tourists and has many hotels and restaurants. There was no problem with drinking the local water because the entire town was served by a separate water system which pumped pure water that was safe for drinking. We did find a bit of the real Mexico in the neighboring small town which was populated by Mexicans who were struggling to sell native goods to the visiting tourists. We spent most of our days basking in the warm sun and swimming in the Pacific and then rinsing off in the hotel's outdoor fresh water pool. The main evening event at our hotel was a Fiesta which consisted of a great variety of delicious Mexican foods. The entertainment consisted of Mexican and Indian singers and dancers in colorful costumes. We opted for the souvenir of the evening - a large mounted photograph of Ray and me wearing oversize Mexican straw hats which we enjoy looking at now and then. The temperature in Ixtapa is a constant 80 to 85 degrees, so it was a perfect time to be there when New York was an icy 5 degrees and full of snow.

We have also been to Costa del Sol in Spain twice (Sam and I had been there three years before), and Paris for a week at the New Year of 1993 (brrrrr). In between these big trips, we have been to New England, Tanglewood, and Brookline where I lived as a child until my marriage. Ray was sweet to take my picture in front of the house where I was born, plus the house in which I studied with Gebhard and met Lenny.

On our most recent cruise from Greece to Turkey, Israel, and some of the Aegean Islands, Ray was asked by one of the passengers if anyone had told him how much he resembled Arthur Miller. In fact someone came up to him at a party a few years ago (he looked impressive in a white suit) and said, "You must be somebody, what's your name?"

Ray got a real surprise birthday cake for the whole table one night on the Mediterranean cruise, with a whole chorus of waiters singing *Happy Birthday*. I had tipped off the head waiter when Ray was busy talking to someone at the table.

For some reason, perhaps because people know that I found my partner for life three years after losing my husband, I have become an authority on how to answer and write a personal ad. Since I met Ray after reading his short personal ad in which he expressed an interest in the arts, I have a strong desire to help others who are in the same boat that I was.

Therefore, I must tell you a story: I happened to meet Kyra, the mother of a former piano student of mine. She is cute and attractive, although she has two grown up daughters. Kyra said she was feeling despondent because she had lost her husband the year before from cancer. When I told her how I met Ray, she asked if I could help her write and answer ads, as she had no idea what to write, or where to look for the best ads. I explained that a personal ad should describe her looks, height, weight, color of hair, and about how old she is. Also it should tell what she enjoys doing, and what she is looking for in a man. Kyra learned how to write an ad so well that she was soon dating two men. One of them she really was in love with, but unfortunately he wasn't able to support her in the manner to which she was accustomed. The other guy was a multi-millionaire (how could he not be attractive?) who lives in New York City. She loved his life style, but after a while she felt that he was too old for her. Kyra was starting to have confidence in herself and this came through in her attractive personality. She said, "Ouida, I have a feeling that the next person I meet will be Mr. Right, and I'm going to place another ad." I had my doubts, but she did put an ad in a magazine and, sure enough, the man who answered was exactly what she was looking for – handsome, retired, financially secure, had a sense of humor, and was a widower! They clicked immediately, and within a month were making plans to marry, sell their own homes and build a ranch house to their liking. Kyra was ecstatic!

Ray and Ouida join Monet's luncheon at the Johnson Sculpture Museum in New Jersey

This scenario doesn't always happen so easily, but it should encourage those who hesitate putting ads in the paper. One has to take chances in life if a dream is to happen. It worked for me and for Kyra.

Ouida finds an ad for a piano player at Montauk,
Long Island – Not quite sure she qualifies

Ouida at Hadrian's Library in Athens

Ray in Old San Juan, Puerto Rico

--- with Shula and Arik Rimmerman in their home in
Natanya, Israel

--- with Sonny and Eva Herr in their bamboo garden

--- with Nahama and Nehemia Rapaport in Tel Aviv

--- with Nehemia and Nahama in Tel Aviv

Ouida at the Wailing Wall

--- at a Bernstein CD ad at the
Opera House in Tel Aviv

--- at the site of the murder of Itzak Rabin

28

LENNY'S SWAN SONG

There are few artists, but anyone can be a critic.
William M. Blatt

One summer, Jerry wanted to use his new camcorder to take pictures of Lenny at Tanglewood, but when he brought the camera through the gate the guard said, "It's not allowed." I suggested he go back to the car to put the camera in its case. Sure enough, he sailed through like a member of the orchestra, and I got Lenny to come out of an auditorium where he had been watching a student of his conduct. When we got outdoors, they tried to stop Jerry from taking pictures, but when they saw the maestro, they gave in, and we got what we wanted. Before Lenny went back in, I asked him if he had read the latest unauthorized biography about him. He replied, "No, I haven't, and I don't intend to." He evidently had heard about it from friends.

It dealt with aspects of his questionable lifestyle, and not as much on his significant contributions to the music of the twentieth century, or his important influence on young people through his programs on TV and in Carnegie Hall and Avery Fisher Hall. Too many so-called authors try to malign our great artists for commercial reasons, and almost ignore their great importance to the world.

In honor of Bernstein's seventieth birthday on August 25, 1988, Tanglewood gave him a four day birthday bash. There was a Prelude on the first day, of songs commissioned in his honor by twelve composers, including Ned Rorem, Harold Shapero, Bright Sheng, Steven Sondheim, Michael Tilson Thomas, Yehudi Wyner, Tredici, Perle, Schat, S. Schwartz, Singleton, and Jamie Thomas (his daughter).

His *Jeremiah Symphony* was played by the Boston University Institute High School students, and his *Mass* was done by the Opera Theater of Indiana University. Ozawa, Michael Tilson Thomas, and Leon Fleisher performed some of his favorite music - Brahms' *Double Concerto* with Midori and Yo Yo Ma, and various works by Stravinsky, Ives, and Mahler.

Almost ten thousand people came to the main concert over which Beverly Sills presided. Gwyneth Jones sang an aria from *Fidelio*, and his old friend Christa Ludwig sang and danced to *Candide*. Rostropovitch (Slava) flew in from Sicily and played Strauss' *Don Quixote*. Lenny and he gave each other a big bear hug.

Steven Sondheim, the lyricist of *West Side Story*, wrote new words for Kurt Weill's *Poor Jennie*, calling it Poor Lenny, who couldn't make his mind up as to what career to choose in life. Lauren Bacall received an ovation from the audience when she sang it in her famous low voice. The song concludes that Lenny decided to do it ALL.

Seiji Ozawa was very grateful to Lenny because he had been helped by him in his conducting, just as Lenny had been helped by Koussevitzky. Ozawa has been the conductor of the Boston Symphony Orchestra for twenty five years, and will be leaving in the year two thousand and two to become the music director of the Vienna State Opera – he had always aspired to work in opera. Seiji ended the four hour gala with this line, "Lenny, we love you, you helped to make our Tanglewood garden glow." Then the whole company sang the closing number from *Candide*. Lenny's three children, Jamie, Alex, and Nina, plus Jamie's husband, David, added to the celebration with the *Seven Oh Stomp*.

Later, when I congratulated Lenny on this marvelous outpouring from his many friends and admirers, he thanked me but added a somber note. He predicted that live audiences for classical music will continue to dwindle, and I must say that his prediction seems to be coming true. Recently, while visiting Ray's brother, Bob, and his wife, Laura, in L.A. we all attended a concert of the Los Angeles Philharmonic at the Dorothy Chandler Pavilion. I observed the sea of wrinkled men and women with hair of gray and silver plus those accoutrements of old age; canes and wheelchairs, coming out of the elevators. It resembled a gathering of senior citizens, with few exceptions. After these ancient and loyal music lovers are gone, who will be left to take their places? Surely not the baby boomers and heavy metal and rock advocates who for years have been supporting the record stores that carry this so-called music. Who will be left to appreciate those talented and industrious instrumental artists who are willing to practice hours and hours to perfect their interpretations of those masters of music, Bach, Beethoven, Brahms, and all the great composers who came before and after?

--- with Lenny at intermission of birthday bash

---with Roddy Macdowell at birthday bash

Lenny hugs Ouida before last rehearsal

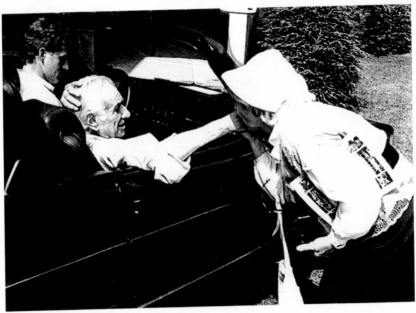

Ouida kisses Lenny's hand at their last goodbye

Lenny must have had this concern in mind when he founded, during his last year, the Pacific Music Festival in Japan, which was modeled after Tanglewood.

Also, before he died in 1990, Lenny established the BETA Fund which supports the Orchestra of St. Luke's Arts and Education Program, established in 1976. This provides free programs of concerts, opera and ballet for thousands of New York City school children.

Alexander Bernstein, who is head of the Leonard Bernstein Center in Nashville, Tennessee, welcomed a new phase of its operation under the GRAMMY Foundation, which is the non-profit arm of NARAS (National Academy of Recording Arts and Sciences). They promote arts education programs for thousands of schools around the country.

LENNY'S LAST REHEARSAL AT TANGLEWOOD, AUGUST, 1990

By Jerry Mintz
(An excerpt from the Roslyn News)

It has long been a ritual for our family to travel every summer from Long Island to the Tanglewood Music Festival in the Berkshires to see Leonard Bernstein conduct the Boston Symphony Orchestra.

This was more than a family outing. Lenny's signed picture has hung on our wall as long as I can remember, along with a photo of Lenny, my mother, Ouida Blatt Mintz, Aaron Copland and the clarinetist, David Glazer, taken at Tanglewood when my mother and Lenny were teenage students of Heinrich Gebhard in Brookline, Mass. In my mind, Lenny has always been a member of our family. Every year we would go to Tanglewood and meet Lenny after the concert. It was always a thrill. Today we once again saw Lenny , but this time it was different.

We had just driven over from Schenectady after visiting my mother's sister, Hester. Lenny had been at her wedding when she married my uncle Morris more than forty years ago in Boston. As usual, our timing was serendipitous. We arrived just as Lenny's car was being chauffeured up to the music shed. Several thousand people were waiting for him to mount the stage to rehearse for the Koussevitzky Memorial Concert on Sunday. We walked up to him as he slowly got out of the car. Mother and Lenny walked toward each other and Lenny gave her a long hug and kiss. "Lenny, how are you," my mother asked.

"Ouida, I'm so sick," he whispered in her ear. "For nine months I've been sick."

Although I've met him many times and he has shown an interest in the work I've been doing in alternative education, it was still difficult for me to ask him, "Have they given you a diagnosis?"

He looked at us, then at the sky. "If only I knew." It was said ominously, sadly.

He left us then to rehearse the Boston Symphony Orchestra for the last time. We went into the shed. Mother was shaken. There were tears in her eyes. "That felt like a farewell," she said to me. And indeed, when he conducted the slow movement of the Beethoven *Seventh Symphony* (often used as a *Funeral March*) it sounded prophetic.

As the rehearsal started, a frail old woman was stopped by the ushers as she tried to make her way to a front row seat. Two women were helping her. After a few seconds of discussion the usher let her through. She was Lenny's ninety two year old mother, come to see her son conduct another Tanglewood rehearsal.

The performance of the Beethoven seemed to be slower and more somber than his earlier interpretations. His conducting was in sharp contrast to his former liveliness on the podium. Mother remembered how long it took the critics to adjust to his dramatic and animated style. They criticized him until they finally realized it was his natural style. It was just Lenny.

During intermission mother met with an old friend, Sheldon Rotenberg, who played in the first violin section of the orchestra. He said, "It was very sad when he started rehearsing *Arias and Barcarolles* and could only get through half of it." One of Lenny's protegées continued to rehearse the piece with Lenny in the audience.

After the rehearsal, we saw him leaving in his car. He stopped, and my mother and he talked for a few moments about old times. Then she kissed his hand and they said goodbye.

Shortly after his last concert, it was announced that Mr. Bernstein would no longer be conducting and performing as he wanted to devote more time to his composing. Of course we knew that he was not well, and for almost as long as I had known him, he had suffered from emphysema. He had tried hard to give up smoking but to no avail.

As we all know, mortality is reality and life is very temporary. Even Lenny Bernstein had to die. I heard that he said toward the end (while holding that inevitable cigarette), "Dear Lord, please give me oblivion." He had suffered enough.

LENNY'S MEMORIAL CONCERTS

The first and most impressive Memorial Concert took place in Carnegie Hall. That concert consisted of music that Lenny had written or was noted for having conducted, played by musicians from orchestras from all over the world. Represented, were: the Vienna Philharmonic, the Israel Philharmonic, the New York Philharmonic, the Tanglewood Young Peoples Orchestra, and others. The most dramatic performance of that concert was Lenny's *Candide Overture* played by the New York Philharmonic without a conductor. There wasn't a dry eye in the house, including mine, as we all visualized Lenny standing there conducting in his inimitable way. Surprisingly, it was a brilliant performance and the ensemble was perfect.

That concert took place on November 14, 1990, which was a significant date for Lenny, who was always fascinated with numerology. One is amazed at the coincidence of so many important events in his life happening on October or November 14th:

Nov. 14, 1900 - Aaron Copland is born.

Nov. 14, 1937 - Lenny sits next to Copland at the ballet - the start of a forty year friendship.

Nov. 14, 1943 - Lenny's debut with the New York Philharmonic (Bruno Walter took ill).

Nov. 14 1954 - CBS - Omnibus Series - Lenny's famous analysis of Beethoven's *Fifth Symphony*.

Oct. 14, 1989 - Birthday of Lenny's grandson, Evan, son of Jamie Bernstein Thomas. (Her daughter, Francisca, was born in 1987).

Oct. 14, 1990 - Date of Leonard Bernstein's death.

I attended the second Memorial Concert about a month after the first. Arthur Laurents had arranged it as a tribute to Lenny for his theatrical work. Appropriately, it took place at the Majestic Theater, and it was exciting to hear excerpts from most of his musicals sung by well known performers and friends of Lenny.

The Cathedral of St. John the Divine was the magnificent setting for the final Memorial Concert. I found it most uplifting to witness this celebration of Peace, which was Lenny's dream for humanity, and was attended by his friends and fellow teachers, composers, and performers. It was a beautiful ending to a life spent mainly in conveying the appreciation of music to people of all ages.

I've read that both William Shakespeare and Leonard Bernstein didn't make the first Millennium List of those who had the greatest influence on humanity. I would like to offer my belated vote for their inclusion on the list; as well as votes for Johann Sebastian Bach, Joseph Haydn, Ludwig van Beethoven, Franz Schubert, Frédéric Chopin, Felix Mendelssohn, Robert Schumann, Johannes Brahms, Antonin Dvorak; none of whom made it.

May I make the case for Lenny, as the qualifications of the others have been known for many years. In addition to a long and glorious conducting career, and spectacular pianistic performances, he has composed notable symphonies and concerti, as well as music for ballets, hit musicals, and superb music for film. But I believe that his greatest impact on human sensibilities has come from his outstanding work in television. First, with his memorable explanations for adults of classical music on numerous "Omnibus" shows, and then with his many Young People's concerts with the New York Philharmonic. The Young People's concerts in particular, I believe, have had a profound effect on a generation. I have heard many baby boomers say that Lenny was the reason they learned to appreciate music.

The reports I've heard could likely be multiplied many times over to calculate the effect Lenny has had on our current parents of young children.

I nominate Leonard Bernstein for the Millenium List.

LEONARD BERNSTEIN'S MOST IMPORTANT COMPOSITIONS

Amberson, the company that Lenny founded during his lifetime, publishes his newsletter, "Prelude, Fugues, and Riffs," which lists performances of his music, as well as essays by well-know musicians.

The following is a compilation of his works:

- In 1939 he wrote *The Birds* at Harvard. Lenny studied composition at Harvard with Edward Burlinghame Hill and Walter Piston, and later with Randall Thompson at Curtis Institute in Philadelphia.
- His first work to be published was the *Sonata for Clarinet and Piano* in 1941, which was performed in Boston a year later. It was influenced by Hindemith's neoclassical idiom.
- In 1943 he wrote *I Hate Music: A Cycle of Five Kid Songs for Soprano and Piano*.
- Soon after, he produced the *Jeremiah Symphony* which was romantic and contained Hebrew arias for a Mezzo-Soprano in the *Lamentation* sung by Jennie Tourel in the first performance. In the Symphony, Jeremiah mourns his beloved Jerusalem, ruined and pillaged after his desperate efforts to save it from destruction by the Babylonians. The New York Music Critics Circle gave the symphony its annual award, and in 1945 RCA-Victor released a recording.
- In 1944 he wrote *Seven Anniversaries for Piano* which were dedicated to his friends.
- In the same year his ballet *Fancy Free*, with choreography by Jerome Robbins was performed in New York by the Ballet Theater. It has a tuneful, jazzy score and was an instant success. The story is about three sailors on shore leave, and on the prowl for girls. This ballet was also the source of Bernstein's first musical comedy, *On the Town,*

which I saw at its premier in Boston in 1944.

- *Hashkiveinu* for solo tenor, mixed chorus, and organ was written in 1945.
- *Facsimile* followed in 1946, another ballet, also choreographed by Jerome Robbins. It has a cast of only two men, involved in fighting for a woman, to no avail. The setting is a beach, where the woman ends up alone and bored. It got excellent reviews at its premier in 1947.
- *Four Anniversaries* for piano in 1948, and in the same year *La Bonne Cuisine: Four Recipes for Voice and Piano.*
- *The Age of Anxiety (Symphony #2 for piano and orchestra)* followed in 1949, which was inspired by W.H. Auden's poem, "The Age of Anxiety." Auden was concerned with the insecurity of our time and was searching for faith. Lenny dedicated it to Koussevitsky. There are several movements, including the *Prologue, the Seven ages, the Dirge, the Masques* (jazzy), *and the Epilogue.* The New York City Ballet presented it with choreography with by Jerome Robbins in 1950. A year before that Bernstein played the piano part with the Boston Symphony Orchestra under Koussevitsky, and it received the Hornblit prize as the best new work that year.
- *Prelude, Fugue and Riffs for Solo Clarinet and Jazz Ensemble* was written in 1949. It was premiered in 1955, and was recorded with Benny Goodman playing the solo part.
- *Peter Pan* followed in 1950 with songs, choruses and incidental music.
- In 1952 came *Trouble in Tahiti*, an opera in one act, which I heard at its first performance, with Lenny conducting, at Brandeis University in Waltham, Mass. He wrote both the words and music and seemed very excited when it was over, and I gave him my usual hug and kiss. The opera took only forty minutes and was about personal family problems. It received a favorable reception, and was repeated on TV, at Tanglewood, and finally on Broadway.
- In five weeks at the end of 1952, Lenny wrote the whole score for the musical, *Wonderful Town*, starring Rosalind Russell, based on the successful play by Joseph Fields and Jerome Chodorov, which later became a movie and a popular radio show. Fields and Chodorov adapted the play for the musical, and the lyrics were written by Comden and Green.

- Two years later Lenny finished his *Serenade for Violin, String Orchestra, Harp and Percussion.* It was commissioned by the Koussevitsky Music Foundation, and was based on Plato's "Symposium," consisting of the ideas of five Greek philosophers. Lenny conducted it at the Venice Festival in 1954, with Isaac Stern as soloist. I heard Midori play this work at Tanglewood in 1989, with Lenny conducting the Boston Symphony Orchestra. She made the headlines that hot and humid day when her three-quarter size violin popped a string, whereupon the concert master slipped her his instrument, and she continued without missing a beat. Believe it or not, she broke another string, was handed another violin and continued without a hitch. She received an ovation, and while the whole orchestra and audience stood up to applaud, Lenny embraced her warmly.
- In 1955 he wrote renaissance-style music, consisting of seven voices, for *The Lark*, Lillian Hellman's translation of L'Alouette, the 1953 play Jean Anouilh about Joan of Arc.
- The symphonic suite from *On the Waterfront* was given its first performance in 1955 when Lenny conducted it at Tanglewood with the Boston Symphony. It was dedicated to his son, Alexander.
- The comic operetta, *Candide*, with a book by Lillian Hellman, based on the satire by Voltaire, was first performed in 1956. A second version, with a different book by Hugh Wheeler, opened in 1973.
- The musical, *West Side Story*, (1957) was dedicated, "to Felicia, with love." The famous theatrical critic, Brooks Atkinson, said that *West Side Story* was Lenny's finest work. Patterned after Shakespeare's "Romeo and Juliet," it was about poverty-stricken Puerto Rican gangs and concluded with the death of the main character- very different from the happy endings of most Broadway shows. Jerome Robbins was the talented director and choreographer, who gave the staging a wild, breathtaking pace. Carole Lawrence and Larry Kert played the leads with great passion. The book was by Arthur Laurents, lyrics by Steven Sondheim, and the sets were by Oliver Smith. It had 732 performances on Broadway. The most successful songs are *Tonight, Somewhere, Maria, One hand- One Heart, America,* and *Something's Coming.*

  Sam and I had decided to invest our meager savings in it, but panicked when we learned from Lenny that it had no star performers. He told us, "We will make our own stars," but we weren't convinced. Too bad we didn't.

- The movie version of *West Side Story* opened in 1961 and earned ten oscars.
- *Fanfares*, written for John F. Kennedy's inauguration in 1961. *Kaddish, Symphony #3*, for orchestra, mixed chorus, boy's choir, speaker, and soprano solo. 1963
- *Chichester Psalms*, for mixed choir, boy soloist and orchestra. 1965
- *Five Anniversaries for piano.* 1965
- *Dybbuk Variations*, a ballet, choreographed by Jerome Robbins. 1974
- *1600 Pennsylvania Avenue*, a musical, written with Allen Jay Lerner. 1976
- *Songfest*, revision of the Kaddish symphony #3.   1977
- *Slava*, overture for orchestra.   1977
- *Divertimento for Orchestra*, in celebration of the Boston Symphony Orchestra's first centenary.   1980
- *Halil*, nocturne for solo flute, string orchestra and percussion. Halil means flute in Hebrew. It is the story of Yadim, a talented flutist, who was killed in his tank near the Suez Canal.
- *Touches: Chorale, Eight Variations and Coda* (for the 1981 Van Cliburn International Piano Competition.
- *A Quiet Place*, a follow-up to Trouble in Tahiti.   1983
- *Jubilee Games*, commissioned by the State of Israel.   1986
- *Arias and Barcarolles*, a suite of six songs about love.   1988

BOOKS BY LEONARD BERNSTEIN

- The Joy of Music   Simon & Schuster, 1959
  Anchor Books, 1994

- Leonard Bernstein's Young   Simon & Schuster, 1962
  People's Concerts   Simon & Schuster, 1970

- The Infinite Variety of Music   Simon & Schuster, 1966
  Anchor Books, 1993

- The Unanswered Question   Harvard University Press,
  1976

- Findings   Simon & Schuster, 1982
  Anchor Books, 1983

MORE

OF MY DAD'S WIT AND WISDOM

AMERICANS

by

William M. Blatt

Children of Teuton, Slav, and Celt,
Children of ev'ry earthly clan,
In many lands and climes they dwelt,
What made them all American?

Not that we live in a certain place
Not that we speak a single tongue,

No, but because we see afar,
Larger than any in the night,
Distant but clear, a single star
Leading us forward to the light.

A hope that peace shall rule the world
And love the barriers shall span,
One brotherhood, one flag unfurled
That makes us all American.

Pencil sketch of her dad by Jo Blatt Pall

A HYGIENE ALPHABET
by
William M. Blatt

(As printed in the AMA Bulletin)

A is for ADENOIDS, troublesome pests,
Have them removed, the physician suggests,
Tonsils included, cut price for the lot,
Septums corrected, or what have you got?

B is for BEDPAN, a clumsy device,
they've got to be used, but they're not very nice.
Why can't a genius think something out
That will work and not fill us with trouble and doubt?

C is for something they call CONSTIPATION,
Most people have it in this splendid nation,
Go off to the bathroom and study the tiles
Or else when you're older you'll suffer with piles.

D stands for the opposite word from the last;
People who have it must move very fast.
Always remember old Socrates' wheeze,-
Those who eat apples should also eat cheese.

E is for ENEMA, useful and good,
Nobody likes it, but all of us should.
It's simple and harmless, effective and sure,
And teaches that all things are pure to the pure.

F is for FOOD which is something to eat,
Once it included potatoes and meat.
Now it means spinach and lettuce and fruit,
Just 'cause fat ladies want to be cute.

G is for GLASSES to help people's sight,
Sometimes you need them to make you see right;
A glass of scotch whiskey will make you see twice,
A glass of wood alky will put you on ice.

H is for HEART, which pumps blood all our lives;
When it beats very quickly we wake up with wives.
Sometimes it's large and then sometimes it's small;
In cheaters and landlords, it's nothing at all.

I is for IODINE, killer of germs.
Use it for bruises, blisters and worms,
Spread it on thick where the microbes may be,
And put quite a lot in your rich uncles's tea.

J is for JAB, which is how you take dope.
Gives you short flashes of courage and hope,
Makes you talk back to your mother in law
And offer to give her a crack on the jaw.

K is for KISS, a disease-spreading vice;
Those who indulge pay a terrible price;
Somehow most people are willing to pay;
Even the Scotchmen are funny that way.

L is for LIVER, which sometimes goes queer,
Have it inspected at least twice a year,
Scrape off the warts and then polish the bone,
And presto your system improves in its tone.

M is for MEDICINE, run for it quick,
Everyone gives it to us when we're sick,
Most of it can't do a darn bit of good,
Lots of it puts us in nightgowns of wood.

N is for NARCOTICS, which makes you go slow.
Like poppy juice extract or Hollywood snow,
A sermon will do, also wood alcohol,
A rap on the jaw is the simplest of all.

O is for OPEN, the window, you know.
Yes, open the window and let in the snow,
The wind, and the rain, and the dirt, and the dust,
'Till you sneeze and you hawk and you cough and you bust.

P, PROPHYLAXIS suggests, does it not?
Well surely it should, or you don't know a lot.
The papers and magazines urge you to buy
All kinds of preventatives. Can you guess why?

Q is for QUININE as bitter as gall.
It cures chills and fevers like nothing at all.
You must gulp the pill whole, even though you should choke,
For it tastes like the day the stock market broke.

R is for RECIPE doctors will write
If you tell them you cough and don't sleep at night.
Twelve bucks to the druggist you hand with the slip,
Then it's stuck on a bottle and worn on the hip.

S is the glorious, life-giving SUN.
Bake in it, stew in it, ain't we got fun!
Take it quite nude, if you possibly can,
Avoiding the cops and the ladies, young man.

T is THERMOMETER, tester of heat
At ninety-eight six there's a notch, small and neat,
If the mercury passes, you're all in the red;
Put on your pajamas and get into bed.

U is for UNDERCLOTHES, worn to keep warm.
Once they enveloped the whole human form.
Somehow the climate is changing, because
Lately the ladies don't even wear drawers.

V is for VITAMINS A, B, C, D.
Good for the kiddies the doctors agree.
Spinach and cod liver oil they must take;
Poor little kids never get a break.

W stands for the WATER we use
To clean, and to drink as a chaser for booze.
It makes a good background right next to a beach,
And to show off the new bathing suit of a peach.

X is for X-RAY by which they can see
Through clothes, skin, and flesh, and just take it from me,
The guy that said beauty is only skin deep
upon the occasion remarked quite a heap.

Y is for YEAST and the very well bred
Declare that without it they would have been dead.
Dissolve in hot water and drink by the glass
But be careful...it sometimes escapes as a gas.

Z is for ZINC and for ZINC OXIDE salve.
Cures certain skin troubles you may have.
Smear on at night with great caution and care,
Wash off the next day and the pimple's still there.

TRUE CONFESSIONS

I love women, large or small
Fat or thin, short or tall
Blonde, brunette or Titian red
Country, town or city bred
Dressed for sea-shore, bed, or dance.
In skirts, or lingerie, or pants.
In winter, autumn, summer, spring,
In rooms or cars or anything,
With make-up or au naturel,
The rich girl and the poor as well
Drunk or sober, frump or smart,
Irish, English, German, Dutch.
Doesn't seem to matter much.
Spanish, Swedish, French or Greek,
Wild or tame or strong or weak.
I can stand a large proboscis
Or a little halitosis
Or a tendency to chatter.
Nothing really seems to matter.
Is she rather plain? Who cares?
If she wears large brassieres.
Any age is right for me
Twenty, thirty, forty, fifty
Pure white hair is clean and nifty.
Ladies, when you want me, call.
Bless your hearts, I love you all.

NO, NOT THAT

Perhaps I'm careless with the truth,
Perhaps I'm frowsy and uncouth,
Perhaps my face is unattractive,
Perhaps my morals are inactive,
Perhaps when I'm asleep I snore,
Or I'm not funny anymore,
Perhaps I hold onto a dollar,
until the eagles on it holler.

———

I may be one or all of these,
Accuse me of them if you please,
I shall be sorry but not sore;
But please don't say I am a bore.

Love, Love, Love.

AT FIRST

The oyster has its pearl,
The head its golden curl,
The wrinkled leaf it's dew,
And I have you.

LATER

The dew drops get the sun,
the flying bird the gun,
The oyster gets it's stew,
And I have you..

A NUN

Once there was a nun
Who done what she shouldn'ta done

TRAGEDY

Sad to see a dame,
at almost any cost,
Trying hard to hold,
what's already lost.

DIG THAT CRAZY PENGUIN

The penguin, male, must seek a wife
When he becomes mature in life.
He then goes searching all around
Until a soul-mate he has found.
But of which sex, to his dismay,
His partner is, he cannot say.
So in his beak he takes a stone
And when he finds his choice alone
He lays it at his loved one's feet,
For what exception it may meet.
If he ignores it, it's a he.
If she accepts it, it's a she.

THE CAMEL

The Camel is an ugly beast,
It bears the burdens of the east,
Its back is just a load of fat,
Here people have for ages sat.
Its gait's a rock and rolling swell
which all but Arabs makes unwell.
Its face is philosophical
And does not seem concerned at all,
But do not stand behind its rear
or you may get a kick, my dear.
For all its patient air, you'll find
The Camel is not really kind.

UNSPORTSMANLIKE

There was a young lady from Blanding
Whose boy friend was very demanding,
In fact it appeared, that just as he feared,
He had ruined her amateur standing.

ROYALTY

The Queen of England has to shit
And wipe her dirty arse.
And that makes pomp
And circumstance
And Majesty
A Farce.

PRAYER

Only a God could see us from any distant star
Only a God would want us, we being what we are.
Only a God could make us, only a God could plan
The weakness and the power that the men of earth call man.
Only a God could change the march of time's unbending will.
    Only a God could grant our prayer—and so perhaps he will.

ODE

You give me a sense of euphoria,
I wish I could see more and moria!

POST-GRADUATE LOVE

by
William M. Blatt

I used to view with consternation
The prospect of romantic thought,
When, it appeared, imagination
Had made one's reason come to naught.
But recently, it seems, my mind
Has undergone a change most strange
In that a certain man, I find,
Affects my diastolic range.

That he expresses admiration
Should not be causative at all
To make my pulse and respiration
Rise wildly, and as wildly, fall.
Should love be biological
Or founded on genetic grounds?
Why cannot it be logical
If love indeed is what I've found?

His hair is thick and brown and curly,
But why should that provoke a sigh?
He's tall and strong and rather burly.
Why should the mind obey the eye?
His IQ's less than "prodigy,"
He has not read too many books,
But Ah! my heart keeps telling me
He has a line, and boy, what looks!

DAVID MAMET AND MY SON, JERRY

David Mamet, who is called America's fiercest, funniest playwright, lives in West Newton, Mass., which is a suburb of Boston. In his twenties, he was a classmate and friend of my son, Jerry, at Goddard College in Vermont. Jerry recalls that David gave him this advice: "Don't wait to be discovered." He certainly lived those words and I'm sure they influenced Jerry.

Although he was born in Chicago, David seems to prefer New England, as he has a summer place — a farmhouse in Cabot, Vermont that has no electricity. For twelve years he lived there with his former wife, Lindsay Crouse, and two daughters, Willa and Zosia. Mamet likes to vary his image with many costume changes, and even disguises. He often wears workboots, bluejeans, and a trimmed beard. Always, there is the crewcut which tops his broad forehead and makes him look rather solemn.

Mamet's present wife, Rebecca Pidgeon, the actress, has converted to Judaism to please her husband. She claims that her husband is a sensitive gentleman and very funny. He is also very devoted to their daughter, Clara, and his other children. Mamet doesn't talk very much, as he'd rather listen. He likes and understands actors as he was one himself a few years ago.

David and his sister, Lynne, who is also a writer and lives in California, were the victims of a miserable upbringing. The bitterness that resulted comes out in his plays, because of his treatment by a violent stepfather. This rage might have destroyed him if he hadn't been able to use it in his creativity. David Mamet has said, "If I didn't become a writer, I would probably be a criminal." It's ironic that he became so successful almost as a result of his negative experiences. "Glengarry Glen Ross," an example of his new style became a tremendous hit, both on Broadway and on film.

A story Jerry remembers involving David shows the generous side of this man. One day in June several years ago, Jerry asked him if he would be the guest speaker at the graduation of his Shaker Mountain School in Burlington, and was very happy that he had agreed to do it. Unfortunately, David later found that he was unable to keep the date, and to Jerry's great surprise he received a letter of apology from Mamet in which he had enclosed a check for one thousand dollars. His note said, "Sorry I can't make it, but here's a couple of dollars." He knew that Jerry needed help with his school, and this was a good chance for him to contribute. David must have had a feeling he would be a success someday. His instincts certainly were right. Today, in his fifties, he has written twenty two plays, many essays, two novels, and fourteen films, and has directed several of them. Mamet is one of the few American playwrights who are successful screenwriters. Three of these movies were running in '97 and '98 at the same time: "The Edge," with Alec Baldwin and Anthony Hopkins, "Wag the Dog," with Dustin Hoffman and Robert De Niro, and "The Spanish Prisoner," starring Steve Martin and directed by Mamet. His latest project is a movie, "The Winslow Boy," Starring Rebecca Pidgeon, his wife, which he directed.

Jerry has dedicated his life to alternative education. He is the founder and director of the Alternative Education Resource Organization, which is nonprofit. His magazine, "The Education Revolution,' tells what's going on in the world of alternative education.

Jerry has assisted many parents in homeschooling their children as well as placing students in alternative schools. He realized at an early age that public schools, with their rigid curriculum and methods of teaching, could easily discourage a student and stifle his creativity. Recently he has become involved in advising alternative schools in several countries in Europe as well as Israel. Jerry has made four trips to the former Soviet Union, visiting the Eureka School and the International Film School in Moscow, as well as the Stork School near Kharkov in the Ukraine, and he has enabled them to receive much needed grants. In dealing with these schools, Jerry has had to depend on interpreters to a great extent in expounding his philosophy of alternative education. In France, he has counseled the faculty of the Autre Chose School in Paris. He has visited schools in Holland and Britain, notably the Summerhill School in Wales.

THIS AND THAT

Memory is the process of making the past a part of the present.
William M. Blatt

THE RUDE MECHANIC

Jerry and I use the same "Car Care" garage for his eleven-year-old Caprice, which had been his dad's, and for my Toyota Camry, which my lovely niece, Ellen Pall, bought for me. One afternoon, when Jerry was out giving a talk at a local high school, I decided to call Car Care to see why my dashboard light was off. A lady answered and asked my name and make of car. When I told her, she said, "Just a minute, Mrs. Mintz, I'll put someone on." I repeated my story and this guy asks, "Can't you fix this yourself? You're pathetic!" I retorted, "I asked my son and he couldn't, so may I come in today?" "Naw," he answered, No openings till next November." After an exasperated pause on my part, he said, "Hey, Mom, don't you recognize your own son's voice—it's Jerry!" His car needed attention too, and while he was there he had picked up the phone when he knew I was on the other end. I couldn't believe that a mechanic would talk to a potential customer that way. When I realized it was Jerry kidding me with his usual sense of humor, I broke out in uncontrolled laughter.

GARAGE "SAILING"

When garage and tag sales became popular, I found myself pursuing them more and more so that it became a Saturday morning habit. Fran, my partner in crime, also became addicted. She isn't as extravagant as I am but she enjoys pointing out things she feels I can't do without. She usually ends up with some small art object that she gives to one of her sisters in New York or Missouri where she grew up. They were very generous to her, and she enjoys showing her appreciation in this way.

Tag sales started at least ten years ago to become a popular sport. Of course, many dealers would show up at 7 a.m. or an hour before the official openings at 9 or 10 a.m. I think I clothed Sam and Jerry in designer clothes from top to bottom. I found what turned out to be Sam's favorite Hush Puppy shoes at one of these sales. There was only one of them in a box filled with other odd shoes, but after digging deeper, the other one turned up. They were dark green and he wore them to a frazzle. Also, he decided slip-on shoes were more convenient than the kind with laces. I remember once when we were visiting Sam's brother, Nelson, in Worcester, Sam was wearing a newly purchased beige cashmere sweater. Nelson remarked that he couldn't afford cashmere. I think it was then that Sam approved of my garage "sailing."

--- with old friends, Fran, and pianist, Ethel,
who lives in Florida

OUR KIDS ARE GOING DEAF

Have you ever been to a Bar or Bat Mitzvah, a wedding or an affair where the so-called music for dancing assaults your ears and drives you crazy with its booming, relentless monotony? Well, I just experienced this harassment at a sweet sixteen party. These days it's impossible to escape the noise. You could eat and run without letting relatives see you, but eventually you will be found out.

I feel the blame falls on the parents who plan and pay for the affair. They should speak up for the middle aged and the older folks who have to endure three or four hours of this torture. It's very sad that kids are not exposed to good music at school or on the radio at home – some jazz, Sinatra, Benny Goodman or, God forbid, some melodic classics. In New York we are fortunate to have WQXR (96.3FM) and WNYC (93.9FM). If children experienced some decent music, they might grow up with better taste in the music they like to hear.

What's most important is that the constant high decibels could produce deafness or, at the very least, impaired hearing. I always carry pieces of cotton to put in my ears when I go to one of these affairs. It helps to soften the blows.

PERFORMING

I performed a group of pieces for REAP (retired people) at the Bryant Library in Roslyn. I hadn't played for an audience in years, except for a piece now and then at Club 88, an offshoot of APTLI (Association of Piano Teachers of Long Island). I remembered a few weeks before I was scheduled to perform, and when I actually played, what a performer goes through. I realized that after my earlier years of performance as soloist, with and without orchestra, that performing was something I didn't really enjoy doing. It was much too stressful, including upset stomach, extra heartbeats and shaky hands during a performance. It made me admire all those soloists who perform successfully many times a year. I did enjoy it more when I had practiced and felt more confident, however. I think you have to hypnotize yourself and learn to focus. Of course, my teacher's method included slow motion (fundamental) practice — especially just before a performance – and it works quite well.

A DATE WITH A YOUNGER MAN

One afternoon, while I was teaching my ten year old student, Frankie Sanchez, I remembered there was a free piano concert that night at "Piano, Piano," a local piano store. I suggested to his mother, Rosa, that she take Frankie. She said it would be difficult as her husband was coming home late and she needed to give him dinner. I volunteered to take him as I was going. Frankie giggled, "Do you mean we have a date tonight?" "Sure," I answered, "but perhaps your neighbor, Steffi, [whom I also teach] would like to come." "Oh," he responded a little sadly, "I guess that would be a double date." Since Steffi had to go out shopping first with her mom, she wasn't able to come until later and we saved two seats for them. On the way to the concert, Frankie exclaimed, "Mrs. Mintz, you can tell Ray that you wanted to try going out with a younger man!" When we reached the concert, I parked the car and he ran around to open my door and insisted I put my arm in his as we walked to the entrance.

MY HOSPITAL EXPERIENCE

Hospitals can be very important when you really need them, but I must tell anyone who feels fairly healthy to do anything he can to stay that way. As my dad said, there are three places to stay out of: the cemetery, jail, and a hospital.

This last Sunday I wasn't feeling quite right, so I called a local hospital and told my symptoms to the nurse who answered the phone. I had felt a little dizzy, my handwriting was off, and my right hand was a bit numb, but it got better after a few minutes. Still the nurse told me I should come in for a checkup as it could be the beginning of a stroke. I didn't feel it was that serious, but I decided to take her advice, and Ray thought it was a good idea.

Well, if I knew what I was in for, I would have hesitated; but thinking it might be an interesting experience, I decided to walk into the ER of this reputable hospital.

The first thing they did was to take my blood pressure, which was much higher than usual, 180 over 115. The nurse said, "You might be getting a stroke so you had better stay overnight. We'll be giving you Heparin to prevent blood clotting." Before I knew it I was spending the night in an emergency room (there was no hospital bed available). They put an IV on my left hand, and an ER tag on my right wrist, along with a number tag. My blood pressure was taken every hour; I was squeezed (hard), pricked (for blood), echo-grammed, x-rayed, catscanned, monitored, and anything else they could think of.

At home, I relax in bed with the TV on while beautiful music (Beethoven, Ravel, etc.) wafts around my ears, and I read or write as I choose. In this tiny room there was nothing to do but stare straight up at the ceiling, as my encumbrances prevented my turning over and going to sleep. It was too late for supper, and no one even walked by. I think you get the idea.

The next morning I was moved to a decent hospital room , where my room-mate was a sweet ninety six year old lady who had fallen down at home.

After the doctors had assessed all the results, the final outcome was this prescription, "One baby aspirin per day!"

DOGS I ENCOUNTER AT LESSONS

There have been a variety of dogs in my teaching life. There is Coco, Frankie's dog, a mixture of golden retriever and something else. He puts his paws on my lap and insists that I say "Hello Coco." He won't leave me alone until I do.

Then there is a big dog, Benjie, who, when he sees us playing a duet, puts his paws on the upper keys and makes it a trio.

Tulie is a large, shiny black dog who constantly puts his head through my arm while I'm sitting next to Jennifer, his mistress. When she is ready to play a complete piece, I sit on a couch away from the piano, and Tulie sits next to me while I stroke her back and whenever I stop for a minute, she puts her paw on my lap asking for more.

Aaron's dog, Lizzie, is a thoroughbred terrier who almost jumps over the gate in the kitchen when I walk in. I wish we all had such enthusiasm.

River and Zachary are two tremendous dogs that belong to Elaine. When I walk in the door, River, who is the size of a small horse, almost knocks me over, so I always run for the nearest chair.

Another medium sized dog, Max, refused to let me leave. After each lesson, he stood in my way and barked fiercely when I got up to leave. They had to put him in his cage before I could escape. I guess he just hated to say goodbye.

MY HERNIA SET TO MUSIC

After enduring a dull pain in my left side every time I took a walk with Ray, I decided to see Dr. Kryle. I told him it didn't bother me when I was lying down. He knew immediately and said, "Let me see your hernia."

My good friend, Fran, told me of a hernia specialist and I made an appointment. He said the only way to "repair" it was to perform an operation, and that I'd go to a "walk in" operating room at North Shore Hospital, and also that I'd be out in two hours. I decided to do it as soon as possible to get it over with.

Ray let me use his walkman with a tape that contained a couple of my favorite Mozart *Piano Concertos* which I was able to listen to during the operation. When I walked into the large multi-operation room I screamed, as it was so large and scary with several procedures going on at the same time and soft "elevator music" being played. It looked like a manufacturing plant. I knew that Mozart would help to calm me down. The scene repelled me because it was to be only my second operation. The first was a tonsillectomy at the age of four. That one left a lasting horrible memory of being pushed down and held. It must have been the ether I was fighting off.

To my surprise, they told me the operation was over before I was aware of having heard a great deal of Mozart, but the fact that I woke up listening to the second of the two concertos told me that the procedure had taken longer than I thought. The operation had been almost painless but the after effects were much worse. When I got home, I had continuous pain but was determined not to let it get me down. I managed to give a lesson at my house the next day sitting on a pillow. The following day I drove to three lessons. At one of them I mentioned to the student's dad, a doctor, that I had just had a hernia operation two days before. He exclaimed, "You must be Superwoman!"

Jerry came home from a seminar on alternative education in Russia shortly after that, and was surprised to learn what I had gone through while he was away.

MEDICAL PROBLEMS

Since Ray miraculously came into my life, after I had practically decided I'd never find my ideal partner, I wanted to make sure he'd be around for a long time.

When he told me he had gone for a five mile hike at Caumset State Park in Huntington with his daughter, Jane, I was impressed. However, when he told me he had never been so completely exhausted as he found himself to be the next morning, a light went off in my brain.

As I had made such a difference in my son Jerry's life by convincing him that he needed a stress test because of his family record of heart disease, I made it my business to convince Ray that he also needed a stress test. His own doctor (a woman) didn't recognize his exhaustion as a symptom of heart disease, but agreed to order the test if he insisted. Sure enough it showed an irregularity in his EKG which indicated some coronary blockage. She prescribed a triple dose of Inderal, which he had been taking to control a minor arrhythmia. That seemed excessive and prompted him to get a second opinion, which led him to a holistic MD, who recommended a regime of vitamins and enzymes to be taken while on a low fat diet. The results have been excellent.

CATARACTS

Another procedure that commonly becomes necessary as one grows older, is the cataract operation, in which the affected lens is removed and a plastic one is inserted in its place. Dr. Charles Kelman of New York developed the accepted technique for this by experimenting on the eyes of stray cats. About fourteen years ago, Ray had the foggy lens of his left eye removed by Dr. Kelman, who performed the operation on closed-circuit TV while a classroom of doctors, learning the procedure, watched a monitor and listened to Kelman's explanation of his moves.

I realized soon after meeting Ray that I would soon be a candidate for a cataract operation, as I was finding it difficult to see clearly when I drove home at night from giving piano lessons. My choice for the operation was a man who, I was told, had magical fingers, Dr. Norman Stahl, who was considered tops in his field and did as many as twelve eye operations in one day at either of his two facilities on Long Island.

I had been told it was a painless operation and I found it to be quite true, but of course there was some apprehension while watching the preceding operation as it was shown on a TV monitor in the waiting room. While Dr. Stahl operated on my eye, I was in a talkative mood, and I saw such beautiful color combinations that I remarked about it. He asked me not to talk so much so he could concentrate, and of course I complied.

The next day I came back for a checkup and asked Dr. Stahl if I could drive to my piano lesson that day and to my surprise he said, "Sure, but wear your dark glasses." How about that for an easy operation? Unfortunately, Dr. Stahl, who had improved the vision of so many, died shortly after, of cancer. It's hard to understand how such tragedies can happen to very talented and useful people.

MY DENTIST

Since this is supposed to be a story mainly about me, I feel it appropriate to tell you about my dentist who has been looking into my mouth for the last forty years. Dr. Stanley Knapp and his wife, Marilyn, were my sister and brother-in-law's friends before she introduced me to them. Stanley became the dentist for my whole family and has had a perfect record for never having pulled one tooth of ours for over thirty years. He also works very fast and is even able to carry on a running conversation about Long Island personalities while our mouths are too full of cotton to respond. If we call him in an emergency, he often answers the phone from Florida and makes an appointment as soon as possible or refers us to his alternate. Stanley is certainly a very sweet guy.

QUISISANA

If someone told you that he had just returned from a resort called Quisisana in Center Lovell (near Portland), Maine and that it had no air conditioning, no TV in the rooms, and mosquitoes, would you want to spend a vacation there? If I told you that you had to make reservations about a year in advance because of the great demand, you would probably wonder why. I will tell you.

First of all, it is on beautiful Kezar Lake with picturesque mountains in the background and colorful sailboats on the water.

Second, the people who go there, including couples and families from as far away as California, Canada and New Orleans, are mostly very interesting and cultured.

Ray and I sat at a table with two other couples and a single woman in her forties when we were there for a week's vacation. She was a career advisor at Boston College and was most friendly and enthusiastic. Another couple lived in New Orleans and the husband was a doctor, Paul Diamond, who loves opera. He is planning to work with the poor and sick in Haiti after he retires at age 65.

We became friendly with a family of four; the father, an orthopedic surgeon, was very proud of his son, David, who at the age of eleven was a pianist, violinist, and an aspiring conductor. He had conducted excerpts from *Carmen* when he was nine. I heard him practicing a Mozart *Sonata* and asked him some questions about music. He knew all the answers, was familiar with many composers, and was unusually enthusiastic. Later I met his dad, Dr. Michael Sermer, his mom and little sister, Rebecca.

It turns out his dad is a frustrated musician who bought a brand new Steinway grand years ago and taught himself to play and sight read.

He just happened to have brought with him the latest biography of Leonard Bernstein by Meryl Secrest in which there is the picture of me flanked by Lenny and Aaron Copland in front of the Tanglewood shed. I was a teenager then. The caption read, "Ouida Mintz with Leonard Bernstein and Aaron Copland." I guess Dr. Sermer and David were very impressed as they seemed to hang on every word I uttered. The doctor even memorized the pages on which I was mentioned. David said he wanted to be my pen pal. By the way, since he complained that he had a small hand, in fact too small at that time to even reach an octave, I suggested and predicted that he would become a conductor. He smiled as if he agreed. Here is a letter David wrote to me;

```
Dear Ouida,
    I am very sorry I didn't write back sooner
but I have tons and tons of work to do for
school. I'm in sixth grade and there's a lot of
work. It's not really hard, it's just very time
consuming. Sometimes I have so much work that I
don't even have time to practice my piano and
violin very much. This week my piano teacher
said that she had too much work and so she's
not giving piano lessons any more. Now I am
looking for a new teacher. My mom called the
Hart School of Music in Hartford to try to get
a good teacher but we haven't heard from them
yet. I am very bored not having lessons and not
```

having any guidance. The last piece I was working on was the Rachmaninoff *Polka Italienne* and I am still working on the Beethoven *Sonata #20*. I am thinking of starting on one of his long *Bagatelles* but I have no one to teach me. Did I tell you I took a long organ course this August? I learned how to play the organ on a beautiful church organ. I played the *Toccata* from Bach's *Toccata and Fugue*. Playing the organ was an amazing feeling because it felt like I was playing every single instrument in an orchestra. My teacher told my mom that I was a natural organist, especially since my hands are so small for my age. Hopefully sometime I can go see you on Long Island. Please write back and tell me if you have advice for me.

Love,
David Sermer

David Sermer with Ouida and Ray

The most extraordinary thing about Quisisana is that after the personable waiters and waitresses serve the most delectable gourmet dinners, they turn into professional singers, actors and dancers at the stroke of nine-fifteen P.M., when the nightly entertainment begins. The staff is carefully chosen during the year from the music departments of various colleges and universities across the country for their special talents in music and acting as well as for their warm personalities and ability to get along with the vacationers. In doing the many chores required to run a resort, including waiting on table, running the office and housekeeping, they have to be down-to-earth young people with a sense of humor. The owner and watchful guide of this venture is Jane Orans. I understand that Quisisana has been operating this way for at least thirty years and has been owned by several people, some of whom are known to friends of mine.

Most guests stay only one week as the nightly programs are repeated each week with few changes. The first night, Saturday, is a preview of the week to come with each performer introducing himself and announcing the college he comes from. Sunday night is Chamber music night which this year featured two flutists, a violinist and a cellist, all very accomplished. The third night was a Broadway musical. Last year it was, *She Loves Me*, and this year we saw *The Music Man* with our waiter taking the part of Harold Hill. What a transformation– seeing our friendly waiter as the star of the show! The fourth night, Tuesday, featured a piano recital by Bonnie Anderson, a charming person and a very fine pianist. She has performed with the Boston Symphony Orchestra and got her PhD. at Boston University. I signed her up to play and speak at a meeting of The Association of Piano Teachers of Long Island (APTLI) of which I am the program chairman. Wednesday night offers a complete opera. Last year it was the *Magic Flute*, this year, *Cosi Fan Tutti* both beautifully sung and acted. Thursday is Cabaret Night where we sit at candlelit tables sipping soft drinks and nibbling snacks. Featured are show tunes sung by a number of performers and a hilariously shortened version of a Broadway musical. Last year it was *The Sound of Music*; this year, *Carousel.* The last night, Friday, is when they sing arias from various operas including solos and duets. The last number is a choral performance by the entire staff of Brahm's *Lullaby*, a tradition at Quisisana for the last music of the week. Beth Gelsinger, our very charming and efficient waitress was an outstanding soloist. The morning after having seen Mozart's *Magic Flute*, we were astonished to see the Queen of the Night serving breakfast at the next table.

We mustn't leave out that basic necessity – food. At Quisisana the menus are most creative, supervised by a chef who is a fine singer and actor and is understandably portly. It's almost impossible to turn down such delicacies as strawberry soup, and a different homemade bread every day. Lobster is served twice a week and the weekly buffet includes Portobello mushrooms, shrimp and scallops a la king. After each lunch and dinner there is a special dessert with artistic flourishes. If you go, expect to gain at least two pounds by the end of the week

"FIDDLER"

One night, before the opening of *Fiddler on the Roof*, I was at a party, sitting at an upright piano with the composer of *Fiddler*, Jerry Bock. I remember he played, among other songs, *Sunrise, Sunset,* and I asked him how he came up with such a beautiful melody. You call on your background and write only what you feel inspired to write, he told me. I've never forgotten that bit of wisdom.

REUNITING WITH LEONARD HOKANSON

Very seldom does one get to reunite with an old friend of one's youth over forty years later, but it has happened to me recently.

After I married Sam, and went to live in Worcester where I had my three children, Jerry, Billy and Lisa, I became a member of the Worcester Music Group. This was a club for talented music lovers which gave them an opportunity to perform for an audience. When one spends a lot of time practicing, it's important to have an incentive, which this club provided. I was president of this group for three years before we moved to New York. One of our members was a twenty year old musician, a great pianist and accompanist who loved German *Lieder.* We all predicted that he would go far in music.

I remember an incident that shows what an accommodating person he was at such a young age. When I had three young kids to take care of, I didn't have too much time to practice, but I had managed to work on the Beethoven *Sonata Opus 10, #3* and planned to play it at the last meeting. I was shocked to hear that Leonard was going to play the same sonata. When I told him of my predicament, he immediately offered to play another piece that was "in his fingers." His magnanimity impressed me no end.

Over the years I have heard recordings on the radio of his performances of obscure pieces by Schubert, as well as his sensitive accompaniment to the great singer, Herman Prey. This summer Ray and I were sitting in the audience at Music Mountain in northern Connecticut listening to a marvelous chamber music concert when I noticed in the program that my old friend, Leonard Hokanson, was to play the following week. A gentlemen sitting next to me, Jack Crockett, overheard me say to Ray that I was sorry I would not be able to hear him and renew our old friendship. This kind person said he would be at the concert and would be glad to give him my best regards. Crockett wrote to me later and told me how great the concert was and described how Hokanson's eyes lit up when he mentioned my name. He was delighted to hear that I had predicted that he would become a great artist. I wrote to him after that.

Hokanson is evidently most famous in Europe, as he has lived there for most of his life. He has performed with such major orchestras as the Philadelphia, Berlin Philharmonic, Rotterdam Philharmonic, and Vienna Symphony. He is a founding member of the Odeon Trio and has been a guest artist with the Vermeer Quartet and the Fine Arts Quartet, and he frequently performs duo recitals with violinist, Miriam Freed, clarinetist, James Campbell, and hornist Hermann Baumann. In song recitals he has played for such artists as Martina Arroyo, Grace Bumbry as well as Hermann Prey. His recent recordings have included collections of *The Complete Piano Works* of Walter Piston, Haydn *Sonatas*, Mozart *Concerti*, Brahms *Intermezzi*, Schubert's *Complete Works for Piano* with Edith Peinemann, Brahms *Sonatas for Clarinet and Piano* with James Campbell, Beethoven's *Complete Songs* with Hermann Prey and Pamela Coburn, as well as previously unrecorded early piano works of Schubert.

One of the last pupils of Artur Schnabel, he also studied with Karl-Ulrich Schnabel, Claude Frank and Jillian Grey. He is currently a professor of piano at the renowned School of Music at Indiana University in Bloomington. He has recorded on the following Labels: Bayer, Denon, Deutche Gramophone, EMI, Naxos, Northeastern, Philips, RCA and Sony.

BRAHMS

Of all the composers I have played and listened to, Johannes Brahms is the one I most revere. I wish I could have met him, though I feel I commune with him when I listen to his music. My teacher, Gebhard, just missed meeting him at the end of the last century but to his sorrow, Brahms died in April 1897 before they could meet. His sublime melodies and harmonies speak to the soul. It's hard to believe that in his time his music was considered too intellectual. It was said in jest that there were signs in concert halls that said, "Exit in case of Brahms." I'm glad he had someone like Clara Schumann to love in his later years and I'm sure it was reciprocated. His love letters to her were in the music he wrote for her to play, which she adored.

When Mozart was asked what his sensations were when he was composing he answered, "The process with me is like a vivid dream." Brahms felt that he had similar feelings. "When I am absolutely alone, I'm in a dreamlike state, and in that condition the ideas flow much more easily. I often get themes when out walking, especially in the country, but I always have to put them down immediately or they quickly fade. Sometimes I let them germinate for years and the original thoughts grow and expand."

He felt inspiration with the spiritual process, but it had to be accompanied by technical skill, and he thought that Beethoven was the perfect type of the creative genius who had lofty inspirations, but was an indefatigable worker.

Brahms was continually torn by an inner struggle. He constantly criticized his own work and only allowed what he considered his worthwhile creations to survive. It is said that he destroyed much of the music he had spent hours writing and felt that his music couldn't stand up next to Beethoven. One day when the Joachim quartet was performing a composition of his, he arose from his seat and growled, "That's too boring for my taste," and left abruptly. Once he described his *D Major Symphony* as a set of waltzes since it contained two movements in three quarter time. He was so modest about his immortal *Fourth Symphony*, which was to be published after its first public performance, that he said, "It's a scandal the work will be printed when its immortality is already finished."

MEMORIES FROM THE PAST

I received a letter from the improbable State of Alabama one day signed by Barbara Cooper, a name I remembered from my childhood. I took care of a three year old girl by that name when I was only ten years old

Barbara's mother had died and I lived on the fourth floor of the same building which my dad owned, so I became her baby sitter for what I thought was a big sum at the time, fifty cents per afternoon.

Well, here's how it happened many years later. A married friend of mine named Al, had gone to Boston from Worcester, Massachusetts, where I started my married life. While in Boston, he was reading the Boston Globe when he came across an ad requesting anyone in the Blatt family to contact Barbara Cooper. It seems she was anxious to get more information about the mother she lost as a child, and hence this random ad which blew me away when my friend mailed it to me.

I wrote a letter to Barbara at the address in Alabama, and thus began a series of letters which brought back many memories, and we became pen pals and friends again after all these years.

OUR VISITORS FROM GERMANY

All's well that ends well.
Shakespeare

When Jerry was on his second trip to Israel to attend an alternative school seminar, he met a fifteen year old boy, Johannes, who had been homeschooled in Austria. He came from a poor, struggling family of twelve brothers and sisters who were managing to survive in two rooms of a cabin on top of a mountain. Jerry, when he heard of his plight, invited him to stay at our house in Roslyn. He readily accepted as he wanted to learn English, and Nicolas, a fellow of twenty-five from Bremen, Germany, offered to bring him. Nicolas was a drummer who happened to find work with a rock band in New York City.

He had a friend, Andreas, of about the same age, who was a bass guitar player from Berlin who also wanted to work in New York. Before I knew it, I had three Germanic boarders living in my house and speaking German among themselves. The two older boys spoke to me and Jerry in English. I was involved in doing their laundry, taking them back and forth from train stations when they went to the city. Jerry, of course, had the job of buying the groceries, and he found himself shopping almost daily.

Nicolas slept on the couch in the den, Andy slept in a bedroom upstairs, while Johnnie slept in a corner of the living room in a sleeping bag. Their clothes were piled up on chairs all over the place. I had never heard so much of the German language since I attended Wagner's *Ring Cycle* as a teenager. They seemed appreciative and a bit awed by our generosity. Before they left, Nicolas and Andreas each took me out to a lovely dinner, which showed me how much they appreciated our hospitality.

HIT SONG

In 1932 my dad wrote material for his good friends, Jack Norworth and his wife, Nora Bayes, when they were performing on Broadway.

They were the people who wrote and sang, *"I'm Looking at the World through Rose Colored Glasses."* They also wrote, *"Take Me Out to the Ball Game."*

The shocker is that they created that world-famous song before they had ever attended a ball game!

Jack and Nora were frequent visitors at our home in Brookline and they created quite a stir of excitement before they came.

STAYING YOUNG

It's so important, I've learned, to keep active and productive as you get older. It's the best way to keep your mind and body young. I think writing this book is a good example of that, and Ray learned how to accomplish the difficult task of typesetting the book as well as it's cover, on his computer.

My son, Jerry, has known a one hundred year old woman, Nellie Dick, a pioneer teacher in alternative education. An example of how sibling rivalry never ends, occurred at her outdoor one hundredth birthday party, which Ray and I attended.Nellie's ninety eight year old sister was sitting next to her accepting the handshakes of people who came over to congratulate her sister. Nellie complained, "You'd think it was <u>her</u> birthday party!"

Jerry made a documentary videotape of Nellie, telling the story of her many years as a teacher in alternative education. The tape is still in demand from people interested in the field.

Another centenarian that Jerry knew was Alfred Leavitt, a fine artist whose oils are found in many important museums, including the Metropolitan Museum of Art in New York. Jerry took a picture of Leavitt holding a newborn baby, and used it on the cover of an issue of his Educational Revolution Newsletter. When Alfred, who was one hundred and three at the time, was trying to figure out why he was living so long, he said, "The Lord has more things for me to do, I guess." At the same time he had a one-man-show on display at Ellis Island in New York. Leavitt had always had a great interest in alternative education, and in his last days was dreaming of being able to start a new alternative school. He lived to the ripe age of one hundred and five.

Guiseppe Verdi wrote some of his greatest operas in his later years. Probably his most successful opera, *Aida*, was written when he was fifty seven. His greatest lyric tragedy, *Otello*, was finished when he was seventy three, and his last opera, *Falstaff*, was completed when he was over eighty, a major accomplishment at such an advanced age. He left most of his fortune to a home he founded in Italy for aged musicians.

MY PERFORMING FRIENDS AT APTLI

Don't wait for applause, keep on playing.
William M. Blatt

I am convinced that music is what makes people feel close to each other. When several people are listening to a beautiful composition together, such as the *Adagietto* of Mahler's Fifth Symphony, I feel something quite mysterious and miraculous happens. A certain feeling of warmth and love of mankind makes one happy to be alive. Most of the slow movements of Mozart's *Piano Concerti* give me that reaction and make me feel that all is right with the world.

I joined a group of piano teachers in about 1968 called APTLI (Association of Piano Teachers of Long Island). We're quite a mixture of people from different backgrounds, but we're all good friends, and are like one happy family. We have monthly meetings on the third Wednesday of every month which feature guest performers. We also have a social meeting each month called Club 88 (named for the 88 piano keys) when we get together in various member's homes and play for each other. Club 88 also has two programs a year for young students to get together and have the experience of playing for an audience. There is an annual concert for which the more advanced students are required to audition. This concert is given on the stage of the hall in the Port Washington Library. At the end of each season we have a special luncheon for the members and their guests. We've been going strong for more than thirty-five years.

I was the APTLI Historian for three years, taking pictures of the guest speakers and putting them in a notebook. I also have played at Club 88 ever since I have been a member. Three years ago I was elected to replace the retiring program chairman, Bernard Kirshbaum. He had the difficult job of selecting performers who could talk about piano teaching as well as illustrate at the piano. One Sunday I heard a wonderful pianist, Linda Laurent, at the Bryant Library and I hired her to play for APTLI. They liked her so much that she now has played three years in a row for us. Last March she brought her outstanding trio from Connecticut. They gave superb renditions of a Mendelssohn trio as well as some very interesting contemporary music by a friend of theirs.

APTLI met for two years at Gillary Gallery. Sylvia and Leo Gillary run a very unique house in Jericho, Long Island, which displays art works on all three floors, and they run six shows a year. The first floor is also a spacious concert hall which has two Steinway concert grands, and they offer about fourteen concert performances each year featuring artists such as violinist Yeou-Cheng Ma (Yo Yo Ma's sister, who has performed with her brother and her guitarist husband, Michael Dadap). These concerts raise money to provide scholarships for talented young musicians. They have been helping to promote young talent since 1976.

Morton Estrin, a Hofstra University music professor and pianist, draws the most people because he jokingly tells his students, "If you don't go, I'll flunk you." You never hear about the teacher of someone like Billy Joel, but Morton Estrin is the one who gave Joel the basics of music. Estrin, has had a long and distinguished career as a concert pianist, recording artist, and teacher. When he played for us recently, he proved to be a very dynamic speaker and performed Brahms and Schumann, which the teachers of APTLI appreciated tremendously. He has made first recordings of Scriabin's twelve *Etudes, Opus 8*, and six *Grand Etudes, Opus 23*, by Anton Rubenstein. He performed the twenty four *Preludes* by Rachmaninov at Alice Tully Hall and at the National Gallery of Art in Washington, D.C.

He has been a professor in the Music Department of Hofstra University for over thirty years. A new association with Sony Classical compact discs should produce more fine Estrin recordings.

Estrin has said about pianists who perform, "If there's going to be a purpose in recreating a given piece of music for the umpteenth time, it is the performer's personality and originality that is going to make the thing come alive."

--- with Sylvia Gillary

Rosabel Lu

Hadassah Guttmann

--- with Thomas Yehuda Tirino

One of my former students who is now pursuing a musical career, Donna Visaya, purchased one of his older Baldwin pianos and had it restored. I'm sure it brought her some luck as it was lovingly played on for twenty five years by Mr. Estrin, and so I'm glad I was the one who brought them together.

When I talk to Sylvia, which I do very often, she just bubbles with all the news of her concerts. She volunteers to play the piano at our Club 88 meetings, which we often hold at her home, and she plays remarkably well for someone who has just celebrated her eighty seventh birthday and has overcome many health problems. There was a concert in honor of her birthday when one hundred friends and performers gathered to celebrate and perform.

Her husband, Leo, has a display of his sculptures in the house, and many of them are scattered in the garden outside. One can see a giraffe's head peeking over the fence as well as other animal heads.

Thomas Yehudah Tirino, born in New York in 1961, studied at Juilliard with Sascha Gorodnitzki. He has won numerous awards including the Gina Bacchauer, the National Arts Club Piano Competition, and under the auspices of Sylvia Gillary, was the winner of the Judith Grayson Memorial Scholarship Award for ten years. His CDs, including works by Ernesto Lecuona, have been widely acclaimed. He is now preparing a documentary for PBS Television.

I got to know him at Gillary Gallery where he played for one of our APTLI meetings. He has a very warm personality and the audience seemed very pleased with his virtuoso performance. The program consisted entirely of the works of Lecuona. A close friend, who is a Rabbi, had suggested that Tom look into the music of this little-played Cuban composer who was best known for *Malaguena*. He was amazed when he listened to the cassette recordings his friend sent him to find over 175 fine piano works as well as dozens of orchestral pieces. Tirino had played all of the classical composers, plus all twenty seven of Mozart's *Piano Concerti* before his love affair with Lecuona.

Tom Tirino has added the middle name "Yehudah" (meaning Jew) to his recital programs lately, and therein lies a dramatic story. Tom's parents brought him up as a true Catholic, and he acted as a choir and altar boy in his church. A few years ago, his mother decided to tell him that it was his father who was Catholic, and that she had kept from him the fact that she had been born Jewish, which meant that he, too, was

Jewish. This late revelation, which had been kept from him, has made a tremendous difference in his lifestyle: He decided to become an Orthodox Jew, and he even keeps a Kosher home. I understand that he is working on an autobiography to explain his feelings when he came to know of his real religion.

Cecilia Gniewek Brauer is a very unusual member and a former president of APTLI. She is one of our most accomplished pianists, and has played Gershwin's *Rhapsody in Blue*, and recently the Rachmaninov *Second Piano Concerto* with the Merrick Symphony. For the past twenty five years, Cecilia has had the prestigious position of pianist and celeste player with the renowned Metropolitan Opera Orchestra under James Levine. With this orchestra she has traveled and played all over the world. Her brother, Raymond Gniewek, is the concert master of the orchestra and his wife is the well known soprano, Judith Blegen. Chronologically, Ms. Brauer qualifies as a senior citizen, and would have every right to retire. But not this lady. As a fairly recent widow, she chooses to live life to the fullest and to continue working and performing at the top of her musical abilities. I'm so delighted and proud to be a friend of hers.

Ms. Brauer has even developed a new career in addition to these accomplishments: she has learned to play the glass armonica and is believed to be one of only five players of this instrument in this country. It was invented by Benjamin Franklin in 1761 and originally consisted of lead glass bowls nested one into another, mounted on a horizontal spindle, and turned by a flywheel and a foot treadle. Many musicians, including Marie Antoinette of France, applied moistened fingers to the rims of the bowls which create its unusual eerie sounds. Many people can get a similar effect by rubbing the edges of wine glasses. Even President George Washington was said to have admired the sound, and attended an armonica concert in Williamsburg, Virginia in 1765. Mozart composed music for the instrument in 1791.

In the 1800s, the instrument's popularity declined because many believed it could cause one to go mad, possibly because of the lead content. Ms. Brauer said, "Today's armonicas are made of quartz crystal, and I had one made with thirty-seven bowls nested inside each other." A few years ago she heard about this instrument on a TV program about a glass blower named Gerhard Finkenbeiner in Waltham, Mass. who made armonicas. She said, "I got in touch with him and, even though I found it cost several thousand dollars, I asked him to make one for me." Ms.

Brauer played her armonica to provide the eerie sound that was featured in the musical score of a Hollywood mystery movie called, "Interview with a Vampire."

Incidentally, Celia has a great sense of humor. She often invites the APTLI group of piano teachers to her home in Merrick. One Halloween, she opened the door dressed as a witch, with a tall pointed hat and even the blackened teeth. She startled everyone, then presented a delicious lunch, and proceeded to play several selections in her inimitable way as part of our informal afternoon concerts.

Another outstanding member of APTLI is Judith Alstader, the director/founder of the Minnewaska Chamber Music Society of Long Island. She has concertized in the United States, Europe and the Caribbean. Judith is a graduate of the Juilliard School and holds a Doctoral Degree from Yale Music School. She has performed at Alice Tully Hall, Merkin Hall, and Carnegie Recital Hall, and has recorded for Musical Heritage Society and Educa records. She is on the faculty of Pace University and of Five Towns College and is director of Judith Alstader Piano Studios. Judith was named Chevalier of the Order of Arts and Letters for her contributions to French music in America, and was honored for her contributions to the Arts in Nassau County, Long Island, by County Executive Thomas Gulotta.

Pat King was one of the first piano teachers to join APTLI over thirty years ago. She is my good friend and neighbor in the Roslyn Country Club. Pat studied pedagogy with Dr. Robert Pace at Teachers College, and gave workshops to piano teachers. Pat is a graduate of Eastman School of Music in Rochester, NY, and says Dorothy Taubman and Edna Golanski have had the most influence on her musical life.

Pat is also a very fine composer and was first prize winner of the Ithaca College Theodore Presser International Choral competition. Her four-part work, *The Hobbitt Suite* was chosen over 180 entries, and is published by Presser.

After Pat won an electronic piano, she began to explore the world of computer labs and has written articles about it. What I particularly appreciate Pat for is the fact that she chose to set the poetry of my beloved sister and my dad to music. There are three beautiful songs as a result - and the lyrics are to be found in this book. They are "Why, Indeed?" by

Pat King, pianist and composer

Carole Montparker's painting of her
Steinway grand piano on Ouida's
living room wall

Cecilia Brauer playing the Armonica

--- with Judith Alstader

my dad, as well as "I Never Knew" and "Sonnet to a Wave" by Jo Blatt Pall.

Rosabel Hsu Lu, who is also a good friend of mine, and a former president of APTLI, was born in Shanghai, China. Rosabel's father, Hsu Chien, was a famous scholar and a high official in the Ch'ing (Manchu) dynasty government. He had been responsible for building up the legal system in China, but, because of the growing corruption in the Ch'ing government, he joined Dr. Sun Yat-Sen's revolutionary group.

After her father passed away in Hong Kong, her mother, Shen Yee-ping, took Rosabel to the United States to pursue her musical studies. Rosabel entered the Juilliard School of Music to study with James Friskin. She graduated in a year and a half, and later finished her post-graduate course in another two years.

She married Hoshen Richard Lu, an aeronautical engineer, and pursued a career as a mother and piano teacher. She has taught countless students and is well known in her home town of Locust Valley, Long Island and surrounding towns. She has occasionally given recitals in Colleges, Universities, and Libraries. In 1967 and 1969 she gave duo-piano recitals at Carnegie Recital Hall with Ann de Pospo.

The newly-formed APTLI welcomed her as a new member almost at its inception. She served on the board in many capacities: first and second President, Treasurer, and in 1989 as President for two years. She started the Student annual recital with Gertrude Barry twenty eight years ago, and this function is still going strong. She is also a member of the National Guild of Piano Teachers, and has served as Chairman of the annual student auditions in her area for twenty years.

Recently, Rosabel gave me some greeting cards that were designed by her mother, many of which had been sold in China, and which Rosabel had found in her attic. I sent several to my friends who thought they were very quaint. Her mother was also a well-known poet in China. Here is an example of her poetry which was translated by Rosabel and Sandra Schorr:

MID-AUTUMN MOON FESTIVAL

Remembering Sher Ling
It is mid-autumn,
Night is on the river.
You and I dwell under
Different skies.

Breezes carry off shadows,
And distant friends
Hunt the same round moon.
In this dense air
With whom can I converse?
We are poor, you and I,
We have only self-pity.
Still, tonight we raise
Our goblets of wine.
In our common moonlight
We shall be virtuous
As trees of bamboo.

Rebecca Levy was a fellowship student at the Juilliard Graduate School where she studied with Olga Samaroff Stokowski and Ernest Hutcheson. She founded the New York Virginal Consort. The virginal is a renaissance keyboard instrument that flourished from 1525 to 1625 and is rarely heard today. The music written for the virginal anticipated the works of Bach, Scarlatti, Rameau and Couperin. Rebecca is a graphic artist and is a past president of APTLI. Herbert Levy, her husband, is a flutist who has been a member of many of the great symphony orchestras, and has served for twenty two years as a professor at Hofstra University.

In my three years as Program Chairman of APTLI, I have become good friends with several fine pianists. One of these is Hadassah Guttman, an attractive young woman, who has become a phone pal of mine, as we are too far apart geographically for frequent luncheon dates. She was asked to give a lecture on the music of the Holocaust at Nassau Community College which was videotaped for classrooms. Hadassah was most recently invited to become a visiting artist for the Annenberg Foundation. The following are some of Hadassah's many accomplishments: She received a B.M. and an M.A. from the Aaron Copland School of Music of Queens College, N.Y.,and a Ph.D. (with honors) in Music from New York University. Her piano teachers have included Nadia Reisenberg and Leon Pommers. She is the author of "The Music of Paul Ben-Haim - A Performance Guide," published by Scarecrow Press. She has been championing the music of Paul Ben-Haim since childhood, and once had the privilege of performing for him. Among the places she has performed are: Merkin Concert Hall, the Carnegie-Weill Recital Hall, radio station WFUV-FM, New York, and recently on cable television. This past summer, she performed a series of live broadcasts on Florida radio station WSBR. Edward Rothstein of The New York Times described her playing as "elegant." Dr. Guttman is on the faculty of the Lucy Moses School in New York City, and Nassau Community College in Garden City, N.Y., where she received the Faculty Distinguished Achievement Award in 1993.

Helene Levey Zemel recently performed for APTLI. When she was 17, she played Books I and II of Bach's *Well Tempered Clavier* in three concerts at Judson Hall in New York. She has a BA in music from Hofstra, and a MA in musicology from Queens College. Helene studied with Nadia Reisenberg and Morton Estrin. She lives in Valley Stream with her husband and daughter, Tara, whom she home schools.

Carol Montparker is a charming and prominent concert pianist, author, and very talented painter. APTLI enjoyed her last performance with us so much, that I decided to call her for a return engagement and she graciously accepted. At the same time, I asked her if she would contribute a short piece about her life that I could use in my book, and this very revealing essay is what she sent me:

At the moment that Ouida invited me to "write something pertaining to my work as a pianist and a writer" for her book, I had just completed the manuscript for my book, "A Pianist's Landscape," which was published by Amadeus Press in 1998. Anything and everything about my life's work in music, had gone into that book, and I felt like an empty vessel. I certainly had no desire to repeat myself, and there has been precious little to report since the book went into production; but one haunting fact may be worth mentioning: a book must end, but a pianist, with some luck, goes on being a pianist.

After submitting a few last-minute items to my editor just under the deadline, I finally had to sadly acknowledge that my work on the book had, indeed, ended (except for the nitty-gritties of proofing, indexing, and so on.) It so happened that I subsequently had a couple of poignant experiences which I would have loved to include in the book. I gave two all-Mozart recitals under tremendous pressures, that were among my most fulfilling concert experiences.

Carol Montparker

Rarely does a musician feel entirely pleased that a performance expresses all intentions and fulfills expectations; and rarely does one feel free enough to be able to take risks and improvise, while staying within the bounds of validity. On these occasions I had health problems, beyond the normal stresses of playing publicly. Yet I came away happy, thankfully, because I had made a decision to take a long sabbatical from solo performance. It is a much preferable condition to quit after one's best efforts.

I have played the piano since I was a toddler. Whether I play for a select group at home, or in a large hall, or even if I don't play for a while, I will remain a musical being. Writing about music is a corridor I veered off into around the time I kept a personal diary (for my own catharsis), of my New York debut recital at Carnegie Recital Hall in 1976. That chronicle became a book, and presto, I was a writer. Since then, with freelance articles leading to a position of Senior Editor at Clavier magazine, hundreds of interviews and feature writing, and a monthly column called "Carillon", I have scribbled happily on, almost as devotedly as I have played the piano.

I imagine it accounts for why this native New Yorker was invited to Ouida's Boston tea party.

Carol Montparker

Ren Zhang appeared at one of our APTLI meetings in 1997 and was sensational. He is one of the most promising young (28 years old) pianists I have ever heard. He was born in Shanghai and began piano at the age of four. At twelve he entered the Shanghai Conservatory of Music and was first prize winner of the 1986 Pearl River in Beijing, and was also a prize-winner in the International Music Competition in Shanghai in 1987 and 1988. In his native country, he perfomed as soloist with principal orchestras and was heard on radio and TV as a featured artist

He became a full scholarship student at the Manhattan School of Music where he received his Master of Music Degree. As recipient of "Artists International's Shura Cherkassky Award," he gave a concert at Carnegie recital hall dedicated to his hero, Cherkassky, who would be proud of him. Some of the major compositions he played were Bach's *Toccata in D Major, Carnaval* by R. Schumann, and several difficult transcriptions of *Études* by Chopin-Godowsky, *Liebesfreud* by Kreisler-Rachmaninoff,   etc.

Ren is such a good-natured and accommodating person that when I had a problem getting an artist to perform for APTLI in September '98, he very kindly volunteered to do it even though he was scheduled to give a whole program in Steinway Hall that night. I refused to let him do it as I knew it would be unfair for him to have to do two concerts in one day.

Ren did actually save the day this September. One of our guest pianists had to bow out a few days before he was scheduled to appear at an APTLI meeting. He had to play the Tschaikovsky *Piano Concerto in B minor*, substituting for a Russian pianist who couldn't make it out of Russia in time.

Naturally I thought of Ren. I knew he had a tremendous repertoire at his finger tips. He chose to play a Mozart *Fantasie* and a Schubert *Impromptu* for us, which he played impeccably. Then he did something that was an eye opener for us. He brought a few rare recordings by great pianists of the Golden Age. Without announcing who was playing, he gave us two selections of Chopin, the *Ballade #1 in G minor*, and the *Minute Waltz*, and then asked if we knew who was playing. I guessed it was Josef Hoffman right away because the selections were played at super speed, and Hoffman was the pianist who played music faster than anyone I had ever heard. It seems that in those days, pianists played in more individual ways, utilizing their own personalities. The interpretations were unique. Leonard Bernstein was innovative in that respect also. He took liberties with tempos and conducted the way he felt would be most effective – faster or slower – not always the traditional way. The results were often sensational, as in the last movement of the Haydn *Symphony #88*, which he took at a very fast tempo.

An interesting note about Hoffman is that after he became successful, Steinway designed a piano to his specifications, as he had short, stubby fingers and needed a special keyboard. He probably could play superbly on the traditional keyboard, but certainly even better on his own piano.

Another sidelight on Hoffman is the fact that he was a recognized inventor and had many patents. His most important invention was the windshield wiper, which they say was inspired by Maelzel's invention, the metronome.

Lucille Felsenthal and Jean Vandersall, who performed a magnificent piano four hand recital at APTLI in the Spring of 2000

--- with Ren Zhang

--- with Leonard Lehrman

Molly Vivian Huang

Leonard Lehrman, who has also appeared at APTLI, is a proponent of contemporary music. He is the president, since 1991, of the Long Island Composer's Alliance. For one of our most interesting meetings, he played the work of fourteen Long Island composers who came to talk about their compositions. He also played music of Morton Gould, who had died shortly before.

Leonard became Elie Siegmeister's youngest private composition student in 1960, at the age of eleven. On his deathbed, Siegmeister told him, "I don't want to say you are my disciple, because I don't believe in doctrine, but you are my continuator." Some of Leonard's other teachers were Nadia Boulanger, Lukas Foss, Leonard Bernstein, Leon Kirchner, and David Del Tredici.

Lehrman also wrote a thesis at graduate school of Cornell University - "Leonard Bernstein's *Serenade* (after Plato's 'Symposium'): An Analysis." He has given lecture/performances at the Gardner Museum in Boston, Carnegie Recital Hall, Steinway Hall, New York University, and the Leningrad Conservatory. Currently he is Laureate Conductor of the Jewish Music Theatre of Berlin, Music Director of the Community Presbyterian Church of Malverne, N.Y., and at the North Shore Synagogue in Syosset, where he is also organist and Composer in Residence.

Leonard is the composer of eight operas, five musicals, four cantatas, and 123 other works that have been heard throughout North America, Europe, Israel, and at the United Nations. We have just celebrated his 50th birthday with him at the Bryant Library in Roslyn, N.Y., where he performed with many of his musician friends, especially including his partner, the soprano, Helene Williams, who has performed in over three hundred concerts with him since 1987.

Their musical programs range from *E. G.: A Musical Portrait of Emma Goldman* to *The Jewish Woman in Song*. Other presentations are: *Memories and Music of Leonard Bernstein*; *A Blitzstein Cabaret*; *Broadway Dreams* (a CD); *Songs of Conscience*; *We are Innocent* (a Rosenberg Cantata); *Remembering Anne Frank, Martin Luther King, Earl Robinson and Edith Segal Memorial Concerts*; *Mozart and Brahms Recitals*; *Heine and Pushkin Bicentennial Concerts*; *Songs of Love*; *A Requiem for Hiroshima*; *The Universal Declaration of Human Rights* (at the U.N.); *Sisters* (at Merkin and Weill Halls); and *Tales of Malamud*.

In August 1998 they performed the first Yiddish song recital ever given in Bayreuth, Germany. Ms. Williams won the Bronx Council of the Arts award, and is director of Accent Reduction in English speech (ARIE) there.

Recently, I attended a memorial program to eulogize the husband of one of our APTLI members, Sonya Burakoff, a talented pianist and accompanist. Gerald, her husband, had died suddenly of a massive heart attack at age sixty-five. Their many grief-stricken relatives and friends filled the hall of the Unitarian Church in Garden City to which they had belonged for over thirty years.

Jerry and Sonya operated a company, Sweet Pipes, for twenty years, dedicated to the recorder in all its various forms, including publishing music for it. Since the recorder is utilized as a beginner's musical instrument in schools, it is a very successful business today.

His friends had prepared a beautiful concert of music for recorders of all sizes. One of the compositions was a trio for recorders by Paul Hindemith. Among the performers was Paul Winter, a prominent musician, who played the saxophone.

It occurred to me how sad it was that this man couldn't hear all the accolades he received from his friends, who often had to stifle tears when they exclaimed, "What a mensch!" (Yiddish, for a man with character), and, "What a guy!" His son, Bill, talked of his great sense of humor and how warm and wonderful a father he had been.

APTLI is a tight-knit, caring group of people; very supportive when any member is in trouble. For instance, Marilyn Hoffman, our former President, and Nancy Cossman each had been suffering with an arthritic hip for months and finally had hip replacement operations. Everyone was very concerned and kept in touch with them for moral support. Marilyn is very dedicated to her piano studies. Recently her husband, Phil, bought a beautiful Steinway Grand for her. Nancy is our secretary and often plays for us.

Sonia Cohen, another member of long standing, and a fine pianist and teacher, had a stroke two years ago. She is on-the-mend with therapy, and encouragement from her devoted husband, Joe, and is writing music for children to play. Members of APTLI visit and play duets with her to keep her spirits up.

Molly Vivian Huang has recently joined APTLI, and often performs for us. She is a graduate of Curtis, where she worked with Horszowski, Bolet, and Galimir, as well as playing with the Guarneri String Quartet. She has appeared as a soloist with the Cologne State Academy Orchestra, China Central Philharmonic, the Phillippine Orchestra, the COS Young Symphonic Ensemble of New York, and she records for the CRS label.

Jeanne Rosenberg, APTLI president, Simone Dinnerstein, concert
pianist, John Perez, and Marilyn Hoffman, former presidents

--- with Herb and Rebecca Levy

Hannah Hsu Wang is a distinguished member of APTLI and a good friend whom I admire tremendously. She came to the U.S. in 1966 and received her music education in the New England Conservatory, and graduated from Yale University with a Master of Music degree.

She has given recitals in New York's Merkin Concert Hall, Carnegie Recital Hall, Alice Tully Hall, and many more all over the world. Hannah has played in Taiwan and also in Suntori Hall in Tokyo. I give her credit for successfully combining her music career with her home life. She is married to a doctor and has three children.

Hannah is also very modest. When she played for a local concert this month, she spotted me in the audience, and at an intermission she came over and asked me, "Am I doing all right?"

One of our most dedicated APTLI members is Vernita Kenney, a good natured, charming brunette in her middle years.She has been in charge of hospitality at our monthly meetings ever since I can remember, and also at Club 88, an offshoot of the main meetings.

A major crisis occurred in Vern's life six years ago, when one of her grown children, a young woman who was nine months pregnant, collapsed suddenly of a brain aneurysm while taking a shower. She was rushed to the hospital and was hemorrhaging so much that they couldn't deliver the baby right away. Unfortunately, the mother died, but the baby survived and was healthy.

From then on, life was turned upside down for Vern and her husband, George. These grandparents suddenly had to take on the role of parents for three motherless children, and Vern, who had studied piano at Columbia University, continued teaching full time as they needed the extra income. The father of the children moved upstairs in the two family house they had to rent, and the children joined him when he came home from work.

Now, after several years have gone by, the family is doing well, mainly due to the sacrifices of this heroic grandmother, Vernita Kenney, and I thought her remarkable story deserved to be told.

One Sunday afternoon, Ray and I heard a most wonderful Russian pianist, Eteri Andjaparidze at the South Huntington Library. We were so impressed with her performance that I decided to ask her if she would like to play for one of our APTLI meetings, which she did the

Hannah Hsu Wang, concert pianist

following season. She talked about the methods of her teacher, Vera Gornostayeva, a pupil of Neuhaus, and played brilliantly for us. She received a standing ovation.

This is a little about her:

Eteri Andjaparidze was born into a family of musicians in Tbilisi, Georgia (USSR) in 1956. She received her first piano lesson at the age of five from her pianist mother. From 1963 to 1974, Eteri studied at the Tbilisi special School of Music for gifted children. By the age of nine, she already had performed with orchestra and had given her first solo recital.

The First Prize at the Transcaucasian Contest in 1972 was a promising beginning to her artistic life, and led to the Fifth Tschaikovsky International Competition in 1974. Fourth Prize was a remarkable achievement for the youngest participant, 17 year old Eteri. The same year, she entered the Moscow Tschaikovsky State Conservatoire of Music and continued her studies under the guidance of Professor Vera Gornostayeva.

In 1976, Ms. Andjaparidze won the Grand Prix at the Montreal International Piano Competition, the first Soviet pianist to do so. Since then, she has performed frequently in the former USSR, as well as in other countries. She has appeared as a soloist with major symphony orchestras and chamber ensembles in Europe, Asia, and North America.

In 1979 Eteri finished her studies, and in 1981 she completed postgraduate courses at the Moscow Conservatory. She accepted the post of Professor of Piano at the Tblisi State conservatory of Music in 1982.

Since 1992, Ms. Andjaparidze has been living in the USA. With concertizing and teaching, she confirms her international reputation as both an exceptionally gifted concert pianist and a fine educator. In 1993, she received the Ambassador Foundation Prize at the Ivo Pogorelich International Solo Piano competion in Pasadena, California.

Eteri was practically unknown here, although she does make CDs for Naxos Records. I asked her if she'd like me to get some library concerts for her in Roslyn. When she agreed, I called the right people at local libraries, and she has played at two of them already.

She played at the Shelter Rock Library in the fall of '94, and at the Great Neck Library the following February. The first work in Great Neck was the *Sonata in A Major* by Mozart, with the *Rondo a la Turka* at the end. The first part with the variations was played in a gentle way with her beautiful touch. Eteri told me she tried to get used to the action of the piano. It wasn't too responsive, although it was a Steinway. What followed was a spectacular version of the *Toccata* by Prokofiev – one of the most difficult pieces in the repertoire. After intermission, she played *Carnaval* by Schumann, one of her great specialities which brings out her variety of tone and whimsy. Of course she got a standing ovation.

When I asked Eteri, in a phone conversation, if she would like to play at our June luncheon, she suggested that we might like to hear a program she was going to play at New Paltz that summer. The APTLI board was delighted to have her try it out for us.

The day for the luncheon at the De Seversky mansion arrived, and when Eteri saw the Steinway, she expected it to be a piano she would enjoy playing, but it turned out to be a nightmare. Candlewax from night club activities had been dripped on the keys, and as soon as I saw it, I started scraping it off with my fingernails. Some of the notes made funny echo sounds and I can't blame Eteri for saying, "Ouida, I can't play Beethoven and Chopin on this piano."

Luckily our APTLI member who is a specialist in tuning and rebuilding pianos, Vincent Izzo, was able to analyze the problem immediately. Realizing what a disaster it would be to have no guest performer for our June luncheon, he rushed out to his car and brought in some tools to try to fix the offending piano.

Like the magician of the piano that he is, Vinnie fixed up the faulty notes with a little tuning and adjusting. The piano miraculously became playable. I glanced hopefully at Eteri as she tried it out with a few runs up and down the piano. Then she gave a slow negative turn of her head.

Suddenly I had a bright idea which I hoped might save the day. I reminded her that she had been planning to play some light music for us by Zez Confrey, whose best known work is *Kitten on the Keys*. Everyone knows it, and would she be willing to play that? Well, surprise, surprise! She not only agreed to play *Kitten on the Keys* but immediately after performing that, she played a whole group of Confrey tunes for us – some with a real jazz beat that no one had ever heard. It was amazing and delightful music and our APTLI audience gave her a standing ovation.

It took a Russian pianist to show us Americans what one of our own composers has accomplished.

Naomi Lehman started her love affair with chamber music in 1971 at a summer workshop, encouraged by her piano teacher, Alida Vasquez, who was also a guitarist and composer, who taught at Mannes College of Music.

Naomi has been the pianist for the Madison Chamber Ensemble since 1991, and was a New York City public school teacher before she started teaching privately in 1995.

Blanche Abrams, who is also an APTLI member and a professor of music at Hofstra University, is the pianist with the American Chanber Ensemble. She became Naomi's coach in 1993, and Naomi credits her intelligent and inspiring instruction for turning her into a "Pro."

One of the distinct advantages of being program chairman of APTLI is that I get to meet many fine artists personally, and one of my newest friends is Eleni Traganas, a distinguished pianist as well as a fine painter and author. A published composer at the early age of twelve, she received prizes in piano and conducting and was accepted at the prestigious Juilliard School, where she received the Master of Music degree. Among her distinguished teachers were Paul Badura-Skoda, Eugene List, Nadia Reisenberg and Beveridge Webster. In Switzerland, she performed in the Master Classes of Mieczyslav Horszowski.

For the past eighteen years, Eleni has lived and concertized in Europe, where she has won many prizes in international competitions. One critic in Bonn, Germany, praised her "astonishing command and limitless range, combined with an overwhelming, unique and individual style." Her piano repertoire is amazing and includes twenty concerti, plus many works of Scriabin and Rachmaninoff, as well as the early masters. Eleni made her Wigmore Hall debut in London, playing an all-Russian Program.

Recently, Simone Dinnerstein performed to enthusiastic acclaim at APTLI for the third time. She has appeared widely in this country and abroad in both solo piano concerts and chamber music. In 1994 she made her London debut playing the Beethoven *Emperor Concerto* at Queen Elizabeth Hall.

Ms. Dinnerstein is a recent graduate of the Juilliard School where she was a student of Peter Serkin. She has won many prizes including that of the New York Kosciuszko Foundation, and she has been a fellow at the Tanglewood Music Center.

Betty Bain, former president; Naomi Lehman
and Simone Dinnerstein, pianists

The Connecticut Trio,
Gerard Rosa, violin, Linda Laurent, piano,
and Julie Ribchinsky, cello

Eleni Traganas, distinguished pianist, artist and author

Courtesy, Museum of Television and Radio, September, 1985

Leonard Bernstein greets Jeffrey Biegel
at Lincoln Center

In 1985, Leonard Bernstein said of Jeffrey Biegel, "He played some fantastic Liszt the other night at the St. Regis Hotel during the dinner in my honor. He is a splendid musician and a brilliant performer." These comments by Lenny helped to launch Mr. Biegel's 1986 New York recital debut as the recipient of the coveted Juilliard – William Petschek Piano Debut Award in Lincoln Center's Alice Tully Hall.

He studied at Juilliard from 1979 to 1985 with the legendary Adele Marcus, whose teachers were Josef Lhevine and Artur Schnabel. Of course that makes me feel that we have something in common, as it means that both Jeff and I go back to Leschetizky.

Jeffrey's concerts all over the world are much too numerous to mention here, but I'll list some of the most important ones:

In 1983, he made his New York orchestral debut, performing Prokofiev's *Second Piano Concerto in G minor* with the Juilliard Philharmonia in Alice Tully Hall. In June 1997, he performed the U.S. premiere of the original 1924 manuscript of Gershwin's *Rhapsody in Blue* with the Boston Pops in Symphony Hall, Boston.

We are so privileged to have such talented people perform for us at APTLI. If we are interested in having them give us a Master Class during the year, they are always willing to oblige.

Another fascinating guest at APTLI was Franz Mohr who had been Vladimir Horowitz's personal piano tuner for most of his performing career, and who had also tuned pianos for Artur Rubenstein, Rudolph Serkin, Glenn Gould and Maurizio Pollini.

Mohr said that Horowitz had his idiosyncrasies. His own piano would accompany him wherever he was scheduled to give a concert, even in Moscow, and Mohr was always there to keep the piano in tune. Horowitz insisted on giving a concert only at four P.M. on a Sunday, and he had Dover sole shipped to wherever he was for his dinner. Another peculiarity was that Horowitz liked the keys to be not too clean so that his fingers wouldn't slide on them. One day Mohr made the grave error of washing them, and when Horowitz found his fingers sliding around he was horrified and insisted that Mohr spray the keys with hairspray to make them grip better.

Mohr said that Horowitz liked a brilliant sound on a piano whereas Rubenstein preferred a deep sound. The pitch of a piano is 440 in the USA but higher in Europe, in Berlin it is 446, Mohr said. During

Horowitz's last TV appearance, which was at his own home, Horowitz was feeling rather cocky and he began to sing. His wife, the former Wanda Toscanini, daughter of Arturo, admonished him sharply, "Don't sing, Play!"

As a singer, Lucille Lewis Bush, a mezzo-soprano, performed on Broadway, did concerts all over the United States, as well as the famous Asti restaurant in New York City.

She met Leonard Bernstein at Tanglewood, where she sang under the direction of Boris Goldovsky. She spent some delightful time with Lenny's parents in Boston. Her admiring husband, Jim, is a local attorney in nearby Garden City. They have two children, Robert and Heidi, and several grandchildren.

A few years ago, Lucille turned down a contract with the Vienna State Opera so she could spend more time with her family.

Ouida's friend, Lucille Bush

Before I end this chapter about APTLI, I must thank Daan and Julie Hu, who have graciously opened their beautiful home on the side of a high hill in Oyster Bay to music lovers. They have promoted the careers of several young pianists including Molly Vivian Huang, and Ren Zhang, who arrived here about ten years ago. They are spectacular performers who have played on the Hu's lovely grand piano many times. There is always a mouth-watering array of fancy baked desserts after the program.

I also want to mention a distinguished member of APTLI, Jane Leslie, who is a graduate of Juilliard. Jane is not only a very fine concert pianist, but a composer of very original piano music. Ray and I always enjoy going to her concerts as well as listening to her CDs.

New president, Jeanne Rosenberg with APTLI officers
(l. to r.) Betty Koontz, Naomi Lehman, Ouida Mintz,
Barbara Riss, Marilyn Hoffman, Gwendlyn Ronis

--- with Eteri Andjaparidze

Jeanine Bryan Briefel has appeared as guest performer on WNYC's "Around New York" and "Keyboard Artists." She was also on WQXR's "Listening Room" with Bob Sherman. Her current piano teacher is Seymour Bernstein, and she has attended the Manhattan School of Music.

Jeanine has served as music director for several Bel Canto Opera Company productions, and her latest article in Clavier Magazine is about teaching children to listen. In 1997, she played in the Town of Oyster Bay's Distinguished Artist Series at the Locust Valley Library.

She lives in Sea Cliff, Long Island with her husband, Dennis, and their three children, and she maintains a piano studio there.

BIOGRAPHY

Alexander Peskanov

"This brilliant pianist can create incredible excitement and knows how to please a crowd," reported The Washington Post when reviewing Alexander Peskanov's Kennedy Center performance of Rachmaninoff's Third Concerto. Mr. Peskanov's American debut as orchestral soloist came with the National Symphony under Rostropovich, and he has since appeared internationally with orchestras such as the London Symphony Orchestra, the English Chamber Orchestra, and the Hong Kong Philharmonic, as well as in the United States with the Baltimore, St. Louis, Houston, Utah, Richmond and Pacific Symphonies. He was also the featured soloist during the six-week tour of tile Polish Chamber Orchestra which included appearances at the Kennedy Center and the Metropolitan Museum of Art in New York City.

Mr. Peskanov has performed at the Wolf Trap, Aspen, Grant Park, Newport and Flagstaff festivals, and in coast-to-coast recitals including the prestigious Van Cliburn Foundation Series in Ft. Worth, Texas, and the Gina Bachauer Piano Festival in Salt Lake City, Utah. Among the illustrious musicians with whom he has collaborated are Maurice Andre, Jean-Pierre Rampal and Yo-Yo Ma. He also appears frequently with his brother, Mark Peskanov.

Alexander Peskanov is also a successful composer of classical works. His "Concerto for Piano Quartet and Orchestra," commissioned by The American Piano Quartet, premiered in 1996 at the Franz Liszt Academy in Budapest, Hungary. Mr. Peskanov is the recipient of three special ASCAP awards.

His recordings include a CD of his own piano compositions entitled "Spirits of the Wind -Peskanov Plays Peskanov" which has been featured in a satellite broadcast on National Public Radio stations. Among other recordings by Mr. Peskanov are Mozart's Concerto in Eb Major, Liszt's Malediction, Beethoven's Concerto in G Major No. 4 and Morton Gould's Concerto Concertante.

Mr. Peskanov graduated from the Stoliarsky School of Music in Odessa, Ukraine, and received his Masters and Bachelor degrees at The Juilliard School in New York. He is also the author of the series of six books entitled: "The Russian Technical Regimen for the Piano," published by the Willis Music.

POST-SCRIPT

Sometimes it seems that the most interesting things that have happened in my life are just coincidences. But when I think about it, I realize I learned from my mother how to take advantage of those coincidences. Also, one has to be lucky. However it happened, it has been a privilege to have known all of the great people I've met; the famous and the yet to be discovered. I have learned so much from them. When I think about my life, I don't know what I might change but, really, I just want to live it all over again.

Printed in the United States
72146LV00003B/1-48